MW00770140

PEARSON LEARNING
CORE KNOWLEDGE

HISTORY & GEOGRAPHY

◆ ◆ ◆ ◆

Edited by E.D. Hirsch, Jr.

Pearson
Learning
Group

www.PearsonLearning.com

ISBN 0-7690-5025-5
Printed in the United States of America
4 5 6 7 8 9 10   05 04 03 02

1-800-321-3106
www.pearsonlearning.com

Contents

HONI SOIT QVI MAL PENSE

Autore Ioanne With
Sculptore Theodoro
de Bry, Qui et excud.

V I R G I N I A

CHAWANOOK

Mongoack

Ramushouuo

Ohanooock

N

Moratuc

Tandaquomuc
Metpeuem

Catokinge

Wataian

SECO

Mascoming

TAN

WEAP

Secota

Cwareuioc

Panauaioc

Neuusiooc

Sectuioc

Cotan

Mequopen

Chepanuu

MEOC

Aquscogoc

Tramasquecoock

Pasquenoke

Promontorium tremendum

Paquipe

Pomeiock

Dasamohquepeu

Wokokon

Roanoac

Trinety harbor

Creatoan

Hatorask

Paquiwoc

OCCIDENS

MERIDIES

ORIENS

Scala leucarum 25

5 10 15 20 25

Scalle of 25 leages

Using Maps

Contents

How Far Is It? Boston, Massachusetts. April, 1775. It's about ten o'clock at night. Paul Revere steps into a boat and crosses the Charles River. An hour later, he reaches Charlestown. There, he borrows a horse. He's on an important mission, and there is no time to lose.

He must get to Lexington and warn Samuel Adams and John Hancock. These two American leaders are in danger. British troops are marching to Lexington to arrest them. But the American colonies need Adams and Hancock, and Revere must get to them first.

As he rides, Revere calls out, "The regulars are coming out!" He wants to let people know that English troops are marching out of Boston to Lexington. The people in the area need to be ready to defend themselves.

About 11:30, Revere reaches the town of Medford. He rides on until he gets to Jonas Clarke's house near Lexington. Adams and Hancock are there, and Revere warns them to flee.

Next, Revere heads toward Concord, but before he reaches his destination a British patrol arrests him. But Revere has done his duty. He had warned Adams and Hancock, and they had gotten away.

All this happened on April 18, 1775. The battles fought between the British and the Americans at Lexington and Concord the next day marked the beginning of the American Revolution.

This map of Paul Revere's ride on the night of April 18, 1775, can be used to measure how far he rode to warn John Adams and John Hancock that the British were coming to arrest them.

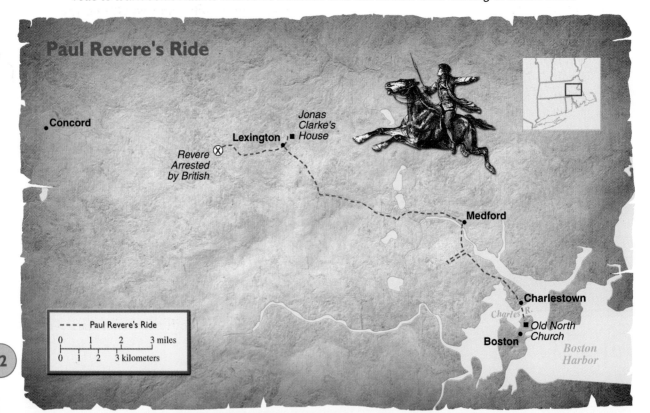

Paul Revere's Ride

Concord

Jonas Clarke's House

Lexington

Revere Arrested by British

Medford

Charlestown

Charles R.

Old North Church

Boston

Boston Harbor

- - - - Paul Revere's Ride

0   1   2   3 miles

0   1   2   3 kilometers

Today, you can trace the route Revere took. You'd need a good map, and you'd need to know your directions.

As you know, a map is a drawing of a real place. A symbol for a road stands for a real road. In the same way, a certain distance on a map stands for a certain distance on the ground.

Look at the map on the previous page showing Paul Revere's ride. In the bottom corner of the map, there's a small box. This is the **map key.** The map key contains information that will help you decode and understand the map. In this case, it tells you that a dotted line stands for the path of Paul Revere's ride. But the key also contains a small picture that looks like a ruler. This is picture shows the map's **scale,** in miles and kilometers. That is, it shows what distance on the map equals, or stands for, what distance on the ground. The picture is called the map scale.

The map scale shows that 1 inch on the map is equal to 3 miles on the ground. How do you know this? Take a ruler and place it under the map scale. Beginning at the left side of the map scale, measure 1 inch. There is a mark at this same place on the scale. The mark is labeled 3 miles.

You can use this information to figure out distances on a map. For example, what if you wanted to follow Revere's route from Medford to Lexington? How far would you

have to walk? First, measure the distance with your ruler. The shortest route from Medford to Lexington measures just about 2 inches. The map scale tells you that 1 inch on the map equals 3 miles in real distance. Therefore, 2 inches on the map equals about 6 miles in real life.

Now see if you can figure out how far Revere rode in all. He began his ride in Charlestown. First he rode to Medford and then to Jonas Clarke's house. After leaving Clarke's house, he rode on toward Concord. He was captured along the way. How far did he ride in total?

Figuring out the distance for the entire ride is a little tricky. It's difficult to measure this distance on the map using a ruler. A ruler is straight, but Revere's route was not. One way to measure the distance more accurately is to use a string. Place one end of the string on Charlestown. Next place the string on the map as close as you can to the exact route Revere followed. Then measure the string. You will find that the string is about 5 inches long. Now look back at the map scale: 1 inch equals 3 miles. Multiply the 5 inches by 3 miles, and you'll find the approximate number of miles Revere rode.

Different Maps and Scales

There are many different kinds of maps. Different maps give different kinds of information. On a map of a small area, lots of smaller places can be shown. For example, the map of Paul Revere's ride even shows where some houses are located. Houses cannot be easily shown on maps of huge areas, such as a country or a continent. Entire cities appear as small dots on a map of the United States.

Travelers often use different maps when going from one place to another. That's because they need different information at

vocabulary

map key a table or chart that helps you decode a map; the key is usually found in one of the corners of the map

map scale the relationship or proportion between the distance as shown on a map and the actual distance on the ground

different points on their trip. For instance, suppose that you and your family live in Barstow, California. You want to travel to San Diego to visit the San Diego Zoo. You might use the two maps shown on this and the next page to make your trip. The map below shows Southern California. The map on the next page shows the city of San Diego. The map of San Diego shows one small part of the map of Southern California. It has a lot of small details. It doesn't show houses, but it does show many smaller streets. Can you find the San Diego Zoo? Find the green area marked Balboa (bal BOH uh) Park. The zoo is located inside this large park. When you get to San Diego, you would use the city map to find your way to the zoo.

There's another important difference between the two maps. The scales are not the same. The map of Southern California is drawn to a scale of 1 inch to 40 miles. The map of San Diego has a scale of 1 inch to 3 miles. Both maps show distance correctly.

But because the areas shown in the two maps differ in size, the scales must be different.

Both of these maps will be useful to you if you are traveling from Barstow to the San Diego Zoo. The Southern California map will help you get from Barstow to the San Diego area. The San Diego map will help you find the zoo once you're in San Diego.

Finding Your Way

The first thing any traveler needs to know is direction. Find on the map of Southern California the symbol with four arrows pointing in different directions. That is called the **compass rose.** It shows you which way is north, south, east, and west. What general direction will you be traveling from your home in Barstow to San Diego? If you said south, you're going in the right direction!

> **vocabulary**
> **compass rose** a symbol on a map that shows directions north, south, east, and west

Use this map to find your way from Barstow, California, to San Diego, California.

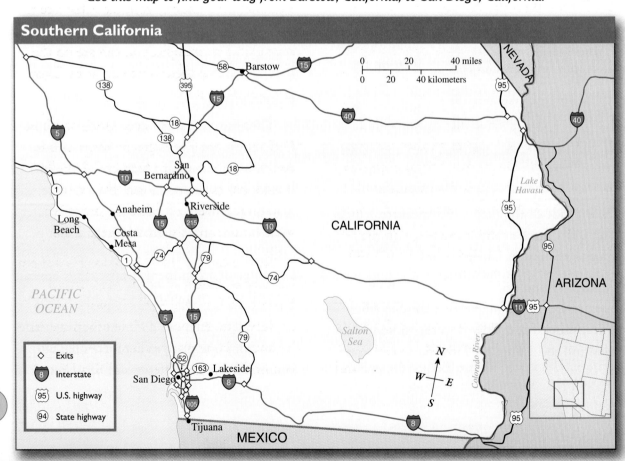

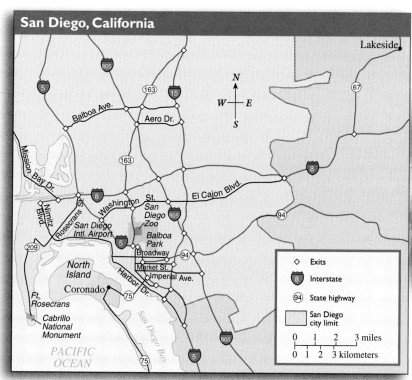

San Diego, California

Use this map to find the way to the San Diego Zoo, where the polar bear shown here lives.

It's nine o'clock in the morning when you leave Barstow. Your mother asks, "What is the best way to get to San Diego?" It's up to you!

First, find Barstow on the map of Southern California. Put your finger there. Then find San Diego and put another finger there. Next, look at the roads connecting the two. What is the shortest way to get from one city to the other?

After looking at the map, you see that Interstate 15, or I-15, goes all the way from Barstow to San Diego. You tell your mother to get on Interstate 15 and go south until she gets to San Diego. After a few hours of driving, you enter the San Diego Area. Now you put away your map of Southern California and get out your San Diego map.

Looking at the San Diego map, you see that the entire yellow area shows you the city limits. As you drive south on Interstate 15, you come to signs marking exits onto Balboa Avenue and then Aero Drive. These landmarks will help you keep track of where you are on the map.

The white squares where I-15 crosses Balboa Avenue and Aero Drive tell you that there are exits leading from the interstate to these roads. But not every road has an interstate exit. For example, you can see on the map above that there is no exit at El Cajon Boulevard for I-15.

Tell your mother to keep going south on I-15. Soon you'll see signs for Interstate 8. Ask your mom to turn west on I-8. Follow it for a few miles to State Highway 163. Then travel south on State Highway 163, which takes you to the San Diego Zoo.

As you can see from the map of Southern California, almost all of the roads from Barstow to San Diego are highways. Some are interstate highways, while others are state highways. How many different routes can you find between Barstow and San Diego?

Where in the World Are You? Water laps against the side of the ship. You can smell the salt in the air. You look around. There's nothing but water in every direction. Where in the world are you? And how does the captain know where he's going?

You've been on this ship for days. You were seasick the first day and couldn't leave your room. Now you don't know where you are. To find the answer, you pay a visit to the captain and explain your mission. He has lots of equipment, like a compass and radar, to help him find his location. But some of his most important tools are maps. He opens up a book and shows you a map of Earth. "This is everything you need to know," he says.

You study the map. If you could just figure it out, you'd know where you were and in which direction you are headed. Read on. By the end of the lesson you'll be able to find any place on Earth.

Making Sense of the Lines

Look at the map of Earth below. The lines running from side to side (from east to west) are lines of **latitude,** also known as **parallels.** You probably already know one of these lines of latitude. The line of latitude that runs around the middle of the earth is called the equator. The other lines of latitude circle the globe to the north and south of the equator.

*Lines of latitude (parallels) show distance north and south of the equator.
Use this map to find the lines of latitude closest to the cities shown on the map.*

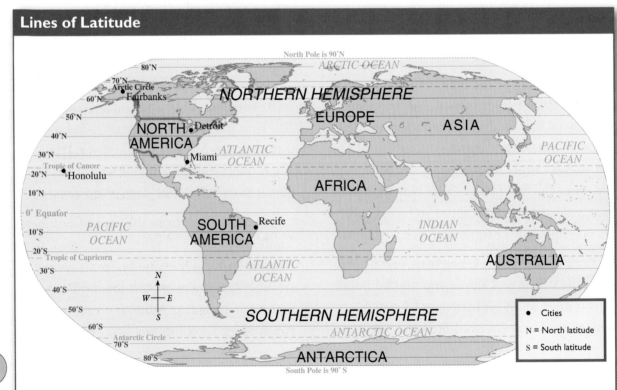

Lines of Latitude

All of these lines are called parallels because they are straight lines that never meet or cross.

On a flat map like the one shown on the previous page, these latitude lines look like straight lines that end when they reach the ends of the map, but it is important to remember that this flat map is meant to represent a round Earth. Since Earth is round, the far right side of the map actually touches the far left side, and the lines that seem to end at the right edge of the map actually continue on the left edge. In other words, those latitude lines that look so straight and flat on a map are actually circles.

In order to understand this better, use a globe. Place your finger on one of the lines of latitude just north of the equator and follow it all the way around the globe until you come back to the place where you started. Then choose a latitude line closer to the North Pole than the equator and follow it around. Can you see that this second circle is smaller than the circle just north of the equator? The circles get smaller and smaller as you move north or south of the equator. By the time you get to the poles themselves, these circles are so small that they are single points!

Travelers like your captain use lines of latitude to identify how far north or south they are from the equator. The lines are numbered in degrees (°) to make it easy. The equator is located at 0 degrees (0°). On the map shown, the first line north of the equator is 10°N. The line after that is 20°N, and so on. The North Pole is 90°N. The parallels south of the equator are numbered in the same way, with the South Pole at 90°S.

The spaces between the lines shown on the map also can be measured in degrees. For example, the point halfway between the equator and the line for 10°N would be 5°N.

What Latitude Tells You

You can tell a lot about a place just by knowing what its latitude is. In general, the farther north you travel in the United States, the colder it gets. That's usually true north of the equator, but the opposite is true south of the equator. On the southern half of the planet, the farther *south* you go, the colder it is likely to be. At the equator, it's usually pretty warm most of the time. At the North and South Poles, it's cold all the time.

Most of the United States lies between 25°N and 47°N. Miami, Florida, is located at about 25°N. The weather in Miami is usually warm. Even in winter the normal temperature is above 70°F. Detroit, Michigan, is located at about 42°N. What do you think the normal winter temperature in Detroit is?

Winters in Detroit are cold. The average high temperature during the winter is about 32°F. That's the temperature at which water freezes. Detroit gets lots of snow and several months of cold weather.

Fairbanks, Alaska, is located at 64°N. Honolulu, Hawaii, is located at 21°N. How do you think the January temperature in Fairbanks will compare to the January temperature in Honolulu?

Now look south of the equator. The tip of South America reaches to about 55°S. It's almost as far south as Alaska is north. The climate there is cold all year long. Farther

In general, the higher the latitude a place has, the colder it is.
These pictures of Detroit (left) and Miami were both taken in winter,
but Detroit is at a much higher latitude than Miami.

north in South America, the weather becomes warmer. The city of Recife, Brazil, is located at about 8°S. The temperature there will be warm all year long. Recife is warmer than Miami because it is so much closer to the equator.

Just now, the captain stops by to tell you the ship is at 40°N latitude. It's winter, and there's a strong breeze. What would you be wearing?

Lines of latitude also help us name parts of the globe. The equator divides earth into two **hemispheres** (HEM uh sfeerz). A hemisphere is half of a sphere. The hemisphere north of the equator is called the Northern Hemisphere. The hemisphere south of the equator is called the Southern Hemisphere.

Lines of Longitude

Now imagine that you and 359 of your closest friends are spread out along the equator, each of you 69 miles apart, so that all of you make a dotted line all around the world. All 360 of you begin walking directly north, heading for the North Pole. For most of your journey, you can't see your friends. But as long as everyone walks straight toward the North Pole, you will gradually get closer and closer together. By the time you reach the pole, all 360 of you will be together, pushing and shoving to stand in the same place.

If you could look back down the way you came and see your footprints, you would see lines of **longitude,** or **meridians.** These are imaginary lines that run from the North Pole to the South Pole. These meridians are equal distance apart at the equator, but they come together at each pole.

Like lines of latitude, lines of longitude are measured in degrees. There are 360 degrees of longitude. The map of the world below shows lines that are 15° apart. In between each of these are 14 other lines that are not shown. At the equator, each meridian of longitude is 69 miles apart. At the poles, all the meridians meet at a single point. You can see this if you look at a globe.

You might think that the lines of longitude would be numbered from 1 to 360. Wrong! They are numbered from 1 to 180 as you go east and then again from 1 to 180 as you go west. The first line of longitude is numbered 0°. It is a special line that runs through Greenwich (GREN itch), England. This is a small part of London. There was once an important observatory in Greenwich. An observatory is a place where scientists study the stars. In the 1800s, it was decided that this place would mark 0° longitude. It is called the **prime meridian.**

The lines of longitude east of the prime meridian are numbered 1°E, 2°E, and so on all the way to 179°E. The lines of longitude west of the prime meridian are numbered from 1°W to 179°W.

Halfway around the world from the prime meridian is another important longitude line. This is the 180° line of longitude. It is not west or east longitude because the lines of east longitude and west longitude meet there. The 180° line is known as the international date line; you'll learn more about it later in this unit.

The Coordinate System

How does longitude help your captain know where he is and where he is going? First of all, lines of longitude, like lines of latitude, are used to help us name parts of the globe. The prime meridian and the 180° longitude line divide Earth into two hemispheres. The hemisphere east of the prime meridian is called the Eastern Hemisphere. The hemisphere west of the prime meridian is called the Western Hemisphere.

Lines of longitude (meridians) get closer together as they go north or south from the equator toward the poles.

Lines of Longitude

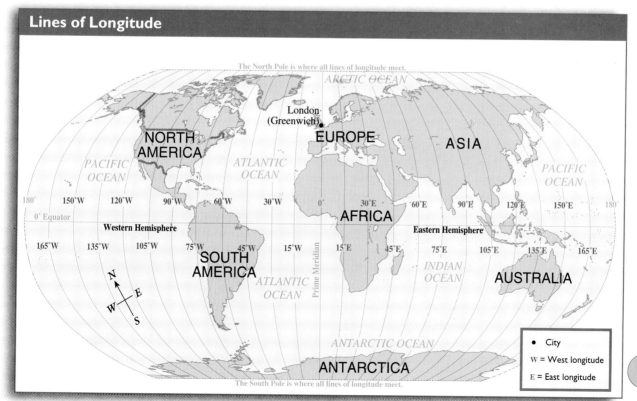

Using Lines of Latitude and Longitude

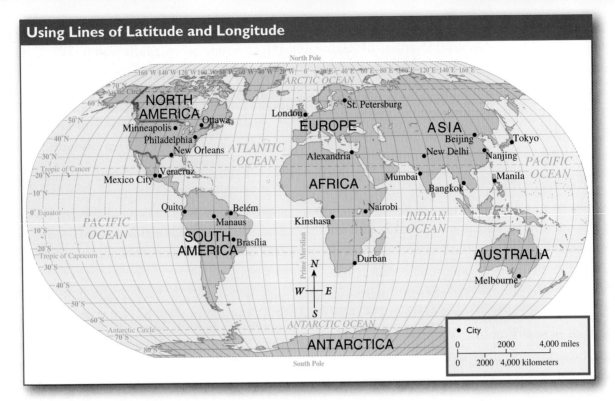

You can find any place on Earth by using the coordinate system created on a map by lines of latitude and longitude. What city lies at 30°N and 90°W?

Longitude gives you east-west information. Latitude gives you north-south information. When you put them together, you can know exactly where you are. For example, your captain knows that the ship is at 40°N and 60°W. These two numbers are called **coordinates** (coh OR dih nihts). These are any set of numbers that help you find your place on a globe or map.

On the map above, find the line of latitude labeled 40°N and put your right index finger on it. Then find the line of longitude that indicates 60°W and put your left index finger on it. Now follow the two lines with your fingers until they come together. The point where the two lines meet is exactly where your ship is. You are sailing across the Atlantic Ocean.

Now you know you're in the Atlantic Ocean. But do you know where you're headed? At that moment, the captain passes by. You ask him, "Do you know where we are going?"

He nods and says, "Sure. We're headed for a lovely city located at 30°N and 90°W. We'll be there in a few days."

Okay. Look at the map. Find the coordinates. Trace the lines with your fingers. Where's your ship headed?

If you found on the map above the coordinates 30°N and 90°W, you would have found the city that holds a great Mardi Gras festival every year.

Crossing the United States Back in the 1860s, building the Transcontinental Railroad was back-breaking work. The workers didn't have any modern equipment. They used hammers and shovels and carried each heavy steel rail by hand.

The rail was placed on wooden ties, and then the workers hammered steel spikes into place to hold the rail. Then the workers moved on, placing more ties, hauling another rail, driving in more spikes.

There were two crews of laborers. One started from Omaha, Nebraska, and built the railway west. The other crew started in Sacramento, California, and built the railway east.

It seemed like an impossible job, but two armies of workers laid mile after mile of track. Finally, on May 10, 1869, the two railroads met. The place was Promontory Point, Utah.

Dividing the Lines

Where on Earth is Promontory Point? Well, it is exactly at 41°38′N, 112°30′W.

You've studied latitude and longitude. You know about degrees. What are the extra numbers in the coordinates? They are called *minutes*.

The first coordinate for Promontory Point is 41°38′N. That is short for 41 degrees, 38 minutes north. Long ago, mapmakers realized that a degree is a very great distance. Sometimes, mapmakers want to measure smaller distances. So they have divided degrees into smaller units. There are 60 minutes in 1 degree. When writing the coordinates, they use the symbol (′) to stand for minutes. So 38′ is read as 38 minutes.

But remember, minutes of latitude and longitude are not units of *time,* they are units of *space.* Don't be confused by the use of the same word. You can't assume that because two points are 2 minutes apart in latitude that it would take you 2 minutes to get from one to another. It might take longer if you walked, or less time if you traveled by railroad!

This scene shows the day the Transcontinental Railroad was completed at Promontory Point, Utah, on May 10, 1869.

The set of coordinates for Promontory Point is 41°38′N, 112°30′W. You can use these coordinates to find the location of Promontory Point on a map. You know that latitude measures distances north and south of the equator. So the coordinate that ends with *N* for *north* or *S* for *south* is the latitude. That would be 41°38′N. Longitude indicates locations east and west of the prime meridian. So 112°30′W is the longitude.

Where the Lines Cross

The map on this page shows what the United States looked like in 1869. You'll recognize most of the states. Many of those west of the Mississippi River had not yet been formed. They were called territories. Somewhere out in the territories is Promontory Point. Can you find it?

This map shows lines of latitude and longitude every 5 degrees. See if you can locate the coordinates for Promontory Point. First look along the left side of the map. You won't find

41°38′N, so locate the line of latitude closest to it. That is the 40°N line. The place you're looking for will be 1°38′ north of this line. Think about it this way. There are 5 degrees between each line shown on the map. So 1 degree is less than half of the distance between the lines. Estimate, or carefully guess, where that place is. Put your left index finger there.

Now look along the top of the map and locate the line of longitude closest to 112°30′W. Once again, this exact line is not shown. But 112°30′W will be exactly halfway between the 110° and 115° lines. Put your right index finger on this line of longitude. Follow the lines with your fingers until the two lines meet. The place where the lines cross is Promontory Point.

Now look at the map and find Omaha, Nebraska. Omaha is located at 41°18′N and 95°57′W. By comparing these coordinates with the coordinates for Promontory Point (41°38′N, 112°30′W), you can see that the

This map shows the United States around the time the Transcontinental Railroad was being built. You can use this map to locate Promontory Point.

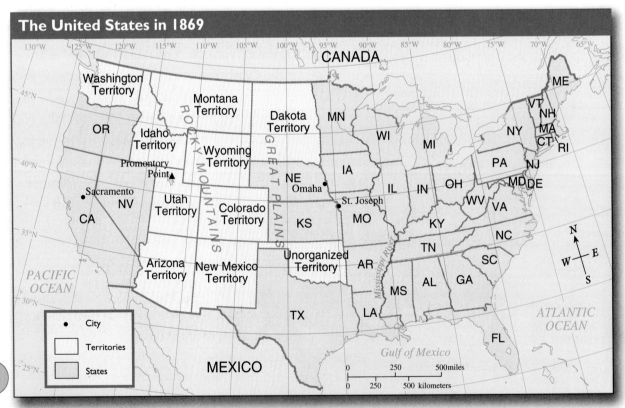

railroad went a long way west and just a tiny bit (20′) north.

Finding an Exact Location

The Transcontinental Railroad linked the eastern United States with the West Coast. Even earlier, the Pony Express accomplished the same thing. The Pony Express was the way mail was sent across the "Wild West." Men on horseback carried the mail along the Pony Express route. They changed horses about every 10 miles. After every 100 miles, a rider handed the mail to another rider, who carried it for another 100 miles. The route ran from St. Joseph, Missouri, to Sacramento, California. It was almost 2,000 miles long. Mail took about 10 days to get from one end to the other.

Today, there is a Pony Express museum in St. Joseph. You can learn all about the Pony Express. You can see pictures of the riders and learn about the dangers they faced.

Let's imagine that your parents or relatives have agreed to take you to the museum. But first you have to find out just where St. Joseph, Missouri, is located.

Start with a book of maps called an **atlas.** An atlas has an index. Look at the sample atlas index below. You can see that the index shows coordinates for St. Joseph and the page where you will find the correct map in that atlas.

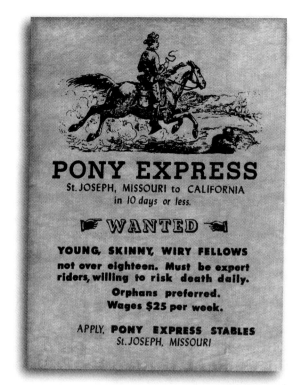

Pony Express riders carried the mail between St. Joseph, Missouri, and Sacramento, California in about ten days.

Using Road Map Coordinates

Let's take a closer look at St. Joseph, Missouri, to learn about different types of co-ordinates that are used on road maps. Imagine that you are on a sightseeing trip with your family. Since you are such a map expert, you have been given the map. Your task is to find the Pony Express Museum on a map of St. Joseph. Instead of looking all over the map, start with the road map index. This is like the index in a book.

> **vocabulary**
> **atlas** a book of maps

It lists all the places shown on the map and gives their coordinates. The index gives you these coordinates: C-2. You're puzzled. These certainly are different coordinates from those for latitude and longitude.

Many local highway maps give coordinates as letters and numbers. They are simpler to use on maps of small areas.

Place	Page	Lat.	Long.
St. George, Utah	119	37°10′N	113°58′W
St. James, Missouri	111	37°99′N	91°61′W
St. Johnsbury, Vermont	109	44°42′N	72°02′W
St. Joseph, Missouri	121	39°77′N	94°85′W
St. Louis, Missouri	117	38°63′N	90°20′W
St. Paul, Minnesota	118	44°94′N	93°09′W

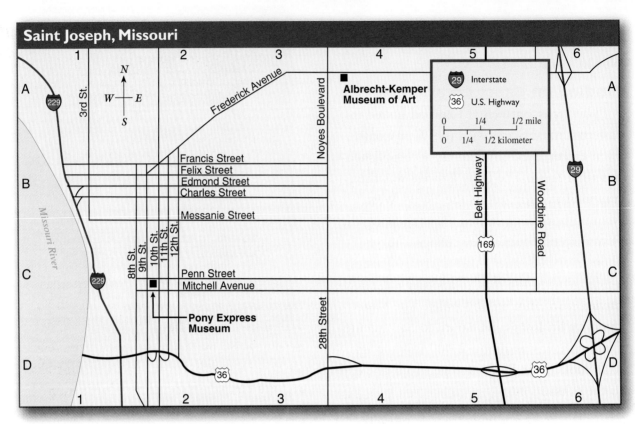

Saint Joseph, Missouri

Instead of using a coordinate system of latitude and longitude, some maps use a system of letters (A, B, C, etc.) and numbers (1, 2, 3, etc.) to create a grid system.

Look at the map of St. Joseph shown above. Notice that the letters run down the sides of the map and the numbers run along the top and bottom. You are looking for the coordinates C-2. But don't look for a line marked C and follow it to where it crosses a line marked 2. Instead, put your finger on the space marked C. Put another finger on the space marked 2. Follow the spaces until they meet. Somewhere close to where your fingers meet is the Pony Express Museum.

You have a great time at the Pony Express Museum. Your mother decides she wants to see the Albrecht-Kemper Museum of Art, but she can't find it on the map. Can you? The map index will tell you that the coordinates are A-4. But how will you get there? And about how far is it from the Pony Express Museum?

The Albrecht-Kemper Museum of Art

A Puzzle About Time

A family is traveling by cruise ship from China east toward Los Angeles, California. The mother is about to have twin babies. At 1:00 A.M. on Monday, January 1, 2001, the ship nears 180° longitude. The woman has a baby girl.

The ship crosses the 180° line of longitude. An hour later, the woman gives birth to a second girl. She has had twins!

The first child gets a birth certificate saying she was born at 1:00 A.M. on Monday, January 1, 2001. The second child gets a birth certificate saying she was born at 2:00 A.M. on Sunday, December 31, 2000.

The baby's father believes there has been an error on the birth certificates. After all, how could the baby born first be given a later birth date than the second baby?

The International Date Line

The puzzle about the two children is easily explained. You see, geographers have drawn an imaginary line from the North Pole to the South Pole. Along that line one day changes to another. If it is Monday on the east side of the line, it is Tuesday on the west side. There is a difference in time of 24 hours. This line is called the **international date line**.

The international date line is the same as the 180° meridian in most places. In some places, it curves around areas of land. If the line ran through countries, people on one side of a street might always be a day behind the people who lived on the other side of the street. Just think how confusing that could be! To solve that problem, the international date line is placed over oceans.

Most people do not notice the international date line. It doesn't have much to do with local events or local time. The people most affected by the international date line are those traveling between Asia or Australia and the United States. People flying from Japan may arrive in the United States hours before they leave. People flying from the United States will arrive in Japan a day later.

> **vocabulary**
> **international date line** an imaginary line that marks the place on Earth where each new day begins

Of course, time is not really lost or gained by crossing the international date line. It takes roughly the same time to fly in both directions. The international date line causes an imaginary loss or gain in time. It was created to solve problems with the calendar for world travelers.

Ferdinand Magellan

Ferdinand Magellan was an explorer in the 1500s. He led the first trip around the world. Magellan and his crew were the first to experience the problem that occurs when travelers go all the way around a planet that is itself rotating.

Magellan and his crew sailed from Spain to the Americas and kept traveling west until they had gone all the way around the world. Actually, Magellan himself did not make the complete trip around the world. He died during the journey, but his crew made the complete voyage. They kept careful records of their journey. When they reached Spain again, they found that the journey had taken one more day than their records showed.

A similar thing happened to people traveling east around the world. They would arrive home a day earlier than they expected.

In order to solve this problem, the international date line was created. It's not a perfect solution, however. Odd things can happen, as in the case of the twins born in "reverse order."

Time Zones

The international date line is easier to understand if you first understand time zones. You may know that other parts of the United States have different times than where you live. Perhaps you've seen it on TV. A program that begins at 8:00 in New York will begin at 7:00 in the Midwest, 6:00 in the Rocky Mountains, and 5:00 on the West Coast.

The United States, including Hawaii and Alaska, is covered by six time zones. Most of the states are in one of four time zones.

When people travel through the time zones, they gain or lose time. For example, suppose you board an airplane in Cleveland. This city is in the eastern time zone. The plane flies to Chicago, which is in the central time zone. The flight lasts about one hour. If you leave at 1:00 P.M., you will arrive in Chicago at 1:00 P.M.

This happens because places in the central time zone are one hour earlier than places in the eastern time zone. So even though you spent an hour flying, you gain the hour back by entering the new time zone.

When you fly back from Chicago to Cleveland, you will "lose" time. If you leave at 8:00 A.M., you will arrive in Cleveland at 10:00 A.M. You fly for one hour. You lose another hour because you changed time zones.

The same change in time occurs every time you travel between time zones. If you travel into the next time zone to the east, you lose an hour. If you travel into the next time zone to the west, you gain an hour.

Look at the map of World Time Zones. What time zone do you live in? What time is it right now? What time is it in Los Angeles? What time is it in New York?

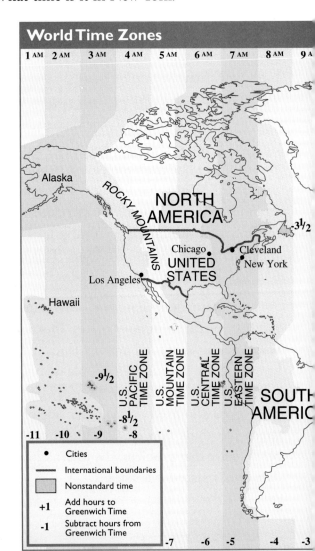

International Time Zones

The time zones in the United States are part of a worldwide system of time zones. There are 24 time zones. Think of the time zones as making up a continuous circle that goes around the world from east to west. Each is 1 hour apart. Each time zone to the east is 1 hour later than the neighboring time zone. Each time zone to the west is 1 hour earlier than the neighboring time zone to the east.

The international date line is in the middle of a time zone. The time on the east side of the time zone is one day earlier than the time on the west side of the time zone. Look at the map. Just to the east of the international date line, it is midnight on Sunday. Just to the west of the international date line, it is midnight on Monday.

Now use what you have learned. If it is Tuesday morning in Los Angeles, California, on the west coast of the United States, what day is it in Australia? This continent is across the international date line from Alaska. Therefore, Australia is one day ahead of California. It's Wednesday there.

Now let's consider time. For example, let's say it is 10:00 A.M. on Friday in Los Angeles. What time is it on the east coast of Australia? Locate Los Angeles on the map. Then count westward through the time zones: 10:00, 9:00, 8:00, and so on. It will be Friday at 6:00 A.M. on the *east* side of the international date line.

Immediately across the date line it will be Saturday at 6:00 A.M. The next time zone will be 5:00 A.M. The east coast of Australia is in the next time zone. It will be 4:00 A.M. on Saturday there.

Now try some time changes on your own. It's 8:00 P.M. on a Tuesday in Japan. What time and day is it in Hawaii?

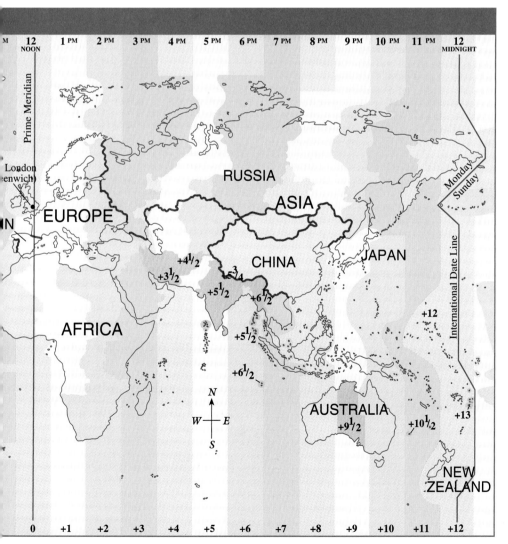

The world is divided into 24 time zones. If it is 9 A.M. where you live, what time would it be in Chicago?

Why Have Time Zones?

You may wonder why people felt the need to set up such a complicated system of time zones. Here's a clue. Earth is divided into 24 time zones. What else is divided into 24 parts?

Did you say a day is divided into 24 hours? If so, you were on the right track. The 24 time zones on Earth and the 24 hours in a day are closely connected. You see, Earth rotates, or turns around, on its **axis** once every 24 hours. This means that different parts of Earth are facing the sun at different times. When the United States and its time belts are facing the sun and experiencing daytime, China and its time belts are facing away from the sun and experiencing nighttime. Time zones were invented because of this rotation. If Earth didn't rotate on its axis, we wouldn't need time zones. But then it would always be daylight in certain parts of the world and always nighttime in others!

But what about the international date line? Why did people feel the need to set that up? This is one of those cases where one thing led to another. Once the time zones were set up, and the time zone in which Greenwich, England, is located had been designated as the time zone on which all of the others depended, the need for a date line arose.

You can understand this by glancing back at the map of World Time Zones. First, find the prime meridian, the 0° longitude line that runs through Greenwich, England.

> **vocabulary**
> **axis** an imaginary straight line that runs through a turning object

Time zones were invented because of the rotation of Earth on its axis.

Imagine that it is 3:00 A.M. on Saturday, June 10, in the Greenwich time zone. What time will it be in the next time zone to the east? 4:00 A.M., of course. Now count over 11 more time zones to the east, adjusting the time as you go. You should end up in a time zone (shaded green) that includes eastern Russia and New Zealand, and, if you have counted correctly, you will say that the time in this zone must be 3:00 P.M. on June 10.

You may say, "That was easy!" But there's just one small problem. If you count your way to this same time zone but go west from Greenwich instead of east, you will get a different answer. Try it and see.

Go back to Greenwich and count 12 times zones to the west, adjusting the time as you go. If it is 3:00 A.M. on Saturday, June 10, in Greenwich, it will be 2:00 A.M. in the next time zone to the west, then 1:00 A.M., then midnight, and then 11:00 P.M. *on the previous day*—June 9. Keep counting until you have ticked off 12 time zones. You should end up in the same time zone you were in before—the green one containing Russia and New Zealand. But what are the date and time? According to this count, it's 3:00 P.M., just as it was before, but it's Friday, June 9, instead of Saturday, June 10!

So which day is it in this time zone— June 9 or June 10? Geographers figured that the only way to solve this problem was to divide this contested time zone into two parts. In the eastern half of this time zone it would be the earlier date, and in the western half it would be the later date. And that's how the international date line came to be!

Physical Maps Show the Easy Route Learning how to read a map makes the job of locating places a lot easier. But once you locate a place on a map, how would you find the best route to get there?

One way to find the best and easiest route to take is by looking at a special kind of map. So far, you've been looking at maps that show roads, towns, cities, and state and national boundaries. These maps tell you where places are located. They also help you figure out how far one place is from another place.

However, these maps do not show you what the land itself looks like. You might want to know about routes that cross mountains and valleys. What you need is a **physical map,** a special type of map that shows the features of the land, such as hills, mountains, and valleys.

All physical maps give information about the **elevation,** or height, of the land. However, there are different kinds of maps that show elevation. Some use lines to show elevation. Others, including the map below, use colors to show elevation.

> **vocabulary**
> **physical map** a type of map that shows hills, mountains, valleys, and other features of the land
> **elevation** the height of something; on maps elevation is shown as the number of feet above or below sea level

This physical map shows elevation in different areas of the United States.

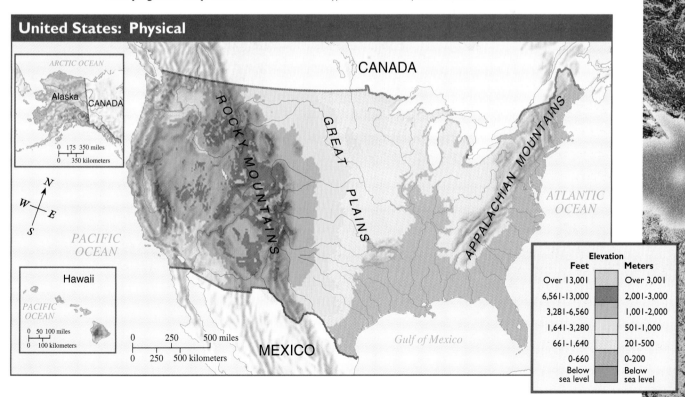

United States: Physical

ARCTIC OCEAN

Alaska CANADA

0 175 350 miles
0   350 kilometers

N
W   E
S

PACIFIC
OCEAN

Hawaii

PACIFIC
OCEAN

0 50 100 miles
0 100 kilometers

CANADA

ROCKY MOUNTAINS

GREAT PLAINS

APPALACHIAN MOUNTAINS

ATLANTIC
OCEAN

0   250   500 miles
0   250   500 kilometers

MEXICO

Gulf of Mexico

Elevation	
Feet	**Meters**
Over 13,001	Over 3,001
6,561-13,000	2,001-3,000
3,281-6,560	1,001-2,000
1,641-3,280	501-1,000
661-1,640	201-500
0-660	0-200
Below sea level	Below sea level

Look at the physical map of the United States on the previous page. From the map you can see that there are two main areas of mountains in the United States. One long range of mountains is in the East. These are the Appalachian Mountains. They run from Maine all the way south to Alabama. The other area of mountains is in the West. There are several ranges of mountains in the West. The biggest is the Rocky Mountains, which run from Canada southward through the American Southwest. You can see that mountains cover much of the western U.S.

These mountains are shown in different colors on the map. In fact, all land areas of the U.S. are shown in color. Places where the land is low are shown in green. Yellow shows land that is higher. Light orange and dark orange mean that the land is very high. Mountain tops—the very highest land— are colored light purple.

Understanding a Physical Map

It is easier to understand what the colors on a physical map mean if you think of how mountains look from the side. Look at the

drawing of the mountain scene below. The lowest part of the scene is a valley. The valley is colored green. Look at the elevation key on the drawing below. The green color shows elevations from 661 to 1,640 feet. That means that the valley is between 661 feet and 1,640 feet in elevation. How high is the part of the mountains that is colored orange?

Now imagine that you are a bird. You're flying, looking directly down on the mountains from above. The picture on the next page shows a bird's-eye view. It shows areas of higher and lower elevation using color.

Notice the part of the mountain that is yellow. This color shows the same part of the mountains as the yellow on the first picture. It shows the part of the mountains that are 1,641 to 3,280 feet high. Now look at the part of the mountain that is colored pink. How high is this part of the mountain?

You can learn useful information by looking at an elevation map. For example, suppose you want to get the best view of the surrounding land. Where would you go?

This view of mountains and valleys uses different colors to show elevation.

Land Elevation: Side View

Elevation

- over 13,000
- 6,561-13,000
- 3,281-6,560
- 1,641-3,280
- 661-1,640
- 0-660

You would climb one of the peaks, of course. These peaks are shown as the three purple areas on the map below. What if you wanted to build a railroad through this area? Where would you put it? You would not put it across the purple areas. That land is steep and high. Instead, you'd build it through the green area. This color indicates that the elevation is low.

So you can see how colors can be used to show the elevation of the land. And you can learn a lot about the land by studying an elevation map. However, this kind of map has limitations. For example, look at the bird's-eye map below. Notice that all three mountain peaks are purple. The purple means the peaks are over 13,000 feet high. But look back at the land elevation map on the previous page. One peak is higher than the others. One peak may be just 13,050 feet high. The other may be 13,500 feet high. You cannot tell the difference on the map below.

Now look back at the physical map of the United States. The elevation key tells you how high the land is. How high are the Great Plains? Most of this area is shaded light green. Therefore, the elevation is between 661 and 1,640 feet high. Which mountains are higher, the Rocky Mountains or the Appalachian Mountains? The Rocky Mountains are higher. They are shaded dark orange and purple. That means much of the land is more than 6,561 feet above sea level, and some of it is more than 13,000 feet above sea level. The Appalachians, on the other hand, are shaded yellow and light orange. They measure between 1,641 and 6,560 feet high.

Finding Your Way on an Elevation Map

You may be wondering how you can use this information. Here's one way. Take a look at the map of Lost Cave Valley on the next page. You and your friends are spending the day exploring the valley and hills. You start at Camp Trout. It's on the west side of the map near the stream. Your goal is Lost Cave. As you can see, there are two trails to Lost Cave. You could take Sheep Trail or Fish Trail. You and your friends can't decide which one to choose.

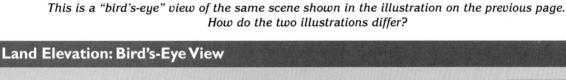

This is a "bird's-eye" view of the same scene shown in the illustration on the previous page. How do the two illustrations differ?

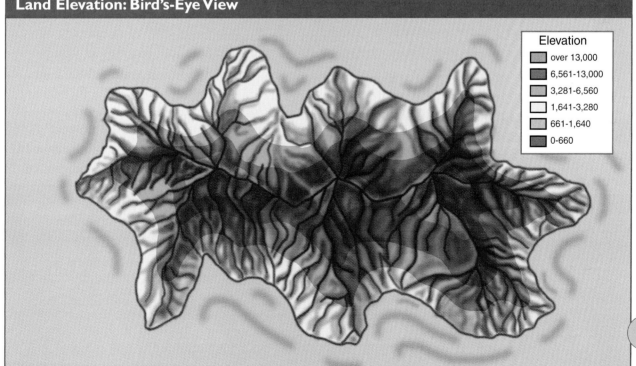

Land Elevation: Bird's-Eye View

Elevation	
	over 13,000
	6,561-13,000
	3,281-6,560
	1,641-3,280
	661-1,640
	0-660

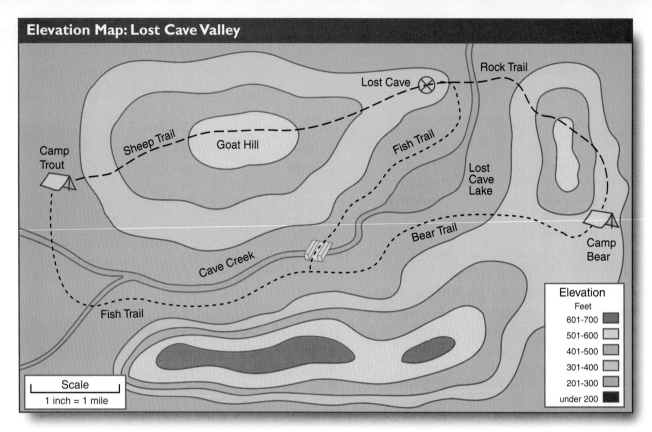

Elevation Map: Lost Cave Valley

Rock Trail

Lost Cave

Sheep Trail

Goat Hill

Camp Trout

Fish Trail

Lost Cave Lake

Bear Trail

Cave Creek

Fish Trail

Camp Bear

Scale
1 inch = 1 mile

Elevation
Feet
601-700
501-600
401-500
301-400
201-300
under 200

By using this elevation map of Lost Cave Valley, you could find the easiest and quickest routes to visit the places you want to see.

Look at your map. What does it tell you about the trails?

On the map, the area around Camp Trout is shown in dark green. Look at the elevation key. Dark green is land that is between 201 and 300 feet high. Sheep Trail goes up Goat Hill. It climbs from the dark green, to the light green, and then to light brown. Next it crosses into yellow. Then it goes back to light brown and to light green. Lost Cave is shown in the area of light green. What this tells you is that you will first be climbing from Camp Trout all the way to the top of Goat Hill. Since the top is shown as yellow, you know the elevation is between 501 and 600 feet. That means that you'll have about a 300-foot climb to the top of the hill. Then you'll have to go down another 200 feet or so on the other side of the hill.

Fish Trail follows Cave Creek. The map is colored dark green almost the whole way.

Only near the cave will you travel into an area that's colored light green. This means your trail will be nearly level most of the way. You may climb about 100 feet up to the cave.

Do you want to climb up the hill and then hike down the hill again to get to the cave? Or do you want to walk along a nearly level trail to get there? Of course, you might also think about the distance. Using a string to measure, you'll find the distance along Sheep Trail is about 4 miles. The distance along Fish Trail is about 7 miles. Four miles with a big hill or 7 miles on a flat trail: Take your pick!

After visiting the cave, you plan to hike to Big Bear Camp. Again, you have a choice of two trails. Which will you choose? Why?

If you can answer questions like these, you will be able to read almost any map you're handed—and the world will be at your fingertips!

22

Glossary

atlas a book of maps

axis an imaginary straight line that runs through a turning object

compass rose a symbol on a map that shows directions north, south, east, and west

coordinates a set of numbers that help identify a specific place on a globe or map

elevation the height of something; on maps elevation is shown as the number of feet above or below sea level

hemisphere half a sphere

international date line the imaginary line that marks the place on Earth where each new day begins

latitude distance, measured in degrees north or south of the equator

longitude distance, measured in degrees east or west of the Prime Meridian

map key a table or chart that helps you decode a map; the key is usually found in one of the corners of the map

map scale the relationship or proportion between the distance as shown on a map and the actual distance on the ground

meridian an imaginary line that runs north-south on a globe or map but measures degrees of longitude east or west of the prime meridian

parallel an imaginary line that runs east-west on a globe or map but measures degrees of latitude north or south of the equator

physical map a type of map that shows hills, mountains, valleys, and other features of the land

prime meridian 0° longitude; the longitude line that runs through Greenwich, England

World Mountains

Contents

O beautiful for spacious skies,
For amber waves of grain,
For purple mountain majesties,
Above the fruited plain!

America the Beautiful, Katharine Lee Bates, 1893

Mount Aconcagua is the highest peak in South America's Andes Mountains.

The Importance of Mountains

Like Katharine Lee Bates, people have long admired the beauty of mountains. Some have even worshiped them, placing offerings on mountain slopes in the hope of good crops, good weather, or good fortune.

Mountains play a part in many religions, perhaps because people feel that being on a mountain makes them closer to their god or gods. Moses, for example, received the Ten Commandments on a mountaintop, and the ancient Greeks believed that their gods lived in the mountains.

Mountains are important in many ways. They affect the earth's climate and weather, they provide a home for many animals, and they contain valuable minerals.

Mountains have historically made trade and travel difficult and have acted as **barriers** to keep out invading armies, or to at least slow them down. More recently, mountains have attracted tourists, skiers, hikers, and climbers.

> **vocabulary**
> **barrier** something that blocks the way

How Mountains Are Made

As you may have learned in science class, mountains are formed in several different ways, most of which are related to activity below the surface of the earth. To understand how mountains are formed, you need to remember that the earth has a crusty shell made up of gigantic plates that can shift, crack, and wrinkle.

Folded mountains are created when the earth's crust shifts so that one piece of rock folds on top of another, like the wrinkles on a scrunched-up table cloth. Some of the Appalachian Mountains (ap uh LAY chun) in the eastern United States are folded mountains.

Fault-block mountains are also created by shifting plates, but in this case pieces of rock are broken off and driven upward by the force of the shifting plates. The Sierra Nevadas of western North America are fault-block mountains.

Dome mountains are created when molten rock called **magma** wells up below the surface of the earth. As the magma presses upward, it makes dome-shaped bumps on the earth's surface. These bumps often look more like hills than mountains. The Black Hills of South Dakota are an example.

Volcanic mountains are formed when a volcano erupts, breaking a hole in the earth's crust. Lava and ash flow down the sides of the volcano and harden into a mountain. Many islands, such as the Hawaiian Islands, are actually the tops of volcanic mountains. Japan's highest mountain, Mount Fuji, is a volcano that last erupted in 1707. The highest mountain in Africa, Mount Kilimanjaro (kil uh mahn JAHR oh), is an **extinct** (ek STINKT) volcano.

Volcanic mountains can be produced by a few days of spectacular eruptions, but most mountains take thousands, or even millions, of years to form. They form so slowly that, in real life, you can't see them changing.

Some of the earth's mountains, such as the Appalachians, were formed more than 200 million years ago. Others, such as the Rocky Mountains in western North America, were formed only about a million years ago. You can often tell whether mountains are young mountains or old mountains by their shape. Young mountains are usually steep, high, and jagged. Old mountains have been worn down by many years of **erosion** (ee ROH zhun).

If you look at the picture of Mount Aconcagua at the beginning of this unit, you'll notice that there is snow on top of the mountain. Most tall mountains are covered with snow, and not just in the winter, but all year long. That is because temperatures decrease with altitude. The farther above sea level you go, the colder it gets. You may have noticed this if you have ever hiked up a mountain or driven to the top of one.

> **vocabulary**
> **magma** molten, or melted, rock deep beneath the earth's crust
> **extinct** no longer active or living
> **erosion** the wearing away of soil and rock by the action of wind or water

Mountain tops tend to be chilly, even when they are located in hot places. Mount Kilimanjaro, in the African country of Tanzania, is snowcapped all year long even though it is very close to the equator.

Major Mountains of the World

Name	Major Range or System	Location	Elevation (in feet)	Highest in feet
Mt. Everest	Himalayas	Nepal/Tibet	29,028	World
Mt. Aconcagua	Andes	Argentina	22,835	Western Hemisphere
Mt. McKinley	Alaska	United States	20,320	North America
Mt. Kilimanjaro	none	Tanzania	19,340	Africa
Mt. Elbrus	Caucasus	Russia	18,481	Europe
Mont Blanc	Alps	France/Italy	15,771	Alps

The chart on this page lists some of the tallest mountains in the world.
See if you can locate all of these mountains on the map below.

Major Mountains of the World

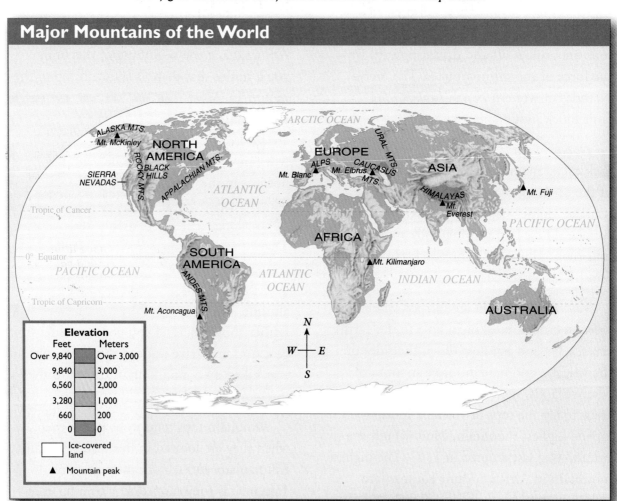

28

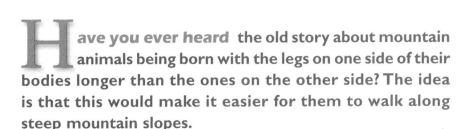

Have you ever heard the old story about mountain
animals being born with the legs on one side of their
bodies longer than the ones on the other side? The idea
is that this would make it easier for them to walk along
steep mountain slopes.

Getting Around

If you think about it, though, there would
be one big drawback to such an arrangement.
The animal could only move in one direction!
If it turned around so that its short legs were
on the downhill side, it would tip over and
tumble down the mountain!

Of course, animals aren't really born with
shorter legs on one side, but animals such as
mountain goats and sheep and other animals
like them do have features that make it easier
to get around. For instance, their hoofs have
sharp edges that help them grip the rocky

earth. While all animal mountain dwellers
are skilled at getting around, mountain goats
are probably the most sure-footed. People
have seen them walk out onto a narrow
ledge, only to have the ledge come to an
end. Since the goats can't back up, they rise
up on their hind legs, pivot around, and
stroll back out.

Surviving the Cold

Since mountains can get very cold,
especially in winter, animals need a way to
survive the cold weather. Animals can deal
with that problem in four ways. One, they

*Mountain goats have little trouble
moving around some of the
world's highest places.*

29

can move down the mountain to where it is warmer and where there is more cover. Two, they can grow heavy coats to keep them warm. Three, they can **hibernate**. Or four, they can find shelter underground or under the snow.

Most large mountain animals choose to spend the winter lower down the mountain side. In the Rockies, elk and bighorn sheep move down below the timberline. There, in groves of trees and bushes, they find shelter from the cold and the wind.

> **vocabulary**
> **hibernate** to go into a sleeplike state during winter while living off body fat

Mountain goats, on the other hand, stay high up. They have two layers of fur to keep them warm—a soft, woolly undercoat and a longer, shaggy outercoat. In the spring and summer, they shed large clumps of these coverings and end up looking rather scraggly.

Some of the smaller animals, such as ground squirrels, survive by hibernating. They spend the summer and fall stuffing themselves with food. Then they go into their burrows and sleep. Slowly their bodies cool off until

This photo of a yellow-bellied marmot was taken in Rocky Mountain National Park in Colorado.

they are about the same temperature as the burrow, about 45°F (7°C) to 50°F (10°C). Their heartbeats and breathing rates slow way down, so their bodies can live off the stored body fat.

This mountain lion, or puma, is found in certain parts of the Rocky Mountains. This photo was taken in Montana.

The meadow vole also stays high up in the mountains, but it does so under the snow. A vole is a small animal distantly related to rats and mice. It digs a maze of tunnels under the snow and goes about its business, while the snow keeps out the wind and extreme cold. A relative of the vole is the pika. It spends the summer harvesting grass and weeds, which it piles up in nooks and crannies around its den. When the pika is hungry, it has plenty of dried food in its pantry to last out the winter.

A Gallery of Animals

In the mountains of North America, the largest meat-eating animal is the mountain lion. Also known as the puma, panther, cougar, or catamount, this animal once roamed all over the continent. Now it is hardly ever found in the lowlands. It was driven to the highlands partly by people hunting it. Also, as people built on the land, the animals that the mountain lions live on died off.

In the Andes of South America live guanacos (gwah NAH-kohz), the ancestors of the llama. As these shy animals graze, one member of the herd stands guard on higher ground. If harm threatens, the guard gives a signal and the herd flees the danger.

An Alpine dweller with a grand set of horns is the ibex. Its horns can grow as long as three feet, and it can scratch an itch on its rump with the tip of a horn. The ibex has long lived in the Alps and its image appears in cave drawings made thousands of years ago.

Mountain animals come in many sizes and shapes. The tiny wolf spider is found in the mountains of North America, while the much bigger Giant Panda makes its home in the mountains of China. Many birds such as eagles and condors soar through the thin air above the mountains of the world.

Probably the most famous animal of the Himalayas is a mythical one. Local people tell stories of attacks by a huge apelike creature called the yeti (YET ee), or the Abominable Snowman. Outsiders have never been able to find proof that there is such a creature.

The mountain-dwelling ibex sports some of the most magnificent horns of any animal.

> **W**hat **spoils my sleep** is not the strength of the enemy, but that immense mountain barrier."
>
> José de San Martín

San Martín Crosses the Andes

In the early 1800s, colonies in South America began seeking independence from Spain. One of the leaders in the fight for freedom was José de San Martín (hoh SAY de sahn mahr TEEN) of Argentina. After leading his country to independence, he knew he had to defeat the Spaniards in Peru, which was the main center of Spanish power in South America. He had one major problem, though. San Martín and his army were in Argentina, on the eastern side of the Andes. San Martín had to cross the Andes to get to Peru.

The Andes are steep and rugged and difficult to climb. Even the **passes** are high. At such elevations it is cold and windy and the air has less oxygen. People who aren't used to being so high up can become confused and sick and even die in the thinner air.

San Martín decided he and his army would cross the Andes into the country of Chile, then go by ship from Chile to Peru. The pass San Martín chose to get through the Andes between Argentina and Chile is nearly 15,000 feet high.

> **vocabulary**
> **pass** a place in the mountains that is lower than the surrounding peaks and that people use to get through the mountains

San Martín and his army set out early in 1817 with 10,600 mules, 1,600 horses, and 700 head of cattle. They also had to get all their supplies, including heavy cannons, over the mountains. The men were lucky—very few of them died. The animals were not so lucky—only 4,300 mules and 500 horses made it to Chile, and none of the cattle were left. The struggle paid off, though. The Spaniards were caught by surprise and quickly defeated. San Martín was also victorious in Peru when he went there.

Getting Over or Through Mountains

San Martín's story highlights the problems mountains pose, not just for armies but for any travelers. Nevertheless, people have managed to find ways around these difficulties. One way is by building roads that go in S-curves back and forth across the mountainside. That way, cars or trucks don't face such a steep climb all at once. More important, they don't have to wear out their brakes on the way down. Even so, traveling these mountain roads is not for the fainthearted!

If you can't go around or over a mountain, you can try going through it. How? By digging tunnels. People couldn't do that until the 1800s, though, because the machinery needed wasn't invented until then. The first tunnel used for travel was a railroad tunnel built

Switchbacks, or S-curves, make it easier for cars to climb steep mountains.

through the Alps between France and Italy. This tunnel took more than 14 years to complete. Today a tunnel for cars, buses, and trucks runs beside the railroad tunnel.

Mountain Passes

No matter whether their goal was to conquer, trade, or settle, people have looked for the lowest places—the passes and **gaps**—to get across mountains that blocked their way. Settlers in the United States followed Daniel Boone through the Cumberland Gap on his way west through the Appalachians. Farther north the Erie Canal was built in New York State through a gap in the mountains. In the West, wagon trains took the South Pass through the Rockies of Wyoming to get to the Pacific coast.

The Cumberland Gap through the Appalachians is very different from the South Pass through the Rockies. The Cumberland Gap is only about 1,600 feet above sea level. The South Pass is more than 7,500 feet high, which is higher than the tallest mountain in the Appalachians. And the pass that San Martín used to get through the Andes is higher than the highest mountain in the Rockies! All this goes to show you that even though a pass or gap is a "low" place in the mountains, in some cases *low* can be pretty *high*.

Mountains and People

Long ago, as people began to choose places to settle, most of them settled in valleys and on plains. But some people chose to settle in the mountains. Why? Perhaps they went there to escape enemies, or perhaps the beauty of the mountains attracted them. Those who settled in the mountains often have had little to do with other peoples. One such group, called the Basques (basks), settled thousands of years ago in the Pyrenees (PIHR uh neez), which are the mountains separating Spain and France. The Basques remained so cut off from other peoples that their language is entirely different from Spanish and French.

A Basque shepherd tends to his flock of sheep high in the Pyrenees.

The Indians living in the Andes Mountains in Peru and the peoples of Tibet and Nepal in the Himalayas live at very high elevations. When lowlanders go that high, they tire easily, find themselves short of breath, and get headaches. Yet the highlanders have no such problems. Why? Because over the hundreds of years that these people have lived on the high **plateaus**, their bodies have adapted to their environment. These people are usually shorter and have shorter arms, legs, and fingers. Their chests are broader and their hearts and lungs are bigger. They even have thicker blood. All these changes help keep them comfortable in the thin air and low air pressure. If mountain people go to the lowlands, their bodies have a hard time getting used to the richer air and higher pressure.

> **vocabulary**
> **plateau** a large area of high but level ground often located between mountain ranges

Mountain people often lead very difficult, rugged lives because of harsh weather and limited resources. However, these people have learned to use the limited resources around them. Many of these people are shepherds. They raise animals like goats and sheep, animals that can adapt to high places.

Mountains have had both positive and negative effects on history. On the negative side, mountains have prevented the spread of new ideas and have made it difficult for people with common interests to communicate with each other. On the positive side, mountains have often made it hard for armies trying to invade countries protected by high mountains.

When the great Carthaginian general Hannibal marched from Spain to Italy in 212 B.C., he had to cross the Pyrenees and the Alps. Hannibal began his march with about 40,000 men. By the time he reached Italy, his army was down to 26,000 men. The mountains had not prevented Hannibal from reaching Italy, but they had taken a high toll on the Carthaginian's army.

I n the 1700s a man named Jonathan Carver explored the Mississippi River. On his travels, Indians told Carver about the Shining Mountains to the west, which were covered with large crystals. Carver thought that these crystals were diamonds.

Mountains and Moisture

In fact, the crystals the Indians described to Carver weren't diamonds; they were crystals of snow that melted in the spring and fed the rivers and lakes of western America.

Most people would be disappointed if they went looking for diamonds and found water, but in the dry West, water is very important. The people of Denver, Colorado, know that very well. Their city is located at the foot of the eastern side of the Rocky Mountains and receives only about 14 inches of rain a year. That is far from enough for a large city. To solve that problem, Denver has tunneled through the Rockies to get water from the western side of the mountains.

Now you may be wondering why the western side of the mountains is wetter than the eastern side. The answer is that the easterly winds that blow in from the Pacific Ocean carry a great deal of moisture. When these winds get to the western side of the Rockies, they are forced to rise up to cross the mountains. As the air rises, it grows cooler. Since cool air can't hold as much moisture as warm air can, much of the moisture falls as rain or snow on the western side of the Rockies. By the time the winds get over the mountains, they have lost most of their moisture.

Mountains and Power

Mountain streams are valuable not only as sources of water but also as sources of power. As streams and rivers travel downhill, they sometimes form waterfalls, which can be used to make power. In the old days, people used the force of the falling water to turn water wheels that operated machinery. The machinery might be used to grind corn or power weaving machines. Today, we more often use the force of the falling water to turn huge machines called generators that make electricity.

Today, when there is no waterfall, people sometimes build a dam to hold back the water in a river. When the water behind the dam is released, it flows downstream rapidly, with at least as much force as water going over a waterfall, often much more. This running water turns huge generators in **hydroelectric plants** that make electricity. All of this may not seem to have much to do with mountains, but if you think about it you'll see the connection: none of this water power would exist if the earth were flat as a pancake.

> **vocabulary**
> **hydroelectric plant** a place that uses the force of moving water to power generators that make electricity

A large hydroelectric plant is at the base of Hoover Dam on the Nevada-Arizona border.

Minerals

It's easy to make fun of Jonathan Carver for thinking that the crystals on the slopes of the Rocky Mountains were diamonds. But in a sense he wasn't as far off as you might think. No one has ever found diamonds in the Rocky Mountains, but the Rockies are bursting with other valuable **minerals.**

After gold was discovered in the Rockies near Pikes Peak in 1858, people rushed to the area to get their share of the riches. Mining camps and towns sprang up overnight. Very few people became rich from the gold, and very little of it is left today, at least near the surface. But the gold rush did lead people to discover other minerals—silver, lead, copper, zinc, and more.

Other mountain ranges around the world also contain minerals. The Ural Mountains in Russia are rich in bauxite, zinc, silver, platinum, chrome, nickel, and tungsten. Miners dig these minerals out of the mountains and send them to nearby factories. Closer to home are the coal mines of Pennsylvania's Allegheny Mountains.

Coal from Pennsylvania's mountains played an important role in the growth of American industry in the late 1800s and early 1900s.

Farming

You might not think of mountains as a places for farming, but people manage to do it. People in the Andes raise llamas (LAH muz) and alpacas (al PAK uz), and the Himalayan people raise yaks. Some Alpine farmers herd goats on the high pastures during the summer. Others use the pastures for cattle. But cattle farming in the Alps is a risky business. A severe winter can destroy a farmer's herd.

People in the mountains also grow crops, though usually just enough for their own use. Swiss farmers raise crops in their mountain valleys. It isn't easy, though—the sides of the valleys are generally too steep for tractors. If the Swiss tried to drive tractors on the sides of the Alpine valleys, they would probably

> **vocabulary**
> **mineral** a naturally occurring chemical substance found in Earth's crust

roll down the mountain. Instead, the people use horse-drawn plows. It takes two people to do the plowing, one to lead the horse and the other to guide the plow. You can see why fewer and fewer people are farming in the Alps!

For hundreds of years the people of the Andes and the Himalayas have used **terracing** to turn mountain slopes into giant staircases, with lots of flat surfaces for growing crops. They built stone walls on the mountainsides and then filled the resulting steps with dirt. The trouble with terraces, though, is that one good mud slide or **avalanche** can wipe out all your work.

Recreation

Today mountains also attract lots of tourists. These tourists come to enjoy mountain sports like tobogganing, bobsledding, snow-boarding, and skiing.

Skiing is an ancient sport. It developed many years ago in the cold and mountainous regions of Europe and Asia. Archaeologists have found skis that they believe were made almost 5,000 years ago! These ancient skis were carved out of bones or wood.

No one knows when skis were first used in warfare, but as far back as A.D. 1200, Norwegian soldiers traveled on skis to spy on their Swedish enemies.

> **vocabulary**
> **terracing** the building of level surfaces on a mountainside
> **avalanche** the rapid downhill fall of a large amount of snow

Over the years skiing evolved from a survival tactic and military skill into a popular sport. It was introduced as an Olympic sport in 1924 and has grown more popular since then. Today, when there has not been enough snow to ski, thousands of skiers practice their sport on artificial snow made by large snow-

Downhill skiing is a favorite mountain sport in many places of the world.

making machines. There are popular ski resorts scattered throughout the Alps and the Rocky Mountains.

Mountain Climbing

People who are looking for something even more challenging than skiing can try mountain climbing. Some people enjoy a hike to the top of a small mountain; others like the challenge of trying to climb the tallest mountains in the world.

The greatest challenge of all is climbing to the peak of the world's tallest mountain, Mount Everest. For many years no human being had ever managed to make it all the way to the top. The frigid temperatures, vicious winds, sudden snowstorms, and thin mountain air combined to foil every attempt. Then, in May of 1953, a New Zealander named Sir Edmund Hillary and his guide from Nepal, Tenzing Norgay, managed to reach the top of the mountain. Later, Hillary wrote about his adventures, describing what it was like to try to sleep in a tent on the mountainside:

> The wind screeches across the ridge and sets the canvas cracking like a rifle range; an awful noise. I'm braced between Tenzing and the tent wall, no room to stretch out. Whenever my head falls back against the roof it's as if I'd run my brain into a [jackhammer].
>
> The other side of Tenzing are Alf Gregory and George Lowe, hunched up in their sleeping bags, twisting, heaving around, trying to find some position less cold and miserable. . . . I keep looking at my watch, wondering if it's stopped.

The hour hand finally creeps around to 4, and I strike a match. The thermometer on the tent wall reads: 13°F. It is still pitch dark.

Since Hillary and Norgay reached the peak in 1953, many hundreds have followed in their footsteps. Some have made it to the top and back, but many others have not. The mountain is littered with the bodies of more than a hundred people who froze to death or were overwhelmed by avalanches while trying to reach the peak.

Why do so many people risk their lives trying to climb Mount Everest and other tall mountains? Surely it is partly because human beings like to challenge themselves. But surely it is also an indication of the fascination that human beings have long felt, and continue to feel, for mountains.

A climber gazes at majestic Thamserku peak in the Mt. Everest region of Nepal. Sir Edmund Hillary and Tenzing Norgay are shown in the inset.

avalanche the rapid downhill fall of a large amount of snow

barrier something that blocks the way

extinct no longer active or living

erosion the wearing away of soil and rock by the action of wind or water

gap a low place in the mountains, often created by a river

hibernate to go into a sleeplike state during winter while living off body fat

hydroelectric plant a place that uses the force of moving water to power generators that make electricity

magma molten, or melted, rock deep beneath the earth's crust

mineral a naturally occurring chemical substance found in Earth's crust

pass a place in the mountains that is lower than the surrounding peaks and that people use to get through the mountains

plateau a large area of high but level ground, often located between mountain ranges

terracing the building of level surfaces on a mountainside

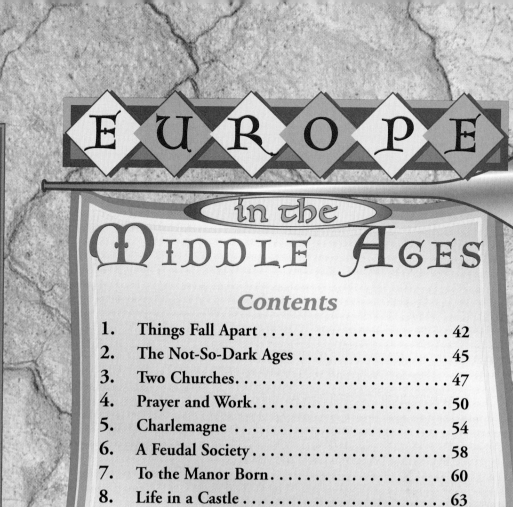

EUROPE

in the

MIDDLE AGES

Contents

Roads Lead to Rome You may have heard the expression "All roads lead to Rome." During the glory days of the Roman Empire, that saying was true. Rome was the center of the empire, and roads from all over Europe led there.

These roads allowed governors and judges to carry Roman ideas about law to the outlying regions of the empire. Messengers also traveled these roads, carrying instructions from the Roman emperor to the Roman governors. Roads allowed goods and taxes to travel from the outlying regions into Rome, too. These goods and taxes kept the powerful Roman Empire running. More important, perhaps, was that Roman soldiers used the roads to enforce the law and put down any rebellions or attacks on the empire.

The roads helped hold the Roman Empire together, but they also played a role in its eventual decline, for the Roman army was not the only army that could use these roads. The same roads that carried the Roman army out of Rome made it easier for outside invaders to march into the city. Beginning around A.D. 200, there were a number of non-Roman tribes that wanted to do just that.

At that time, Rome was still a vast and powerful empire, but it was facing some serious problems. Powerful Roman generals had been fighting each other. Each general wanted to gain enough power to become emperor. This was terrible for the health of the empire. A main purpose of the Roman government was to provide law and order so that people could conduct business and live in safety.

At its height the Roman Empire covered parts of Europe, Africa, and Asia.

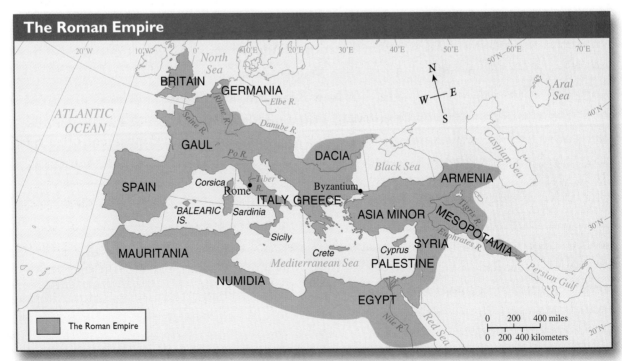

However, the wars between the generals undermined Roman law and order and interrupted business, trade, and government.

During these wars, so much money was spent on armies that Rome had less money to maintain roads and buildings. With poorer roads, trade decreased, and some of the people who had depended on trade to earn a living went out of business.

The Roman Empire grew weak enough in the 200s and 300s that it began to attract the attention of various tribes that lived on the fringes of the empire or outside its boundaries. Rome had conquered some of these tribes and had sent armies to guard the borders against others.

The Romans, who spoke Greek and Latin, looked down on these people and labeled them "barbarians." *Barbarian* was a Greek word for someone who spoke no Greek. The Romans dismissed non-Greek- and non-Latin-speaking barbarians as primitive, uncultured, and vastly inferior.

This was a classic example of something that happens all the time in history. However, many of the barbarian tribes were not uncivilized. Many tribes had skilled metalworkers who created beautiful jewelry and coins. Their languages belonged to a German language family rather than to Latin.

People on the Move

The Romans lumped a number of tribes into the barbarian category, including the Angles, the Saxons, the Huns, the Vandals, the Goths, the Ostrogoths, and the Visigoths. Several of these tribes were Germanic tribes who lived in northern Europe. The Angles and the Saxons lived in what is now Denmark and northern Germany. They eventually drove the Romans out of England. The Goths and Vandals attacked and eventually sacked the city of Rome itself. The Vandals caused so much destruction that, even today, we still use the word *vandalism* to describe acts of destruction.

However, the barbarians who left the longest memory of fear and destruction were not Germanic tribes. They were a nomadic people from central Asia called the Huns. The Huns lived on the steppes, a flat, grassy, treeless area that stretches for thousands of miles in what is now Ukraine, southern Russia, and Kazakhstan.

The Huns raised sheep, cattle, and horses on the steppes. As the seasons changed and the available grasses dried up, the tribes moved in search of new grazing lands for their livestock.

The Huns were amazing horsemen and experts with bows and arrows. They learned to ride horses as children, at the same time they learned to walk. So good was their horsemanship that one Roman historian described the Huns this way: "They are unable to put their feet on the ground. They live and sleep on their horses."

In the 300s the Huns, tired of trying to maintain themselves on the steppes, began to move westward across Europe. Due to their skill in warfare and their excellent horsemanship, the Huns easily conquered other tribes and moved onto their land.

Attila the Hun

Mysterious and terrorizing, the savage Huns struck fear into Romans and other tribes alike. But the most feared and notorious of all barbarians was Attila the Hun. For about ten years, Attila and his brother Bleda shared the throne as rulers of the Huns. But Attila wanted to rule alone—so badly that he killed his brother and became the sole king and leader of the Huns.

Attila became known as a brilliant but cruel general. He led the Huns westward, conquering other tribes and leaving devastation in his wake. The Huns crossed the Danube River and crushed a Roman army in eastern Europe. Then they invaded what is present-day France. At one point a Roman army combined with another barbarian tribe, the Visigoths, to defeat the Huns in a bloody battle in Gaul (present-day France). But that didn't stop Attila. It was to be his only defeat.

Next, Attila turned his attention on Rome itself. In 452 he blazed a path of destruction across northern Italy. In hopes of saving Rome, Pope Leo I, the bishop of Rome, rode out to meet with the feared Hun general. Most Romans thought that was the last they would see of Pope Leo. But in a dramatic face-to-face meeting, Attila thought he saw a halo around the pope's head. The cruel conqueror who feared no army was afraid of one man who seemed to have a power Attila knew nothing about. He decided to spare Rome. Soon after this meeting, Attila became sick and died. Without their leader and weakened by disease, the Huns retreated into eastern Europe.

The End of the Roman Empire

You may have heard the expression "Rome wasn't built in a day." It means that it takes a long time to accomplish a big task. It took hundreds of years before the Roman Empire reached its peak, and then it lasted for hundreds of years. At one point the Roman Empire was split into two parts—the Western Roman Empire centered in Rome and the Eastern Roman Empire ruled from Constantinople.

Finally, in 476, a German king called Odoacer (oh doh AY ser) attacked Rome and killed the emperor. Since no new emperor was named, the date 476 is accepted as the official end of the Western Roman Empire. The Eastern Roman Empire, which was not conquered, lasted for almost another thousand years.

In the next several lessons, you will read about a different way of life and government that came about in western Europe.

This painting shows Pope Leo on the left, protected by angels, meeting Attila who is on the black horse in the center.

ife as Usual Today, we usually say that the Middle Ages began in 476, when the western half of the Roman Empire collapsed. However, to the people of the time, especially those who lived outside of Rome itself in areas that are now part of France, Germany, or northern Italy, there probably wasn't any difference between life in 475 and 480.

Even though the Roman government ceased to exist, day-to-day life went on as before for most people. Many people probably did not even hear about the barbarians or the fall of Rome. And even in areas where the barbarians took over, many aspects of life remained more or less unchanged. Many of the barbarian tribes respected Roman ways, so the language and the relative positions of different types of people in society remained the same. Religions, customs, and laws did not change all of a sudden. People kept doing the things they had always done. Most people did not really care whether a Roman or a Germanic leader ruled the region they lived in, so long as law and order were preserved and they could feed themselves and their families.

Gradual Change

Over time, however, things did begin to change. Many roads and aqueducts built by the Romans to carry people, goods, and water began to fall apart. Although there were many local governments, there was now no central government with

money to fix the roads. Even if a ruler in one region decided to repair the roads that crossed his land, there was no guarantee that the roads in the next region would be any better.

Over a long time, trade dried up. During the time of the Roman Empire, there had been lively trade among the outposts in Europe and northern Africa, as well as the eastern Mediterranean regions. Those networks gradually stopped working, and around 600, it was nearly impossible to sell Europe's goods to northern Africa or to the eastern Mediterranean.

The Romans built well. This aqueduct still stands over the River Gare in France.

With the decline of trade, cities also began to shrink. Merchants who had depended on trade no longer had much to sell. The governors who had once carried out Roman laws were gone. Without stores and government offices, there were fewer places to work in the cities. Some cities got smaller. Others just disappeared entirely.

Most people survived by farming or soldiering. With no government to pay for big public buildings or ships, artisans couldn't practice their skills. Today, we have many books that explain how to do different things. In those times, when few people could read or write, skills were passed from a skilled worker to a younger worker. When the skills were no longer used and passed on, people simply forgot how to do things. People forgot how to build domes and large ships because there was simply no use for these things during this time.

The Dark Ages

Because people forgot some things that were known by the Greeks and Romans, this period from about 500 to 800 was once called the Dark Ages. You may wonder why the terms *barbarian* and *Dark Ages* were ever introduced.

There was a rivalry between the Middle Ages and the period that followed—the Renaissance. Many Renaissance scholars tended to look down on the Middle Ages and dismiss them as dark ages when there was no learning. Because many modern people admired the artists and scholars of the Renaissance, people tended to accept what the Renaissance writers said about the Middle Ages.

Today, historians present a more balanced view, admitting the shortcomings of the Middle Ages but also noting its strengths. It is true that some valuable skills were forgotten during this time. Since travel was difficult and potentially dangerous, most people tended to stay in their own areas. The Middle Ages also had its fair share of violence. However, today historians agree that the Middle Ages were probably not any more violent than the time of the Roman Empire or the Renaissance. Modern historians see these years as a time of change and growth, contributing to the rise of Western civilization in many ways.

Spreading Out

The history of western Europe in this period may seem very distant. But in the years following the fall of Rome, nations that would play important roles in European history were being created.

Remember the destructive Visigoths who sacked Rome? They continued to move westward, into present-day France. Then they crossed the Pyrenees mountains and moved into Spain and Portugal, where they settled into a life of farming. Another related tribe, the Ostrogoths, moved into central Europe, the present-day Czech Republic and Hungary. The Huns were absorbed by other ethnic groups. The Angles and Saxons moved across the sea to England, whose name comes from the Angles—"Angle-land."

History is a little like making a cake. Many ingredients go into it—and something very different comes out. In these years the tribes that brought down the Roman Empire began the process of creating a new and different Europe.

The Bishop of Rome Although the city of Rome was much smaller after the fall of the Roman Empire, it was still a city. People living in the city still needed food and other supplies.

It is very difficult for people who live in cities to grow the food they need. Food has to come from farming areas outside the city. However, now there was no one to take charge and arrange for these kinds of supplies to be brought into Rome. Who would perform those duties now?

Remember when Attila the Hun almost attacked Rome? The person who talked him out of doing that was Leo. He was the bishop of Rome. There was still an emperor at that time, but the power of the emperor was fading fast. The power of Rome's bishop, however, was growing.

The Victors Convert

The Germanic tribes had conquered the Roman lands. And yet, in a sense, these tribes had been conquered too, though not by the Roman army. The Germanic tribes were conquered by the Roman church. Remember that Rome

During a time of disease and famine, Pope Gregory I, the bishop of Rome, leads a procession to pray at St. Peter's Basilica.

was a Christian empire by 476. Nearly all the tribes who took Rome's lands eventually became Christians themselves. They took on both the religion and the customs of Rome.

In addition, many of them began to speak the language of Rome. That is why French, Italian, and Spanish, the languages spoken in southern Europe today, are called Romance languages. They are more closely related to the Latin language of Rome than they are to the Germanic languages of the people who conquered Rome.

Even though newcomers had conquered Rome, they admired what it stood for. It had been the center of the most powerful empire of their world for hundreds of years. Many Roman laws and customs, the Latin language, and the Roman religion were respected and preserved by these victorious invaders.

When there was no longer an emperor, the bishop of Rome became the most important official in the city. Pope Leo believed that his power as bishop of Rome extended far beyond the city of Rome itself. Leo said the bishop of Rome was the most important official in the Christian Church. He felt that his power extended over all other churches throughout the lands of the Roman Empire and beyond.

What reasoning did Leo use to support his claim to power? He claimed that the power of the bishop of Rome came from Jesus himself, through Saint Peter. Leo said that Jesus had chosen Peter, one of his followers, to be the head of the church after the death of Jesus. According to Christian belief, Peter left Jerusalem after Jesus was crucified and went to Rome. Leo and his supporters believed that Peter became the first bishop of Rome and that all the bishops of Rome after him were heirs to his position as head of the Christian Church.

Using this argument, Leo and other bishops of Rome who followed him claimed that the bishop of Rome was the *papa*, or father, of the Christian Church. The former Western Roman Empire was broken up into many smaller kingdoms and territories. As leader of the Church in all these regions, however, the bishop of Rome claimed power throughout Europe. Do you know what the bishop of Rome is also called today? If you said *pope*, you are right.

The Eastern Empire

There was just one problem with this idea, or, rather, there were four problems. You see, there were four other bishops who also viewed themselves as leaders of the

Christian Church. These were the bishops of Constantinople, Alexandria, Antioch, and Jerusalem. These cities were all located in the Eastern Roman Empire.

Remember how the Roman Empire was divided into two parts? One part was the Western Roman Empire, centered around Rome. The other part was the Eastern Roman Empire, also known as the Byzantine Empire. The Emperor Constantine, the first Christian emperor of the Roman Empire, in

the early 300s built a new capital at the ancient Greek city of Byzantium. He named this new capital Constantinople. While the Western Empire was weakened by internal problems and eventually destroyed by invaders, the Eastern Empire survived.

However, the Eastern Empire was much less Roman than the parts of the empire that had been conquered by the Germanic tribes. The eastern part of the empire was more Greek than Roman. Most of its people did not speak Latin or languages that were influenced by Latin. Do you think the bishops of Alexandria, Antioch, and Jerusalem would be more influenced by the bishop of Constantinople or the bishop of Rome?

If you said Constantinople, you were right. Over time the differences between the Christians in what had once been the western part of the empire and the Christians in the eastern part of the empire got stronger. There

Hagia Sophia, the Church of the Holy Wisdom, was built in the sixth century in Constantinople as the main cathedral for the Eastern Empire.

Over the centuries they had developed a very different tradition of governing the Church and its religious customs. They did, however, accept the belief that the bishop of Rome was the heir of Saint Peter.

During this time, the bishop of Rome took on more power and demanded that the eastern bishops accept his authority. In 1054 the differences came to a head between the bishops of Rome and Constantinople. After some major disagreements, the two churches separated.

Two Separate Churches

Christian bishops in the Eastern Empire, including Bulgarians, Serbs, Russians, Syrians, and Egyptians, chose to join with the bishop of Constantinople. People on both sides of this argument expected that the division between the two parts of the Church was just temporary.

Over time, however, the two sides did not get back together. In fact, they found more reasons to disagree. Today, the church that is headed by the bishop of Rome (the pope) is known as the Roman Catholic Church. The church in the region that was ruled by Constantinople (now Istanbul, Turkey) is generally known as the Eastern Orthodox Church. In the rest of this unit, we will study mostly the lands of the Western Church.

had always been some differences, of course. Even though both groups were Christians, they spoke different languages and had different cultures. More and more disagreements sprang up between the two groups. Some of these disagreements may seem trivial today, but they were passionately debated in the Middle Ages. For example, Christians in the former Western Empire used flat bread made without yeast in their holy ceremonies. Christians in the Eastern Empire used bread made with yeast in their holy ceremonies.

More important than such issues was the larger issue of who was in charge of the Church. Bishops in the Eastern Empire did not like accepting the rule of the bishop of Rome as the final word on all Church matters. They were used to ruling in a more cooperative manner, in which each bishop had a vote.

Saint Benedict of Nursia Just about the time of the fall of the Western Roman Empire, a boy named Bennet was born in the mountain village of Nursia, northeast of Rome. He was a very serious child who thought a lot about right and wrong. He was described as having "the mind of an old man" in a young man's body.

Bennet's parents sent him to Rome to study, but he was upset by the sinfulness he saw around him. Bennet was shocked by the lying, cheating, and dishonesty he saw in the city. He left Rome and decided to live as a monk, devoting himself to a religious life. At that time there were many monks in Asia, but there were very few of them in Europe.

The European monks who did exist lived isolated from the world as hermits, denying themselves the comforts of life for religious reasons. Many of them did things that were harsh and painful to themselves, like going without food or living in a cave for years on end. That is what Bennet did at first. He spent three years living in a cave.

Benedict's good works and holiness made him one of the important saints of the Catholic Church.

Eventually, Bennet, now called Benedict, decided that it was not enough to pray in a cave. He believed that monks should serve God and people. Benedict's years in a cave spread his fame as a holy man. A group of rich monks invited him to become the leader of a **monastery**. Benedict accepted, but things did not go very well. When Benedict tried to get them to serve God by helping other people, they refused. It got so bad that the other monks even tried to poison Benedict.

Benedict saw that to realize his bold new ideas he would have to start his own monastery. He moved to the town of Monte Cassino and wrote a book that is known today as *The Rule of Saint Benedict*. This book contained a list of rules to be enforced in the monastery. Instead of urging people to seek holiness through pain or fasting—going without food and water—Benedict urged monks to find God in ordinary, simple, and useful work. Work was balanced with prayer and reading, sleeping, and eating. He also emphasized the importance of working with and getting along with everyone in the monastery, especially those who were annoying or difficult to get along with. He felt that finding the ability to see Christ in everyone was the path to God.

> **vocabulary**
> **monastery** a community of monks

Monte Cassino was destroyed during World War II and has been rebuilt.

Self-Sufficient and Hard-Working

Monte Cassino was a successful monastery, and Benedict's fame spread. Soon other monasteries were created to follow his rules.

Monasteries following Saint Benedict's rules were called Benedictine monasteries. These monasteries tried to be self-sufficient. That means that the monks grew and made almost everything they needed themselves. They had gardens in which they raised their own vegetables. They kept chickens and goats to provide eggs and milk that they used to make cheese. They also baked all their own bread, sewed their own clothing, brewed beers, and made wines.

Does it seem strange that deeply religious people made beer and wine to drink? This is a good example of how customs change over time. In the Middle Ages almost everyone drank small amounts of beer every day. Beer was considered a healthy drink because of the grains used to make it. There was just one meal a day, with a cold snack in the evening. Meals consisted of bread with eggs, cheese, or fish. The monks ate at assigned places. There was no conversation during the meals, but one monk read aloud from the Scriptures or a religious book.

Benedict also required monks to follow a shared schedule. When the bell rang for prayer, everyone in the monastery stopped whatever he was doing and went to the chapel.

A day in the monastery was divided into three general work periods. Monks spent about six hours in prayer, six hours doing manual work such as gardening, cooking, or sewing. And around four hours were spent in studying and writing. Monks slept seven to eight hours a night. Saint Benedict's rules are interesting to read in today's busy times. Monks worked hard and were productive, but they also lived healthy, balanced lives.

The **abbot** made the rules in the monastery, and all monks had to obey him. Monks were required to show hospitality to all guests, whether invited or not, and to treat all the monastery's possessions—whether gardening tools or precious altar pieces—with care and reverence.

Missionaries, Hospitals, Schools, and Libraries

The Rule of Saint Benedict had a great influence not only on Benedictine monasteries but also on other types of monasteries that developed later on, as well as on **convents**. Altogether these religious institutions had a great impact on the history of Europe.

Monasteries took on the role of supplying missionaries to bring Christianity to people who followed older non-Christian religions. Saint Benedict himself spread Christianity in the area around Monte Cassino. One of the most famous missionaries was Saint Patrick, who brought the Christian religion to Ireland. Saint Augustine, another famous missionary, brought Christianity to the Anglo-Saxons of Britain. Saint Boniface converted many of the tribes in what is now Germany.

Saint Benedict also saw the role of the monastery as helping the poor. During this time, government provided no help for poor people. What help was provided came from the Church, from priests, monks, and nuns who saw caring for the poor as their Christian duty.

Monks and nuns also ran hospitals for the sick who were too poor to hire their own doctors, and schools for children training to become monks and nuns.

One of the most important things that monasteries and convents did for Europe was to set up libraries. In the early Middle Ages,

books were rare and expensive. Every book that existed had been written or copied by hand! Although there were important Islamic libraries in Asia and Africa, in Europe almost all the libraries that existed were in monasteries.

Most people in Europe had little need for reading. Some went their whole lives without ever seeing a book. Information was passed along several ways. Most people learned by watching and doing. Children would watch their parents make things, take care of animals, and farm. Once they learned to do these things, they would get married, have children, and pass these skills on to their children. For more skilled crafts, such as shoemaking, barrel making, and others, young men would work alongside master craftspersons and learn the craft.

> **vocabulary**
> **abbot** the leader of a monastery
> **convent** a community of nuns, or women who devote themselves to religious life

Few people learned how to do things from reading books. People learned about the Bible from listening to a priest, monk, or nun. For the most part, the only people who knew how to read were priests, monks, and nuns. There was no mystery to this. Practically the only schools that existed were religious schools. And most of the students there were in training for a religious career.

Reading was an important activity in many monasteries and convents, but few people sat and read silently to themselves. Most of the time one person would read aloud to a group. If people wanted to make an oath, it was considered more important to say it out loud than to write it down and sign it. The ability to read and write was so unusual and so highly valued that many people believed that it was a special gift from God to the servants of God. Even those of us who read well today would have had trouble reading manuscripts from the early Middle Ages, though. Practically all of them were written in Latin, and the writing was hard to follow.

Even after the fall of the Roman Empire, the Latin language that had been used in the empire remained the official written language in Europe. Any document that had religious, legal, or scholarly significance was written in Latin.

In the early Middle Ages (and also in ancient Rome), reading was difficult because words were not separated or punctuated.

NOWONDERITWASHARDFORME
DIEVALPEOPLETOREADTHEYDIDNOT
HAVECOMMASPERIODSORSPACES
BETWEENWORDS

Imagine reading a whole book that way! That was why around the year 800 monks began to put spaces between words, mark the end of sentences, and invent the small letters we use today.

Monks worked to copy the texts of books that did exist. Most of the books they copied were longer than the book you are reading now. Think of how long it would take you to copy every word in this book by hand. Monks didn't just copy the words, either. They also decorated the important first letters and borders of their manuscripts. Maybe you can see now why books were so rare and expensive. Think of how long it would have taken to make one! Today, these handwritten books from the Middle Ages are considered valuable works of art.

Monasteries still exist in the modern world, and monks and nuns continue the work they have done for more than a thousand years. Today, however, there are thousands of schools, universities, hospitals, and libraries all over the world. That is why it may be hard to imagine how important the work of the Benedictine monasteries was to the lives of Europeans. For many centuries, the monks and nuns were the teachers, writers, librarians, book publishers, doctors, and nurses for all of Europe.

Knowledge was kept alive by monks who would spend enormous amounts of time copying books for monastery libraries.

**Head Above the Others** Monks and monasteries spread Christianity through much of what was Europe. In the late 700s, however, one man would come along who was not a monk but who would do more than any other person to spread Christianity and strengthen the Western Church.

That man was Charles, the king of the Franks. The Franks were a tribe that lived along the Rhine River in present-day Germany. Charles was not just the king. He might have been the tallest man in his kingdom. Charles was 6 feet 3 1/2 inches tall. (We know that because his bones have been measured.) Even by today's standards, that is tall. But in the 700s, when Europeans were much shorter than people in Europe or the United States today, it was really tall. Charles towered about a head above everyone else.

Charles was not only tall but was healthy and energetic as well. He followed health advice you've probably heard all your life! He ate healthy foods, exercised every day (he loved to swim), and got plenty of rest (he took a nap every day). He was a hard worker, too. He started having meetings the minute he got out of bed, before he had finished dressing. His advisors would come into his bedroom and ask him questions.

Charles's greatest talent was organizing and managing people. He knew how to inspire armies to fight, and he also knew how to move them quickly from one place to another. This was an important skill for a leader in a time when there were no reliable maps. He didn't give up, either. Once he started something, he finished it and he expected the same of his men.

Charles enjoyed being king. Like most rulers, he enjoyed the power of ruling. But unlike some kings, he had goals beyond gaining power for himself. He wanted to spread Christianity, and he wanted to foster learning and culture. These noble goals and Charles's ability to make them happen

This gold and jewel-encrusted statue is a symbol of the importance of Charlemagne as a ruler.

combined to make him one of the greatest rulers Europe had ever known. Charles became so great that "great" became part of his name. By the time he died, people were calling him *Charlemagne* (SHAHR luh mayn), which means Charles the Great, and that is what historians today call him.

To the Rescue

The Frankish army was an impressive sight. Strong and disciplined, they wore leather vests and light armor. Their most important weapons were their swords, and Frankish soldiers treated their swords with care. Many of them had scabbards, a case for a sword, decorated with silver, gold, and even jewels.

The Frankish army was very successful in battle. These strong soldiers with their glittering weapons conquered much of the territory that had once been part of the Western Roman Empire. The Muslims (called Moors by Europeans) controlled central Spain, but Charlemagne took parts of northern Spain, as well as most of what is now France, Germany, Switzerland, Holland, Belgium, and Luxembourg and united them into a Frankish empire. He also took northern Italy from the Lombards, a Germanic tribe.

In an earlier lesson you read about how the bishop of Rome, also known as the pope, was trying to exert more leadership after the fall of the Western Roman Empire and that the bishops of Constantinople, Alexandria, Antioch, and Jerusalem didn't like that very much. But Pope Leo III had enemies closer to home. Powerful princes from the lands around Rome grew jealous of the Church's wealth and power. The pope's enemies actually attacked him as he was walking through the streets of Rome! They pushed him to the ground, pulled off his robes, and beat him up. He woke up covered with cuts and bruises.

The pope fled from Rome and appealed to Charlemagne for help. Charlemagne did not let the pope down. He sent an army to escort the pope back to Rome, where his soldiers punished the pope's enemies.

The following year, Charlemagne went to Rome for two purposes. He wanted to make sure the pope was safe from any more attacks, and he wanted to celebrate Christmas with the pope. It was A.D. 800, the beginning of a new century, a special year, and Charlemagne wanted to celebrate it with the pope in St. Peter's Church.

Emperor of the Romans

The celebration proved to be much more special than Charlemagne had dreamed possible. According to Charlemagne's biographer Einhard, Charlemagne prepared for a traditional Christmas mass. He planned to wear his usual Frankish clothing, but the pope asked him to wear a Roman toga and sandals instead. Out of respect for the pope, Charlemagne agreed. When he arrived at the cathedral, he found it packed with people from all over his kingdom. Romans, Franks, Bavarians, Greeks, Lombards, and Anglo-Saxons were gathered there. Even Charlemagne's children were there.

When Charlemagne reached the front of the cathedral, he knelt in prayer. After a long time he stood up, and the pope placed a crown on Charlemagne's head. The people in the Church broke out in a cheer. "Long life and victory to Charles Augustus, crowned by God, great and peaceful emperor of the Romans," they cried.

Reading this today, it is hard to believe that Charlemagne was totally surprised by being crowned by the pope. But that's the story that has come down through the ages.

The crowning of Charlemagne as emperor accomplished three things. It gave the Romans an emperor for the first time since 476, it gave Charlemagne the blessing of the pope, and it established that Charlemagne agreed that the pope had the power to crown an emperor.

A Great Ruler

Charlemagne expanded his kingdom through warfare. However, what made him great wasn't what he did on the battlefield but was what he did with his kingdom after he won it.

Charlemagne built a beautiful capital city, Aachen (AH ken), in what is now northwestern Germany. He built a palace and a chapel. He also had a great library. He even built a huge swimming pool out of marble. The pool was filled with water from natural hot springs and was big enough for 100 people to swim in at once. He started a school in his palace and allowed the sons of poor people to attend as well as the children of nobles. Charlemagne believed that women should be educated as well as men, an unusual view for his time. He even tried to provide free education to all his subjects.

Charlemagne was a good manager in times of peace as well as in war. He improved communication and management throughout his empire. He sent teams of ambassadors chosen for their good character to enforce laws and solve conflicts in the kingdom. Like the Romans, he built roads and bridges to make trade and travel easier.

When Charlemagne first began conquering the Saxons and other tribes, he tried to force them to become Christians. At first his rule was very harsh. People who would not convert to Christianity were killed. Later in his life, however, Charlemagne realized that force was not the best way to win souls. By the 790s he allowed his conquered subjects to make their own choices about Christianity. He also rewrote many laws to make them fairer.

In 800, Pope Leo III crowned Charlemagne emperor of the Romans.

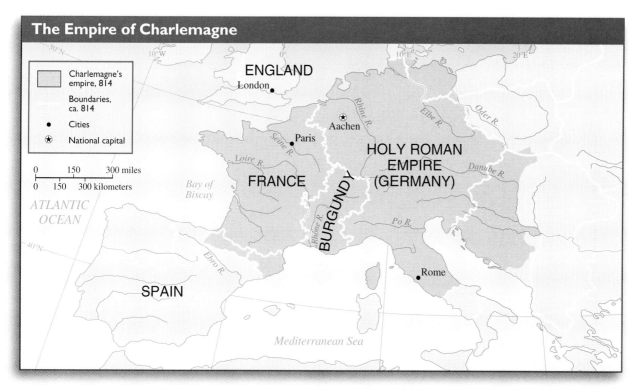

The Empire of Charlemagne

Charlemagne's empire, 814

Boundaries, ca. 814

• Cities

✪ National capital

0   150   300 miles
0   150   300 kilometers

ENGLAND
London

ATLANTIC OCEAN

Aachen ✪
Paris •
Seine R.
Loire R.
FRANCE
Bay of Biscay
Rhine R.
BURGUNDY
Rhône R.

HOLY ROMAN EMPIRE (GERMANY)
Elbe R.
Oder R.
Danube R.
Po R.

Rome •

Ebro R.
SPAIN

Mediterranean Sea

Charlemagne ruled a vast area that included many different people.

Charlemagne died in 814. None of the rulers who followed had his gift for leadership. The empire that Charlemagne created did not last. However, it set a new standard for learning and management. It brought the people of many tribes together and helped form some of the modern countries of Europe.

The Franks originally spoke an early form of German. By the time of Charlemagne's death, however, many Franks were speaking a new language that was influenced by Latin. This language became known (to English speakers) as French and the country where it is spoken as France. Over the next 200 or 300 years, the French-speaking part of Charlemagne's empire broke away to form the kingdom of France.

The Holy Roman Empire

Charlemagne's empire continued in various forms for centuries. Part of it was expanding toward the east. It still included Rome, however, and there was a strong alliance between the pope and the rulers of this German-speaking empire.

In the 1200s the Hapsburg family took power over this German empire. It was at this point that it became known as the Holy Roman Empire, having been blessed by the pope. This empire now included the areas that are today Germany, Holland, Belgium, Switzerland, Luxembourg, Austria, the Czech Republic, western Poland, northern Italy, and eastern France. It stretched roughly from the North Sea and Baltic Sea in the north to the Mediterranean in the south and from the Rhone River in the west to beyond the Oder River in the east.

New Society Who do you think is the most important person in your town? In every society there are certain people who are more important and more powerful than others. In the United States today, power and importance often come with money, some special abilities, or elected office.

In the Middle Ages there were no political elections and few offices that one could get by having special abilities. Money didn't make you important in the same way it can today. The important people in the Middle Ages were those who controlled land, especially the kings and the lords and knights who fought for the kings.

With the end of the Roman Empire, everyday life for most people continued much the same. But the nobles—the important people of the Roman Empire—lost some power. Powerful soldiers who conquered Germanic tribes were awarded more power. These warriors became the new nobility of a new society that continued for more than a thousand years. The system that developed around these new leaders is usually called **feudalism**.

A Special System

Feudalism appeared first in France after Charlemagne's time, and later it spread to some other medieval kingdoms. It arose because kings needed warriors to fight for them and therefore made deals with powerful fighters. The fighter (or lord, as he was now known) would become the king's **vassal**. The king would give him a large amount of land, called a **fief,** and each would make certain promises to the other. The vassal would swear to fight loyally for the king; the king pledged to protect and be loyal to the vassal.

Feudal government was not like modern government. During the Middle Ages there were no

vocabulary
feudalism a system of government in which land is exchanged for loyalty and services
vassal a person who receives land from a ruler and in return promises aid
fief a plot of land exchanged for loyalty to a ruler

The feudal system was based on the relationship between the lord, who could be the king, and his vassals.

nations in the modern sense—no central governments with bureaus, branches, and departments. There were only networks of lords and vassals under the supervision of a king. However, the oaths that vassals swore held these networks together. The interlocking links between vassals and lords encouraged people to think of themselves as part of a larger whole. Eventually, some of these networks of lords and vassals evolved into modern European nations.

A feudal agreement was meant to be a long-term arrangement. In the Middle Ages it was arranged by kings and priests and sealed in a church. The ceremony in which a man became a vassal was called an act of homage (HAHM ihj). *Homage* is the French word for "honor" or "respect." Let's time-travel back to the Middle Ages and watch as a medieval lord pays homage to a king.

"Kiss of Peace"

Imagine we are in a cathedral lit by hundreds of flickering candles. There are beautiful windows of stained glass and paintings and sculptures. The altar is made of beautifully carved wood. Sitting in the cathedral are all the great lords of the kingdom and their families dressed in their finest robes and jewels. At the front stands the king, waiting to receive his vassal.

A lord walks slowly down the center aisle of the cathedral. When he reaches the king, he falls to his knees and recites an oath that might have sounded something like this:

> Lord, I become your man. From this day forth, I will love what you love and loathe what you loathe, and never by word or deed will I do anything that will grieve you.

Then, the king raises the kneeling man to his feet and announces that he was bestowing land upon the lord in exchange for an eternal vow of loyalty and other services. The king kisses his new vassal on the cheek in a "kiss of peace."

What made feudalism work was that it was not limited to the king and his lords. The king's lords would divide up part of their land and grant fiefs to vassals of their own. The king's vassal might rule a large area called a duchy or a county. That made his title duke or count. The dukes and counts would grant portions of their to land lesser lords and to other soldiers called **knights**.

Feudal Government

Feudal loyalties usually preserved law and order within a kingdom, but there were few laws across kingdoms. Individual lords made their own laws and enforced them in their own fiefs. The one law that extended across

> **vocabulary**
> **knight** a military servant of a feudal king or other superior

Europe was the sacred oath of loyalty that a vassal took. If a vassal failed to serve his lord or betrayed his lord, he became an outlaw, shunned and persecuted by other lords.

Over the years these titles and arrangements became hereditary—they were handed down from father to son. The families who held fiefs became the nobility of central and western Europe in the Middle Ages. As nobles they had special privileges that other people did not have. In the next several lessons, you will read how feudalism provided a way for people to make a living and how it also created its own culture of knights, battles, and honor that is still remembered today.

Self-sufficient Village You might be wondering what happened to the land that the vassals received from their lords. You probably know enough about dukes and counts and other nobles to know that they weren't likely to be out milking cows and planting crops.

On the other hand there were plenty of people living during the Middle Ages who needed to eat but who did not receive fiefs from a king.

In much of northern Europe, each lord lived in a castle or **manor** house, surrounded by the land on which food was grown and where the people who worked in the fields lived. The manor estate was a lot like a village. Nearly everything that people needed was grown or made there. In addition to their food, people who lived on the estate made their own soap, candles, furniture, leather, tools, and cloth. Most of the people who lived on the estate farmed, but there were a few specialists, like blacksmiths who made things out of metal.

In addition to the manor house and cottages of people who lived on the estate, you would probably also find a church building on a manor estate. Sunday worship, baptisms, weddings, and funerals were conducted there. Next to the church there would probably be a graveyard where people from the estate were buried when they died.

Exchanging Labor for Land

The lord of the manor allowed **serfs**, farmers who were bound to the lord's land, to use his land. The serfs grew food on the land, raised animals that grazed on the land, and used the wood from the forests. The lord also

provided a mill to grind the grain grown on the manor, large community ovens for baking the grain into bread, costly equipment like plows and wagons, and teams of oxen to pull the plows and wagons.

vocabulary
manor the estate over which a lord had control; also the lord's house on an estate
serf a farmworker who was bound to live and labor on his lord's land

Manor

Pasture

Worksh[op]

Serfs' Houses

Barn

Third Field

The lord of the manor had other responsibilities. The lord provided the serfs with law and order and protection. The lord could spare a serf for stealing if he felt like it. Or he could punish him severely. The lord was limited in these matters by the law of the church. In other words, he could not punish or kill someone without a reason.

The lord also protected the people who lived on the manor. If an enemy were to attack, the lord's army would protect his people. The lord did not provide these important services without getting a lot from the serfs in return. The serfs had to spend about three days a week working in the fields that grew food for the lord of the manor and his household. During certain times of the year, like the planting and the harvesting seasons, the amount of work required could be increased.

A manor house, a church, and a mill were all part of a typical village of the Middle Ages.

Serfs also had to give part of everything they grew for themselves to the lord of the manor. They had to give the lord a portion of all the milk they got from their goats and cows and of the eggs they got from their chickens. If they collected firewood in the forest, they had to give some of it to him, and if they used the lord's mill to grind their grain into flour, they had to give the lord some of that as well.

In addition, the serfs had to provide other services to the lord. For example, the serfs had to keep the walls of the lord's manor repaired. If heavy barrels needed to be stacked or moved, the serfs had to do it. If war broke out, serfs had to help defend the lord's land. If the lord had guests, serfs might have work in the stables taking care of the extra horses or in the kitchen to help prepare the food. This meant the serfs had little time for their regular chores.

You might wonder why serfs would agree to give the lord so much. The answer is that they had little choice. In the Middle Ages, power determined who ruled. The lords had all the power. They had the weapons and the knowledge of how to rule. The times were violent, and no peasant family could survive without some lord's protection. The Church supported the feudal arrangements, so almost everybody went along with them. As you might guess, serfs did not have easy lives. They had to work very hard just to get enough to feed their families.

The Three-Field System

Despite all this hard work, there was not always enough food for all the people who worked the land and their families. The soil in England and the parts of Europe north of the Alps was rich, but the growing season was short and rainy. People had to make the most of what they had.

In the Middle Ages, people had little of the scientific knowledge we have today. But they did know something about farming. Working in the fields every day, people learned that if a field was farmed year after year, it lost its ability to grow healthy crops. They came up with a solution to that problem: the three-field system. In this system, all the cropland on an estate was divided into three parts. Each year, one part was planted in the spring, one part was planted in the fall, and one part was left fallow, or unplanted. Thus a particular field would be used differently in different years. One year it might be used to grow crops planted in the spring, like wheat and rye. The next year, it would be used to grow crops planted in the fall, like oats, barley, and beans. The third year the field would be left fallow. This gave the soil a chance to recover.

The three-field system allowed the soil to keep renewing itself. The crops that were planted in the spring used different nutrients than those that were planted in the fall.

A lord of the manor instructs the workers in his gardens. Note the differences in the clothing of the lord and the serfs.

The fields that were fallow had a chance to recover nutrients as old matter broke down and replenished the soil.

Cooperation Was the Key

People on a manor estate had to cooperate with one another. They lived closely together. They had to share pastureland. They had to cooperate about when to plant wheat and oats and when to leave fields fallow. People cooperated to create goods for trade. Certain things were not available on a European manor estate, like salt and iron, so everyone had to cooperate to trade for it.

Cooperation was essential to survival. It wasn't just voluntary. A smart lord took care of his serfs and tried to keep them happy. Yet the lord was always the boss. In the society of the Middle Ages, he was superior to the serfs—and no one questioned that.

The residents of the manor came together for special holidays. Christmas and Easter and many other religious holidays were celebrated together. The lord, his family, and serfs would attend church together. There would be a feast, games, and celebrations for holidays during the year. In this way, serfs and their lord formed a community that endured through the centuries of the Middle Ages.

**astles: Dream and Reality** You've probably heard fairy tales about kings and queens and castles. There's always something magical going on in fairy tales. Wizards, witches, and fairy godmothers are likely to be hanging around the castle casting and breaking spells.

Castles are real, however, even if some of the characters in these stories are not. Even today you can see castles all over England, Spain, France, Germany, Portugal, and other parts of Europe. In this lesson you'll learn why people built castles and what it was like to live in one.

Castle Fortress

Castles were fortresses. Lords built castles to defend themselves and their manors against attacks. The forts were usually built on high ground. This way the defenders could look down on the attacking enemy. In the early Middle Ages, people built forts out of wood. A big ditch called a moat was built surrounding the wooden fence.

If you were attacking such a fort, what would you do? If you answered "Burn it!" you would have made a good general in the Middle Ages. Wooden castles were easy to build, but they provided no protection against flaming arrows.

Lords realized they needed to build castles out of stone to get any real protection from invaders. So that is what they did. It was certainly a lot more work. But by the year 1000 stone castles were spreading across Europe.

What did a stone castle look like? What was it like to live and fight in one? Read on and find out!

Castle Construction

Put yourself in the place of a lord in the Middle Ages. You need to build a castle. What's the first thing you're going to think about? If you answered "location," you get an "A" for good thinking.

A castle needed to be in a place that would be easy to defend. Ever wonder why so many castles are built on hilltops? A hilltop was easy to defend. Soldiers could see their enemies coming. The enemies had to get up the hill while soldiers looked on them from above. Castles had high watchtowers for spotting approaching enemies.

Most castles were surrounded by tall walls and a water-filled moat. Some castles had more than one moat and more than one wall. Drawbridges could be lowered or raised to create or remove a roadway over the moat. These extra walls and moats provided additional lines of defense. Some castles also had underground tunnels for moving soldiers between different parts of the castle. On top of the walls there would usually be walkways from which soldiers could fire arrows or dump boulders and hot oil down on the attacking enemy.

The center of the castle was called the keep. Some of the area in a castle's keep was open courtyard; other areas were covered to provide protected living and working space.

The keep was built to hold out for a long time against an enemy who surrounded the castle. In the keep there were stables, workshops, a large oven, and a kitchen.

There was a well for water and stalls for farm animals. There were storerooms where grains and other foods were kept as well. These stores were not unlimited, however. Many people—nobles, servants, and soldiers—lived inside a castle. Eventually, all the grain would be used up. The chickens would stop laying eggs, the cows would stop giving milk, and all the pigs would have been eaten. Still, people could survive behind a castle's walls for many months.

Castles in War

Castles were strong forts; but well-armed, patient attackers could take a castle. Attackers dug tunnels under the stone walls. Then they stuffed the tunnels with gunpowder and set them on fire, causing the walls to collapse.

Since castles were so strong, direct attack rarely worked. Most attackers relied on siege, or blockade, to win the battle. In a siege an attacking army would surround the castle so that no food, weapons, or supplies could reach the people inside. Castles were prepared

for sieges. But after weeks they would use up their supplies. Only then would the attackers attempt to take the castle, since the defenders were weak from hunger.

Attackers used siege towers, tall wooden towers that rolled on wheels and could hold soldiers. These towers were rolled up to the castle walls. Soldiers inside the tower climbed up the tower and over the castle walls.

The battering ram was another method used by attackers. Many soldiers were required to hold up a huge log that was banged against the heavy, ironclad castle doors until the doors broke open. Battering down the door was difficult. Castle doors were strong. And the men holding up the battering ram were under constant attack from defenders high on the castle walls.

Attackers also shot flaming arrows into the keep. The walls may have been stone, but castles still had buildings made out of wood, plus hay in the stables, and other items that could catch fire.

Still, a castle was a strong fortress. A small army could hold out against a much larger force.

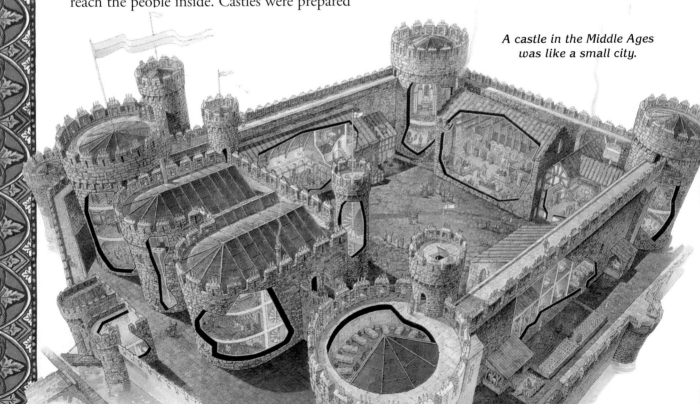

A castle in the Middle Ages was like a small city.

Sometimes, what decided the battle was action outside the castle. A lord under siege would try to get word to other vassals to come to his aid. An army surrounding the castle had to be prepared to fight both the castle troops and another army.

Life in a Castle

Castles were very expensive to build, but that doesn't mean that they were nice to live in. In fact, living in an early castle was more like living in a cave than in a mansion. Castles were usually cold, drafty, and dirty places.

Many people lived in the castle, but few of them had their own rooms or apartments. Most people lived and ate in the Great Hall, the largest inside room in the castle. In early castles the lord and lady might have had a bed in a corner of the hall. Everyone else slept on the floor, often piling any clothes they happened to have under and over themselves for warmth.

The Great Hall was also used for meals. Again, the lord and lady would probably have had chairs to sit in, but everyone else would have sat on long benches alongside tables. After everyone had eaten, the tables were put aside to provide room to sleep. Some early halls did not even have fireplaces. An open fire was built in a stone hearth in the center of the room. You can see why it was a lot like camping in a cave!

It was hard to keep these castles clean. Dogs were allowed to run free in the Great

A rich lord might hire a jester, also called a fool, to entertain his guests by telling funny stories.

Hall. There were no flush toilets, just closets built into the edges of walls. Wastes fell into pits or moats along the outside of the castle. Lords and ladies occasionally took baths and washed their hands, but servants did not have many chances to wash.

Over time, castles did become more comfortable, especially for the nobles who lived in them. Fireplaces were added. More people had beds and their own bedrooms. Cold stone walls were hung with tapestries or even paneled with wood to cut down on drafts.

The Great Hall was still a center of activity, though. Musical performers, storytellers, and jugglers entertained people while they ate and after dinner, especially during the winter when it got dark early and the only light in the castle might come from the fire in the Great Hall.

Castles were so well built that many still stand nearly a thousand years after they were built. Castle building changed along with weapons and warfare during the Middle Ages. During the early Middle Ages, foot soldiers used bows and arrows as their main weapons. You can see how thick castle walls would be a good defense against the bow and arrow. But toward the end of the Middle Ages, the use of cannons in battle made it easier to break down a castle's walls. The coming of the cannon brought the great age of the castle to an end.

Knight in Shining Armor Close your eyes. Imagine a column of knights on horseback marching out across the drawbridge of a castle to fight a distant enemy. It's a bright sunny day, and the sunshine glints off their armor, creating a dazzling sight.

Mounted knights were important figures in the Middle Ages. In military terms an army of knights could turn the tide of any battle. And knights were also important figures influencing the songs and stories of the Middle Ages.

How did one become a knight? What was a knight's training like? What did knights do when they weren't fighting battles? Read on and find out.

Pages and Squires

Most knights were the sons of noblemen. They began training to become knights when they were even younger than you are now. By the time a lord's son was seven or eight years old, he would be sent away from the castle or manor to live with a relative, such as an uncle, or with his father's overlord—the person who had granted his father a fief. Why was he sent away?

It was here, in his new home, that the young boy started his training as a knight. In the first stage of training, the young boy served as a pageboy. A pageboy had to wait on tables and learn the manners of a nobleman. Most important, the pageboy was required always to be courteous to those of higher rank. Pages practiced their riding skills and fighting with toy swords. A knight had to know how to fight when tired and in pain, so pages practiced until they were exhausted.

When a page was about 12, he would become a squire. A squire was a personal servant to a particular knight. He went everywhere with the knight, cleaned the knight's armor and weapons, and cared for his horse. One of his most important jobs was helping the knight into his armor!

Becoming a Knight

Depending on his rank, the squire might be knighted any time between the ages of 16 and 20. Often a young man of high rank was knighted at an earlier age. Normally, a young man was knighted in a solemn ceremony. He stayed up all night, praying that he would be a worthy knight. Then he would be presented with spurs, a sword, a shield, and a helmet. His sponsor, usually the lord who had taken him in as a page, would tap him lightly on the shoulder with a sword and dub him Sir Something-or-Other.

During wartime the ceremony might not be so elaborate. There would be no time to stay up all night and pray. A young man simply might be handed a helmet and a sword, be tapped on the shoulder by a higher-ranking man, and sent into battle.

Not all knights were born into noble families. The rank of knight was one of the only positions of nobility that a poor man could hope to attain. Since nobles were usually desperate for good fighting men, a soldier who showed bravery in battle would occasionally be made a knight as a reward.

Life of a Knight

An armored knight on horseback was a great fighting machine. Arrows from enemy archers could bounce harmlessly off the steel plates. The armor also protected him from an enemy knight's sword and lance, a long wooden, metal-tipped pole.

In the early Middle Ages, armor was made of sheets of chain mail—metal rings—reinforced with plates of steel in key areas. A shirt of chain weighed about 25 pounds. Under the mail, the knight wore a shell of thick, hard leather.

By 1400, chain mail was replaced by hinged and fitted steel plates that covered a knight from head to foot. A suit of armor could weigh as much as 65 pounds. It was not easy to move around in these metal suits. That's why knights needed help getting into the saddle by their squires. But learning to move quickly in armor was a skill that knights had to learn if they were going to survive. On horseback, a knight was a dangerous soldier. If a knight fell off his horse, however, he was a sitting duck, unable to stand up quickly without help. After a fierce battle, a knight would sometimes need the help of a blacksmith to get his dented helmet off his head.

Tournaments and Chivalry

Knights had to stay in shape to face the challenges of battle. During peacetime, knights held **tournaments**.

A tournament was a festive time for everyone on the lord's manor. Colorful banners would blow in the breeze on the tournament grounds. Knights painted colorful and complex designs on shields and banners to identify themselves and their families. A tournament would often attract knights and guests from surrounding castles. Lords and ladies wore their finest robes as they watched their favorite knights charge toward each other on horseback. The goal of the competition was to use a lance to knock the opposing knight off his horse. This was called jousting. Nobles and serfs alike would bet money on their favorite knight to win the competition.

> **vocabulary**
> **tournament** a staged battle fought by knights for money and honor without the intention to wound or kill

Tournaments were staged battles where knights could show how skillful they were.

Men of Honor

In the early Middle Ages, some knights could be a problem for their lords. After all, they were armed, violent men who settled arguments with their swords. They were the lord's vassals, and their job was to protect the lord from his enemies. But often lords felt threatened by their own knights.

To control the knights and their dangerous behavior, lords created a set of rules that knights should follow. These rules were called the **Code of Chivalry**. Knights were supposed to be generous, courteous, loyal, and honorable.

The Code of Chivalry required knights to follow certain rules of fighting. If a knight surrendered, he couldn't try to escape. He had to fight fairly. He could not cheat.

Chivalry also required knights to be courteous to women. A part of the code called for knights to show courtly love to a lady. A knight would pledge his honor to a lady and would perform acts of bravery to win her approval. The knight called himself his lady's vassal, placing himself below her just as a vassal placed himself below a lord. A knight who fought in a tournament would often tie his lady's scarf to his helmet to show that he was fighting on her behalf.

People loved to hear romantic stories about the adventures of knights and their ladies. **Troubadours** wrote long songs that told the stories of courtly lovers, and minstrels traveled about, singing and performing these songs for those who would pay to listen.

> ### vocabulary
> **Code of Chivalry** a set of rules for knights
> **troubadour** a person who composed poems that were set to music

A knight was also expected to pledge his honor and respect to a lady.

The End of the Mounted Knight

What happened to knights? Remember you read earlier that castles became useless as armies started using cannons. The same thing happened to knights. Steel armor was fine protection against arrows and swords. But it was useless against cannonballs and bullets. However, knights did not disappear completely. Rulers continued to offer knighthood to men who had provided services to their kingdoms other than fighting. Explorers, artists, and scientists could become knights for outstanding achievements in their fields. Indeed, in Great Britain famous people are still awarded knighthoods today.

The Medieval Majority Before the 1300s, most people in medieval Europe were not lords or knights (or their wives). The vast majority were serfs. As you learned, serfs were the common people who lived on the manor estates and worked the land for the lord.

In fact, serfs came with the land. If a manor changed hands, the serfs who lived on the land went with it. If you bought the turf, you got the serfs, too.

If you're thinking that being a serf sounds something like being a slave, you're on the right track. Serfs were a little like slaves. One important difference was that a serf had the right to keep what was left over after paying whatever he owed to his lord. Also, serfs could pass their land on to their children.

Slaves had been common in the Roman Empire. However, as more and more members of the barbarian tribes became Christian, the church began to complain about slavery. The church at this time was not absolutely opposed to slavery, but it was opposed to enslaving Christians. As a result, many people who had been slaves were freed. These men were known as freedmen.

Unfortunately, these freedmen were not in a position to make much use of their freedom. Since they had been slaves all their lives, they generally had no money. Even if they could have purchased land, they probably would not have been able to protect themselves against warring tribes and powerful lords. Therefore, many freedmen decided to trade freedom for security by placing themselves under the protection of a feudal lord. They became serfs.

Indeed, even free peasants who may have owned their own land often gave up their independence to become serfs. Like the former slaves, these small landowners were outside the feudal support system and had no way to protect themselves from bandits, invaders, and neighboring lords. So, many of them willingly became serfs of a powerful lord. But not all peasants gave up their freedom.

All serfs led a hard life. Lords were supposed to protect their serfs, but if a lord treated a serf unfairly, about all he could do was abandon his land and flee. Serfs had to work extremely hard, and they kept little of what they grew or made.

The Life of a Serf

Serfs "belonged" to the land, and they lived close to the land. They spent their days digging in the soil to grow things. They had no soap to wash themselves, so their hands and bodies were often covered with dirt. They often had only one set of clothes, so they didn't wash their clothes, either. They wore the same clothes, no matter how caked with dirt and mud they became, until the clothes fell apart.

The house of a serf was typically made of earth. By around the year 1000, wood was hard to come by in parts of Europe. So serf houses were made of a frame of wood, with a mixture of mud and straw spread in between the wooden beams. The roof of the house was made of straw, and the floor was dirt. In wet weather, the floor was mud.

Serfs slept on the floor, perhaps with a layer of straw to provide a little bit of cushioning and warmth. They lived with their animals—chickens, sheep, and pigs. There was no fireplace—just a hearth in the middle of the floor, with smoke drifting up through a hole in the roof. The huts were smelly and smoky.

The life of a serf wasn't all work; there was time for fun and games.

Serfs spent many of their days working for the lord of the manor: plowing his fields, planting his seeds, harvesting his crops, and stomping his grapes to make wine. Women were often in charge of smaller livestock. They would shear the master's sheep, spin the wool into yarn, and weave it into cloth. Women also had the job of tending the family vegetable garden and caring for the children.

While the serfs prepared food and goods for the master, their own lives were very poor. They lived mostly on bread, vegetables, and ale or beer. As time passed, medieval serfs probably ate less meat, although women's

diets improved after about the year 1000. This helped them live longer and bear more children, causing Europe's population to grow rapidly.

If serfs got sick, they depended on village healers, who used local herbs for healing. (Lords might have a professional physician, though his cures probably didn't work much better.) But serfs who didn't feel well didn't get much time to rest—they could be fined or whipped if they didn't work hard.

All peasants—serf or free—faced many difficulties. But there were still some good times in their hard lives.

Holidays

Just as we enjoy holidays today, people also enjoyed them in the Middle Ages. In fact, the word *holiday* comes from the "holy days" that were part of the calendar in the Middle Ages. Remember, the Church was a part of everyday life on the manor. People celebrated many more holidays than we do today. With Sundays, saints' days, and other holy days, there were about 100 days when everyone did little work.

On the holy days, the whole manor attended church. But there was usually more to these holy days than worship. The knightly tournaments you read about earlier were often held on holidays. People held parties, danced, and participated in sports such as bowling and wrestling. They watched jugglers and magicians and listened to traveling troubadours and minstrels. These sports and hobbies gave villagers something to look forward to and lightened the load of serfdom.

Serf Goes to the City Now that you've read about the difficulties of a serf's life, you will not be surprised to hear that many serfs ran away from the manors to live in the cities. Imagine a serf who has lived his early life on a manor in the French countryside.

He spends his days in the field, working side by side with other serfs. Then one day this serf—let's call him Peter—is sent to the city to sell some firewood from the manor and bring the money back. He leaves the manor with a cart filled with firewood.

Before the trip Peter has heard many stories about life in the city, but he has never really believed them. Anyway, no stories can prepare him for the reality of the city.

For a young man who spends his days in open fields, the crowds of people pressing against him on all sides are a terrible shock. Peter would never have guessed that the whole world contained this many people. Walking with his horse and cart through the streets,

Peter feels as if he is being pushed and shoved all the way across the city.

Peter is astonished by the gangs of children at play, the women carrying baskets of fruit, and the men pushing small herds of sheep before them. And yet none of these people pay any attention to Peter whatsoever!

The city is filled with many churches. From all the churches you might think that the people who live here are very holy. That's what Peter thinks at first. But then he realizes they aren't. Instead, everywhere he looks, he sees thieves and beggars.

Peter watches as a group of actors present versions of Bible stories for people on the street. Is this a religious

The hustle and bustle around shops and shoppers added to the excitement of city life.

experience? No, Peter sees, as they pass the hat for people to put in money after each performance.

Even though it is a sunny day, Peter can't tell what time it is because the streets are shadowed by the rows of buildings. He listens for the toll of church bells to know the time.

Peter is excited by all the new sights, but he is also horrified by some of the new smells. As a serf, he is used to a certain amount of odors; but the city smells worse than anything he has encountered. People dump wastes from animals and people into open drains and ditches. Rainy weather has turned the dirt streets to stinky, messy marshes and mud. People selling meat and fish throw their unsold, rotting foods into the streets. Dogs and pigs roam around, trying to make a meal of such garbage. The river is filled with all kinds of garbage too, including dead animals. Nevertheless, Peter is fascinated with the city and city life.

After selling his firewood, Peter begins to make his way home to the manor. Peter cannot stop thinking about the alluring sights and sounds of the city. Then, he makes a decision. He will run away to live there. As he continues home, he begins to make plans. After a few weeks back on the manor, Peter escapes for the city and freedom.

What is Peter going to do in there? He is a farmer. How can he make his living in the city? Peter isn't sure, but he knows that much of the excitement in the streets is due to people selling and buying wares and services. The streets are crowded with shops of tailors, barbers, furriers, grocers, carpenters, cobblers, leather tanners, and bakers. These shops are more like market stalls opening right onto the street. In the back of the shops people make items to sell in the shops.

Peter wants to find a way to work in a shop. He goes from shop to shop, talking with shopkeepers and clerks about how the system works.

Guilds

In his discussions with shopkeepers and clerks, Peter discovers that each type of business is organized into a guild. For example, there are guilds for shoemakers, carpenters, hat makers, tailors, clockmakers, and jewelers. Master craftspersons, members of a guild, work together to make rules for operating their craft in the city. The guilds set standards for products and services that protect customers and workers alike.

Guilds require would-be members to train for a certain number of years with a guild member. Most start out as apprentices when they are children, helping the master at work.

When an apprentice learns some of the skills, he is promoted to **journeyman** and is allowed to make parts of the product. Finally, a journeyman will produce a "masterpiece," which is his finished product. For example, a shoemaker's masterpiece is a pair of finished shoes. The masterpiece is proof that a journeyman is competent to become a guild master himself.

Peter is too old to start as an apprentice, but he might look for work in the growing trade between cities. Merchants need people to carry their goods to other towns to sell. Trade has increased since the year 1000, as Europe has become somewhat safer from bandits and outlaws. For several centuries before, there was not very much travel or trade between areas in Europe.

The Growth of Trade and Cities

Many people preferred life in a town to life on a manor estate. Cities in Europe grew along with trade and business. London, Paris, Venice, and many other towns began to expand into larger cities. Still, even the largest (Paris) had fewer than 50,000 people.

The growth of towns and cities had an impact on local government as well as business. Unlike people on a manor, people in a town did not have a lord. French or English townspeople owed loyalty directly to the king. To establish a government, towns offered their king a sum of money for a **charter**. Charters granted townspeople permission to elect their own mayors, sheriffs, and other officials. However, the only people who could vote in these elections were the powerful merchants.

After 1000 the feudal lords began to lose power to the kings. Kings used the wealth from these towns and cities to become more powerful. And out of this change came some nations we know today—England, France, and Spain. The whole process took centuries. But the decline of feudalism and the erosion of the power of feudal lords began with the growth of middle-class power in the towns and cities.

> **vocabulary**
> **journeyman** an apprentice who is considered qualified to work in a particular trade
> **charter** a document given by a government or ruler to a group of people or a company

Churches, government buildings, guild halls, shops, and houses crowded behind the safety of city walls during the later Middle Ages.

12 Women in the Middle Ages

How **Women Lived** Most of the people we've been talking about so far in the Middle Ages were men. There is not as much information about the lives of women in Europe during this time. However, a few women became very famous.

Most of the women of this time, like most of the men, were peasants and serfs. They had the same hard lives as their fathers, husbands, and brothers. Like boys, girls began doing farm work when they were about seven. They had to haul water, take care of younger children, and care for animals.

Adult women spent their days weaving, cooking, tending small animals, and caring for children. During busy times, women and men worked together in the fields, trying to grow enough food to pay their lords and keep their own families fed.

Poor Health

People in the Middle Ages did not know as much about medicine as we do today. Many died from diseases, and few lived as long as the average American today. Nobles and wealthy townspeople tended to be healthier than serfs just because they got enough to eat. But everyone suffered from lack of knowledge about germs, poor sanitation, and bad medical practices.

Women were at a special risk because of childbirth. Today, having a baby is a routine medical procedure. But in the Middle Ages it was very dangerous. Many mothers and their babies died in childbirth. To make matters worse, many of the children who survived the delivery did not make it to adulthood. So, there was much sadness and tragedy in life for women in the Middle Ages.

The Four Virtues—Fortitude, Prudence, Justice, and Temperance—are shown here teaching nuns how to take care of the sick.

Convent Leaders

Convents were like monasteries; the members, who were women, devoted their lives to God. And just as monasteries had a big impact on life in the Middle Ages, so did convents. Women in convents devoted their lives to prayer and to helping people. In the religious world of the Middle Ages, sending a daughter to a convent was thought of as an act of religious devotion.

The leader of a convent was called an abbess. Some leaders of convents became famous for their writings and even for their success at negotiating peace agreements among warring nobles. Matilda, the daughter of Holy Roman Emperor Otto I and the abbess of a convent, brought peace to much of Europe during her lifetime.

Hildegard of Bingen

One nun became famous in her time and her fame has lasted to our time. Her music is recorded frequently on CDs and can be found in most record stores and on the Internet. She is the earliest composer in history whose life story is known to us. In 1998, people in Vermont, California, Massachusetts, and Germany had parties to celebrate her 900th birthday. That's right—900th! Why was this woman so remarkable?

Some of Hildegard's visions such as this of the tree of life were described and illustrated in books during her lifetime.

Hildegard of Bingen was born in 1098. She was a religious person from her earliest days. She began having religious visions when she was only three. When she was eight years old, her parents sent their religious daughter to live with a famous holy woman who was to be her teacher. In just a few years, though, people began hearing about Hildegard and her remarkable visions. Soon, a small group of young women came to live with Hildegard and Jutta, her teacher. This group started a convent.

Throughout her life, Hildegard had remarkable visions. Today, some people think that her visions may have been caused by migraine headaches. But what made Hildegard special was not what caused her visions but what she did with those visions.

She had a vision when she was 42 in which "the heavens were opened and a blinding light of exceptional brilliance flowed through [her] entire brain. And so it kindled [her] whole heart and breast like a flame, not burning but warming . . . and suddenly [she] understood the meaning of expositions [explanations] of the books [holy books]. . . ."

Visions like this one and many others inspired Hildegard to write beautiful music that is still performed and recorded today.

She wrote poems and books based on her mystical visions. She wrote two medical books that were used for hundreds of years after her death.

Eventually, Hildegard started a new convent in the German town of Bingen. Her works were admired by the pope and by many other religious and political leaders. Arguing that women and men were equal in the eyes of God, she wrote, "God receives in baptism both sexes at all ages."

Trade and Learning

Many women went into business with their husbands, and others either began businesses by themselves or continued working alone after their husbands died. Historians have found records of women who worked as brewers, glassmakers, weavers, **coopers**, and **smiths**. Some women carried on these trades after the deaths of their husbands.

One important change during the Middle Ages that did not affect women was the development of universities. Universities sprang up in several big cities. The first ones were started in Paris and Bologna (Italy) in the 1200s, but other cities such as Padua, Prague, and Oxford soon followed their example. These universities advanced learning in many fields, but women were not allowed to go to them. This made it almost

> ### vocabulary
> **cooper** a person who makes barrels
> **smith** a person who works with metals, such as a goldsmith, silversmith, tinsmith, or blacksmith

These women are selling the shoes and boots they made.

impossible for women to work in fields like law and medicine.

Women in convents, though, continued to share knowledge. Certain convents trained women to teach young children, and others trained women to provide health care and help to families.

Despite restrictions, a few women managed to leave a mark on the world. Margaret of Denmark and Matilda of Tuscany were two women rulers whose political skills brought them land and power. Rosvitha von Gandersheim (rahs VEE tah vahn GAHN durs hym) was a nun in Germany in the 900s. She wrote comic plays based on classical Greek and Roman dramas. Marie de France was a writer in France in the 1100s. We know very little about her except for the long poems she wrote about knights and courtly love.

Christine de Pisan

Christine de Pisan (krihs TEEN de pye SAHN), born in Venice in the 1300s, also wrote. Christine's family moved to Paris while she was still a baby. Her father was a famous scholar and was invited to work for the king of France. This was a great honor, for the court of the king of France was a very learned place. The move to Paris provided Christine with an opportunity. Unlike most women of her time, she was given the chance to get a very good education—and she took it. It's a good thing she did.

At first her life seemed to be going the way the lives of most young women went. She got married and had children. But then her husband and father died quickly, one after the other. Suddenly, Christine had three young children, a mother, and two younger brothers who depended on her. The king didn't offer to help Christine and her family with money, but she was allowed to keep

using the king's library. That was a big help, because without a husband or father, Christine had to do the only thing she knew how to do. She began to write.

She started out with poems. Then she wrote about religion and history. She was especially interested in writing about women of the Middle Ages. Her most famous book was a history of women called *The Book of the City of Ladies*. Christine de Pisan also wrote a military manual. Her view was that armies should be used only for defense. It was a strange opinion in those warring times, but the book was read by many people.

She wrote books arguing that universities should accept women as students. "There is no doubt," she said, "that Nature provided [women] with the same qualities of body and mind found in the wisest and most learned men." If women did not receive an education, however, they could not develop those qualities.

Pisan's books were very popular. Her writings were translated into many languages. She hired women artists to illustrate her books, and she became the first European woman to earn her living as a writer.

After 29 years of writing, all the people Pisan needed to support were either grown up or dead. She retired to live in a convent. However, she wrote one book before she died—a long poem about Joan of Arc, a French woman who lived at the same time. Later you'll find out why this famous author broke her retirement to write about this remarkable young woman.

Christine de Pisan is kneeling to present one of her books to the queen of France.

illiam of Normandy In the 1000s, in a part of France called Normandy, there lived an eight-year-old boy named William. One day, William was a happy child, the son of a powerful lord, the duke of Normandy. The next day, William's father was dead.

Young William was named duke. Now, you might think that being a duke would be fun, but not for William. What it meant for him was that other powerful lords in Europe, men who had been friends of his father, wanted to kill him.

What was going on? Why would his father's friends want William dead? In the world of politics in the Middle Ages, the death of a great lord often was the cause of violence. As his father's oldest son, William was the rightful duke. But that didn't stop others from trying to kill him to become the duke themselves. William survived, thanks to help from the king of France.

Why is this story important? Because William, duke of Normandy, fought and won one of the most important battles in the Middle Ages, the Battle of Hastings. This battle changed the history of a nation and helped create the English language you are reading right now.

The Battle of Hastings

If you locate Normandy and the English Channel on a map, you can see that the English Channel is the body of water that flows between England and Europe. Normandy lies along the English Channel, just across from England. Today, Normandy is a section of France, but in the 1000s it was a duchy, a territory ruled by a duke. The king of France, who was the duke's feudal lord, had little real power there.

In 1066 the king of England died. Several people claimed that they should be the next king of England. One was an English lord named Harold, who had himself crowned king. Another person with a claim to the throne was William, duke of Normandy.

In late September 1066, William and his army of knights and foot soldiers crossed the English Channel. King Harold was in the north of England, having just defeated another king who wanted to rule England. He and his army marched south and met William and the Norman forces on October 14, 1066, near the coastal town of Hastings. The English soldiers were in a line on a hillside. They turned back the first Norman charge. But when the Normans retreated, the English soldiers broke ranks and chased them. This was just the break William needed. He turned on the disorganized English army and

soundly defeated them. King Harold was killed in the battle.

William marched his army to London, the capital, and was crowned king. Now William, duke of Normandy, also became King William I of England. He is better known to history as William the Conqueror.

A New Language

William's conquest of England has had a big impact on our lives, even if we may never have lived in or even visited England. Before William arrived, most people in England spoke Anglo-Saxon (Old English). This was the language of the Germanic tribes who had arrived in England after the fall of the Roman Empire.

The Normans spoke an early form of French. At first, the common people of England spoke Anglo-Saxon and all the nobles (most of whom were the relatives and friends of William the Conqueror) spoke French. Eventually, the French and Anglo-Saxon languages blended. That is why English includes a mixture of French and Germanic words. Sometimes we even have two words for the same thing, one from the French and one from the Germanic languages. So it is with *cow* and *beef*. When we talk about cows, we are using a Germanic word that the Anglo-Saxon people used before William came to

England. When we sit down to eat beef, we are using a French word that was brought to England after the invasion of William and his knights.

Historical Documents

The Middle Ages were a long, long time ago. There are many people and events that we know very little about because there are few surviving records. But we know a good deal about England in the time of William the Conqueror because several important historical records have survived. Two of the most significant of these historical records are the Bayeux (bye YOO) Tapestry, part of which is pictured below, and the Domesday Book.

Sometimes, when a new ruler takes over, he leaves things pretty much as they were before. Not William! He started to change England from top to bottom. William threw many of the Anglo-Saxon lords off their lands and estates and replaced them with Norman friends who had fought with him at Hastings.

William wanted to know more about his new country. He ordered that a list be made of all the people and valuable items in the kingdom. The king's agents went all over England, visiting even the smallest villages and most distant settlements. They recorded

It is believed that one of William's brothers ordered the creation of the Bayeaux Tapestry as a record of the Battle of Hastings in pictures and words. Because of the tapestry, we can picture in our minds a battle that happened almost a thousand years ago.

the name of the lord of each territory, as well as the number of small landowners, knights, and serfs serving each feudal lord. They counted pigs, sheep, and other livestock and made notes about the forests in each region. If there was a mill or some other business in town, William's census takers made a note of it. They even kept a record of how many beehives there were in each territory.

The Domesday Book

This survey of William's kingdom was called the Domesday Book. It took several years and a lot of money to finish. But it was worth the expense, for the book let William know exactly who lived where. It allowed him to keep track of all the rent and taxes that were due to him.

But the Domesday Book was about more than taxes and money. William made sure that every lord listed in the book swore an oath of loyalty to him as the king of England. Anybody who did not cooperate with William's agents or refused to swear loyalty to the king was severely punished. The Domesday Book is a treasure for historians of the Middle Ages. It gives an accurate picture of a feudal kingdom over 900 years ago. For example, we know that there were two million people living in England during the reign of William I.

This is the Tower of London today.

One final item: What about the name, *Domesday?* It is actually an old-fashioned spelling of the word *Doomsday*. Some people think it was called that because people who did not cooperate with the king's agents were killed. But that is not the real reason. In fact, it was probably called the Domesday Book because doomsday was the biblical day of judgment and accounting. That was exactly what William's agents did when they arrived in a town—they counted up the people and judged how much everyone and everything was worth.

The Tower of London

William was also responsible for one of the most famous buildings in London, the Tower of London. A few months after winning the Battle of Hastings, William had a castle of earth and wood built on the north side of the Thames (temz) River in London. William's son added to this castle, and by 1100 it included a stone tower. Later kings continued to enlarge and fortify the castle. Over the years the Tower of London has been used as a fortress, a prison, a royal residence, and a place for storing treasure. Today, tourists visit it. It is one of the most famous symbols of the nation William helped build.

Weak Kings and Trouble in the Land William died in the year 1087. Several kings followed, all of them ruling England and parts of France. None of these kings were as strong as William the Conqueror, though, and that caused trouble in England.

Other nobles, seeing that William's successors were weak, tried to seize power. This led to constant warfare and a general breakdown of law and order. Without a strong king to hold them in line, the great lords just below the king made war on the king and each other in an effort to grow more powerful.

For serfs and people in towns and cities, these were hard times. Invading armies robbed people and killed anyone who resisted. Lords needed money to fight their wars, so they increased taxes on everyone. It was bad for business because trade could not be conducted safely. Towns and villages had to pay protection money to avoid being attacked. Then, they would be attacked by that lord's enemies anyway.

Henry II is shown here with all his royal symbols—holding the scepter and orb and wearing the crown.

A Strong King Makes Order

Once again, as in 1066, a hero arrived from across the English Channel. Henry II was the great-grandson of William the

Conqueror. But since he was only two when his grandfather Henry I died, the throne had been taken by one of his cousins. Even as a boy, Henry was involved in struggles over the throne of England. At first, his mother fought on his behalf. Finally, when he was 21, he won the support of some dissatisfied nobles. Henry was crowned King Henry II in Westminster Abbey, the greatest church in London, in December of 1154.

Bright and well educated, Henry spoke French and Latin, but he did not speak much English. Usually he was good-natured and gentle, but he had a terrible temper. It is said that once, when he was enraged with jealousy because someone had flattered one of his rivals, he ripped the covers from his bed and began to chew on his straw mattress!

A Man of Pleasure

Henry loved to hunt, and he loved to go hawking. Hawking was a sport that used trained falcons and birds of prey to capture other birds. These hunting birds were treated with care, like expensive hunting dogs. Henry loved to travel around with a favorite bird perched on a leather glove. He and his nobles often brought their trained birds to the banquet hall and fed them treats and morsels.

The King Is Number One

Henry was full of energy and ideas. As king, Henry had one goal. He was determined to end the wars that had plagued England in recent years and to make the king the strongest lord in England. Henry may have been an informal man of pleasure, but as king he dedicated his life to crushing his rivals and making sure the king would always be stronger than the lords. Henry did not waste time. One of his first acts as king was to take to the field of battle and go after lords who had grown too powerful.

Law and Order

Henry soon realized that he needed more than a good army to be a strong leader. He needed laws and government to make sure

It took patience to train a hawk, which is being allowed to fly free, to return with its prey.

the kingdom ran in an orderly manner. Henry turned his attention to the way the laws and courts worked in England.

The court system was very confusing. Lords were in charge of courts for certain types of crimes in certain places. The king was in charge of other courts, and the church was in charge of still other courts.

There were also different types of trials. In these trials people accused of crimes might be forced to "prove" their innocence through combat; or they might be forced to pick up a red-hot piece of iron in their bare hand. If the hand didn't heal quickly, he was guilty.

What a mess! Henry II set up a group of administrators who could run the legal system. Henry wanted to organize the system so criminals could not escape trials and punishment. He held several conferences with nobles and church leaders. In these meetings, Henry ordered a fairer legal system and the right to trial by **jury**. The job of people on a jury is to hear evidence in a trial and then to vote in secret whether they think the person accused of a crime is guilty or innocent. The jury system Henry began is still in use in England and the United States 900 years later.

Other Improvements

Henry made many other changes in his effort to make the king more powerful. Remember how vassals owed their lord military service? It was a centuries-old tradition of feudalism. But Henry realized it was not working. Lords who were not fully behind the king would take their time responding to the king's call for soldiers. Then, they would not send as many soldiers as they were supposed to.

Henry decided to change the law and started the *shield tax*. This meant that the lords had to send money instead of soldiers. Henry could then use the money to hire his own soldiers, who would be ready to fight and loyal to the king.

Henry also started a program of rebuilding castles. Henry built stone castles and made sure everyone understood that these were the king's castles. And the king could decide who lived there.

A Long Line of Kings

Henry and the kings who came after him were known as the Plantagenet (plan TAJ uh-niht) dynasty, or rulers belonging to the same family. The name *Plantagenet* probably came from a yellow flower called *Planta genista* that Henry's father liked to wear as a sort of badge or emblem. Henry II was the first Plantagenet king of England and is considered

Setting up a uniform system of laws and courts was probably Henry II's greatest accomplishment.

> **vocabulary**
> **jury** a group of people who hear evidence in a trial and then vote on the guilt or innocence of the accused

to have been the greatest of his line. All of them were known for their intelligence, energy, creative drive, quick anger, and strong sense of justice.

Henry's strong will and quick temper helped him accomplish all that he did as king. But these traits also caused problems. In the next lesson you will learn how Henry's hot temper led him into conflict with the most powerful priest in England.

Hard-Working Man Henry II depended on a group of trusted advisors to help him run his large kingdom. The one he relied on most was named Thomas Becket. (You sometimes will see his name written Thomas à Becket.)

Becket was not born in a noble household. He was the son of a merchant. Becket became a priest, and through hard work and intelligence he began to rise through the ranks of the Church. At the same time, he also began to work his way up in the world of politics.

In 1154, one of the first acts of the newly crowned King Henry II was to appoint Thomas Becket to the job of chancellor. The chancellor was the king's highest advisor.

This was an important job. Becket worked hard, but he also enjoyed his hard-earned position. His household soon became as grand as any in the kingdom. In fact, Becket's house in London became known as the place to be. King Henry didn't care much for hosting fancy feasts. But everyone, including the king and queen, went to Becket's for a good time. He had a grand banquet hall with a high ceiling. In those days, people thought that eating raw fruit was unhealthy and that vegetables were for the poor. So, for the rich, meals consisted of meat, poultry, and breads.

But what meats and poultries! These nobles didn't live on chicken and roast beef. The platters in Becket's household carried starlings, seagulls, herons, and storks. Peacocks were roasted and presented with their spectacular tail feathers inserted in the roast. A roasted swan was arranged on a bed of green-tinted pastry so that it looked as if the bird were gliding over a pond.

Thomas Becket knew how to throw a good party. Most of his friends thought of him as a man who loved fun and a good time. But in his personal life, he remained a serious, devout priest. He also worked hard at his job to help King Henry bring order to the kingdom.

Archbishop of Canterbury

Working closely together, Becket and Henry became good friends. Becket was 15 years older than Henry, but they got along well, and Becket gave the younger king lots of advice that helped him run his kingdom well. You already know that Henry was trying to solve some problems in the legal system of England. He wanted to get rid of some of the loopholes created by the separate court systems of the Church. When the man who was the archbishop of Canterbury died, Henry thought it would be a good idea to tell the pope that his good friend Thomas Becket should be appointed the archbishop of Canterbury.

Being the archbishop of Canterbury was a great honor and a big promotion. There was only one problem: Becket didn't want the job. It may have been a great honor, but Becket saw the trouble that would lie ahead.

Since the king and the Church were often in conflict, he knew that Church officials would see him as on the king's side instead of theirs. He also knew that if he were going to do his job well, he would have to take positions that opposed the king.

But when a king asks you to do something, it's hard to say no. Becket became archbishop of Canterbury. At first, he and King Henry got along despite some minor conflicts about the Church courts. To everyone's surprise, Becket took his new job very seriously. Most people did not know about the serious side of Thomas Becket. Now they saw who he really was. The big parties and banquets came to an end. Becket put aside his fancy robes and furs and wore simple clothes and coarsely woven shirts. He spent a lot of time praying, meditating, and studying the Bible.

Trouble and Tragedy

King Henry was surprised by the change in his friend's behavior. But he grew truly alarmed when Becket opposed the king on questions about the role of the Church in the legal system.

King Henry proposed a new law that took a great deal of power away from the Church's courts and gave it to the king. Henry let Becket know that he expected him to support the new law. Instead, the archbishop opposed the king.

Hot-tempered King Henry was enraged at the actions of his former friend. This was the beginning of a feud that, thanks to Henry's bad temper, just kept getting worse. Henry charged Becket with violating the law. He took some of Becket's castles and lands away. Becket felt so threatened he left England secretly and spent a few years living outside the country. Twice they tried to end their conflict, but again and again they quarreled. Eventually, the pope ordered the king to end his quarrel with the archbishop or face **excommunication**. Henry gave in because he could not risk the anger of the pope.

Becket Returns

Becket felt it was safe to come back to England. King Henry was known for his bad temper, and Becket for his stubbornness. This was a recipe for trouble. And the trouble came soon enough. Shortly after he returned to England, Becket excommunicated some powerful nobles who were friends of the king.

> **vocabulary**
> **excommunication**
> the punishment of not allowing someone to continue as a member of the Church

This caused Henry to explode again. One night in December of 1170, Henry was at a castle in Normandy. In a fit of anger, he cried out, "Will no one rid me of this upstart priest?" No one really knows what Henry meant by these words. Were his words a casual expression of anger, or did Henry really want to be rid of Becket?

It so happened that four young knights, hotheaded and eager for the king's favor, heard the king speak. And they took his words as a serious call for action.

Slipping out of the castle that night, the knights found a boat to take them across the English Channel. At the cathedral in Canterbury, they found Becket conducting a religious service. The heavily armed knights expected Becket to be afraid and beg for his life. Becket did not run. He only began to struggle when the four rowdy men tried to drag him out of the cathedral. He declared himself "ready to die for my Lord," and then the knights hacked him to death, right there in the cathedral.

Thomas Becket was murdered on the altar of Canterbury Cathedral.

Reaction

The murder shocked all of Europe, but few were more upset by the crime than Henry himself. Just as Becket himself had done on becoming archbishop, Henry removed his fine clothing and dressed in sackcloth, a rough, uncomfortable cloth made of the hair of animals and other coarse fibers. He poured ashes over his head. Like dressing in sackcloth, this was a way to show sorrow. He refused to eat or sleep. He exiled himself for six months and then asked to be whipped.

Finally, he made a **pilgrimage** to Canterbury. When he was three miles from the cathedral, he got off his horse and removed his shoes. The king walked the last three miles barefoot. By the time he arrived, "his footsteps . . . seemed to be covered in blood . . . for his tender feet being cut by the hard stones, a great quantity of blood flowed from them on to the ground."

vocabulary
pilgrimage a journey undertaken for a religious purpose

Three years after his murder, Becket was made a saint by the Church. His tomb in Canterbury Cathedral became the most popular shrine in England. Henry was rid of his "upstart priest," but he had also lost one of his best friends. Yet Henry would find even more trouble before his rule had ended. This time, the source would be someone who was even closer to him than his old friend Becket.

People who visited and prayed at Becket's shrine often wore a badge like this one to show that they had been there.

Queen of France Eleanor of Aquitaine was a woman who had everything. She was beautiful, charming, intelligent, and came from a powerful family. She could read and write (unusual for a girl in the 1100s), play the harp, and ride a horse as well as a boy.

But the most important thing that Eleanor had was land. She was the duchess of Aquitaine (AK wih tayn), one of the largest and richest regions of what is now France. Aquitaine was a region rich in rivers (its name came from the Roman word for "land of waters"), olive groves, vineyards, wheat fields, orchards, and forests.

As duchess, she was a vassal of the king of France; but she controlled more land than he did.

Still, she had to do what the king said. So when the king told the 15-year-old Eleanor that she was going to marry Louis, his 16-year-old son, whom she had never met, she didn't even question it. Eleanor had always known that she would marry a young nobleman some day and that her marriage would be based on land rather than love. Shortly after her marriage, the old king died and Louis became king of France. Eleanor became the queen.

At first, the two teenagers got along quite well, but disappointments followed. Eleanor produced two girls instead of the son the king needed to follow him on the throne. She hated the royal castle in Paris, which struck her as a cold, dreary place compared with sunny Aquitaine. Louis was not as bold and dashing a knight as Eleanor's father and grandfather had been. To make things worse,

Louis got more and more interested in religion, and life in Paris became more and more dull for Eleanor. Was she looking around for a new husband? No one really knew, but one day a young nobleman named Henry came to Paris.

The End of a Royal Marriage

You've met Henry before. The young man Eleanor saw was the same handsome, energetic, and charming man who later became Henry II. When Eleanor met him, he wasn't yet king of England. He was Henry of Anjou (ahn ZHOO), and he controlled the lands north of Eleanor's Aquitaine. The king of France saw Henry as his chief rival for power. Little did he know how much of a rival Henry would be.

Shortly after she met Henry, Eleanor asked for an annulment, or a cancellation, of her marriage to Louis. King Louis was sad that she wanted to end the marriage; he still loved Eleanor. But Louis was unhappy about the marriage, too. Their failure to produce a son was a serious issue. The religious king wondered whether that failure was a sign of God's displeasure, as Eleanor claimed. After 15 years of marriage, the marriage was annulled, and Louis and Eleanor went their separate ways.

Eleanor returned to Aquitaine. Even if she had wanted to remain unmarried for a while, Eleanor soon saw that it was impossible. She was simply too valuable. More than one knight tried to kidnap her and force her to marry him. Eleanor needed the protection of a husband.

Queen of England

No one knows for sure when or how Henry and Eleanor agreed to marry or who made the first proposal. Yet, two months after the annulment of her marriage to Louis, Eleanor and Henry were married.

These two were far better suited to each other than Eleanor and Louis had been. Henry and Eleanor were both intelligent, bold, and spirited people who admired learning and literature and enjoyed power. In the first 13 years of her marriage to Henry, Eleanor had eight children with Henry, including five sons.

Together, they were the most powerful couple in Europe. The combination of their lands gave Henry the knights, ships, and power he needed to sail across the Channel and claim the throne of England.

For 14 years, Henry and Eleanor ruled together over their kingdom that stretched from Scotland to Spain. Look at the map to see what lands they controlled.

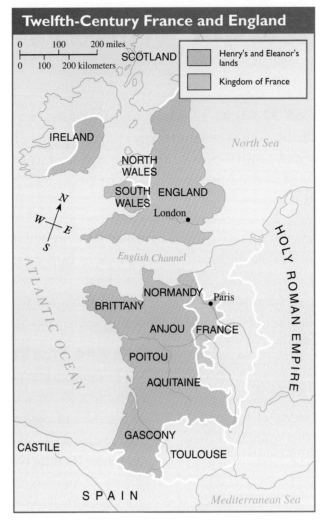

Twelfth-Century France and England

You can see how much land Henry and Eleanor controlled.

Eleanor was 11 years older than Henry, and at last their marriage began to fail. Eleanor returned to Aquitaine with her children. It wasn't long before some of her sons were teenagers. The young sons were impatient for power of their own. Henry gave them titles but no power. Eleanor encouraged her sons to think about the day when they could oppose their father.

Meanwhile, Eleanor held court in Aquitaine. She hired the best poets and troubadours to entertain her and her castle full of teenaged children and their friends. She favored stories of courtly love in which brave young knights performed feats of courage for their ladies. She encouraged her sons to be brave and dashing, but she also demanded courtesy and witty conversation in her court. It was the most civilized place in Europe.

Royal Rivals

The murder of Thomas Becket was a turning point in Henry II's rule of England. Many powerful nobles in England blamed Henry for Becket's murder. Eleanor saw an opportunity and encouraged her sons to take advantage of the king's new weakness and rebel against him. With their mother's help, the sons were able to get the help of several powerful nobles eager to strike back against the king. Remember, it was King Henry who had just recently stripped them of their power.

The sons, with the help of several nobles, did lead a rebellion against their father. But Henry was still a master warrior. Henry put down the rebellion and placed Eleanor under house arrest, making her a prisoner in one of his castles. There she stayed until his death some 15 years later.

King Richard I

At Henry's death, his and Eleanor's eldest son, Richard, became king. Richard immediately had his mother freed. The new king was very close to his mother. And Eleanor saw many of the same qualities in Richard that she had first admired in Henry. He was dashing, handsome, adventurous, and energetic. Richard would have been a great king, except for one important thing: He did not have his father's gift for governing. Henry may have been quick to anger, but he was a gifted ruler who knew how to solve problems.

During his ten years as king, Richard the Lionhearted, as he was called, hardly set foot in England. He was too busy leading crusades against the Muslims, having adventures, and fighting wars. At one point he was taken prisoner and held for ransom. Eleanor raised the money to get him out of prison.

If the king was away so much, who ruled England while he was gone? His mother, Queen Eleanor, that's who. As Henry II had done, she worked on solving problems in England. She introduced a system of uniform coins, weights, and measures. She also did away with some unfair rules. These reforms made her popular with her subjects.

When Richard was killed during one of his adventures, Eleanor was heartbroken. She was nearly 80 now and ready to take a rest at the end of a rich and long life. Eleanor retired to a convent, where she died at the age of 82.

The statue of Queen Eleanor on her tomb is holding a book, which shows just how unusual a woman of her time she was.

he Landless Son The youngest child of Eleanor of Aquitaine and Henry II was a boy named John. Although John would become Henry's favorite (perhaps because he was not as close to his mother as the other boys), Henry had already given his most valuable fiefs to his other sons.

As a young man, John was given the nickname "John Lackland," because he did not have any land of his own. No one expected John to become king because he had so many older brothers who would come to the throne before he did. In fact, when John was very young, he was sent to be raised in a monastery. Like Hildegard of Bingen, he was supposed to dedicate his life to God. All of that changed, however.

Except for Richard, all of John's older brothers died before reaching the throne. When Richard died, the 32-year-old John was the sole surviving son of Henry II, so he became king of England.

For many centuries, John was considered the worst king in English history by historians. Nowadays, many say that he wasn't such a terrible king, but he did make some mistakes. Like other Plantagenet kings, he was intelligent and hard-working, with a strong sense of justice. Nonetheless, people did not seem to trust him, and intelligence and hard work were not enough to win wars.

A Series of Defeats

Five years after John took the throne, the king of France attacked Normandy and Anjou. These were the lands that Henry II brought to his marriage with Eleanor. John was unable to defend the lands. One reason was that his nobles did not like or trust him enough to fight for him.

It was bad enough that John lost important lands to the French king, but now he wanted his nobles to pay higher taxes to cover the costs of the war. He raised their taxes. If nobles refused to pay, or could not pay, he took hostages. In other words, he might hold a relative or important servant prisoner until the baron paid up. King John also demanded taxes from people who lived in cities, especially wealthy merchants. This put the merchants on the side of the nobles, or barons.

John seemed to have a special talent for making enemies. Now that he had the barons and powerful townspeople angry with him, he made enemies with the pope. King John refused to agree to the man the pope wanted to become archbishop of Canterbury. It was not a wise decision on John's part. The pope, Innocent III, was probably the most powerful man in Europe at this time. He fought back with all the weapons he had.

After John seized property that belonged to the Church, the pope ordered all the churches in England closed. Priests refused to perform any sacraments, or holy ceremonies. No weddings, funerals, or baptisms could be performed. People could not confess their sins and be forgiven. And it was all King John's fault! Then, Innocent excommunicated the king. John had no choice but to give in. This was a costly defeat. First, he agreed to recognize the pope's choice as archbishop. Then, John surrendered England to the pope and became his vassal. The pope returned England to John as his fief. It was humiliating.

A Great Charter

Peace with the Church did not satisfy the demands of the angry barons and townspeople. In 1215 they prepared a list of demands known as the Magna Carta, which is Latin for "great charter." It laid out rules for what the king could and could not do to nobles, citizens, and the Church. The barons said they would go to war against John if he did not sign the document. When he saw he could not defeat them, John agreed to meet the demands of the barons.

At a meeting in a meadow outside London, John signed the Magna Carta. Copies were made by hand and carried all over the kingdom. John died the next year of a fever as a new war raged through his kingdom. Over the next eleven years, the charter was revised several times. The final version was signed in 1225 by John's son, Henry III.

Why is the Magna Carta important? It is an important document in the history of the rule of law. In the Magna Carta a king agreed that he had to rule according to laws. Some

This is a nineteenth-century painting of a very important event in English history—the signing of the Magna Carta. One of ten existing copies of the Magna Carta is shown here.

of the Magna Carta's principles lasted through the centuries that followed.

A few ideas in our Constitution can be traced back directly to the Magna Carta. Modern democracy, with its emphasis on freedoms and rights, was still a long way in the future, but one of the first steps was taken when a group of barons got King John to sign the Magna Carta in a field outside the city of London.

London Bridge

King John is also remembered for the construction of the first stone bridge across the Thames River in London. The bridge was completed in 1209 and stood for 600 years. It was not just a way to get across the river; it included two rows of houses and 140 shops. More than 500 years would pass before another stone bridge was constructed across the Thames in London.

ngland's First Parliament King John died the year after he signed the Magna Carta. His son Henry III was only nine years old, so England was ruled by a council of barons until Henry was old enough to rule.

During these years of rule by the council, barons settled their disputes in discussions rather than by going to war. Instead of hard times, England enjoyed peace.

Henry's grandfather, Henry II, had created a system of government that worked well. For centuries, England had been divided into counties. Under Henry II's system of government, each county had a sheriff who managed local affairs. The whole country was divided into six **circuits**, or districts. Each circuit had three judges. All the judges enforced the same laws, which made the country seem more unified.

> **vocabulary**
> **circuit** an area or district through which a judge travels to hold court sessions

Once Henry III was old enough to rule, there were problems. He forgot things. He didn't get things done that he was supposed to do. He also gave many jobs in the government to his wife's friends and relatives. Once again the barons rebelled, as they had against Henry's father, King John. They demanded that the king allow a council of barons to rule. At first, Henry agreed. Then he changed his mind, and war broke out between the king and some of the barons.

England's First Parliament

After capturing King Henry III, Simon de Montfort, the leader of the barons' revolt, tried something new. He called a meeting of land-owning nobles, leaders of the Church, knights, and citizens from the towns to pass laws and run the country. Since it was not practical for everyone to come, Montfort had each group vote for representatives who would come to the meeting.

This historic meeting was the first time that representatives from all classes, except serfs, met together to make decisions. This was the beginning of England's parliament system. More than 100 people met for two months. Although it was not democratic by modern standards, it was a new idea. This first parliament was an exciting but short-lived affair. King Henry escaped from capture. His army defeated the rebels and killed Simon de Montfort. The parliament was disbanded.

The Model Parliament

The next king, Edward I, learned from the mistakes of his father, Henry III, and his grandfather John. Edward was fighting a war to keep Aquitaine from being taken away by the French. He was building expensive castles in Wales, and he was also trying to conquer Scotland. These projects cost a lot of money. Instead of ordering people to pay taxes the way King John had, Edward decided to try something different. Using the idea of Simon de Montfort's parliament, he called together representatives from throughout his kingdom. He hoped to win their cooperation in raising money for his projects.

In 1295, what became known as the Model Parliament met in Westminster, now part of London. It included two knights from each county and two citizens from each city and town. These representatives were elected, not appointed. Also attending were representatives sent by priests, as well as barons, nobles, and bishops. The Model Parliament included some prominent women as well as men. It has become known as the Model Parliament because every Parliament in England since then has been based on the model of this one.

King Edward, surrounded by a king of Scotland, a prince of Wales, Church leaders, and representatives of nobles and townspeople, presides at the Model Parliament.

Edward was a wise king. He concluded that he would be more likely to get the money he needed and avoid bad feelings if he directed his requests to the representatives in Parliament. His plan worked. Parliament agreed to give the king the money he needed. But once Edward started asking for money from Parliament, things began to change.

People began to expect the king always to ask Parliament for money. Eventually, the idea sprang up that the king couldn't impose taxes without first getting the approval of Parliament. This was not the king's idea of what should be done. Friction developed between the king and Parliament.

Parliament's power continued to grow. In the 1300s, Parliament divided into two houses. The representatives from the towns and cities formed their own section that became known as the House of Commons. The barons and nobles became the House of Lords.

England was not the only country that had a council to represent the people and to limit the power of rulers. In most countries, though, these councils eventually disappeared under rulers who wanted to keep as much power as possible.

In England, Parliament has continued in much the same form through the centuries. Well into the 1600s the king and Parliament continued to struggle over power. Sometimes, Parliament held the upper hand. Other times, the king was stronger.

Parliament Today

Today, the House of Commons has 650 elected representatives. Both houses of Parliament meet in the Great Palace on the Thames River. This building was rebuilt in the mid-1900s, but it includes Westminster Hall, built in 1099. The houses of Parliament are among of the most famous landmarks in London.

An Unstable Situation Sometimes, being closely related can be a cause of confusion and even conflict. That certainly was the case in England and France during the Middle Ages. For many generations the rulers of England actually spoke French.

Henry II, for example, was one of the great kings of England. He spoke French much better than he spoke English.

As strange as it sounds, the king of England and many of the powerful English nobles were also vassals of the king of France. You see, many years earlier the ancestors of these English nobles had received large grants of land from the king of France, and this meant that they and their heirs owed loyalty to the king across the English Channel.

This became a very big problem when the kings of England and France went to war. Many nobles were vassals of both kings and owed loyalty to both.

Here was another complicated part of feudalism: All these nobles and monarchs could only marry other monarchs and high-ranking nobles. Therefore, the kings and dukes of almost every part of Europe were related to one another. This caused some serious confusion when a king died. In fact, most wars were fought over the succession, or the order in which people took the throne. Remember the Battle of Hastings?

In the 1300s the king of France died, leaving no sons to take his place on the throne. The mother of the king of England had been the sister of the king of France who had just died. That meant that the king of England,

Edward III, was the nephew of the recently deceased king of France. The English king claimed the throne of France, but nobody in France accepted his claim. In fact, the French throne had previously been claimed by Philip of Valois (vah LWAH), a nobleman. This conflict over the French throne was the event that started the Hundred Years' War.

A Misleading Name

The Hundred Years' War is a misleading name in at least two ways. First of all, the Hundred Years' War lasted more than a hundred years. It lasted 116 years to be exact. Second, the Hundred Years' War was not a single war. It was several smaller wars fought between England and France. War did not go on all the time during the 116 years from 1337 to 1453. There were **truces** that lasted up to 25 years.

When the Hundred Years' War began, France was by far the richest and most powerful kingdom in Europe. It was rich in farming and grazing land. French castles and churches were the marvel of Europe.

England, on the other hand, was a small island with a harsher climate, fewer people, and much less wealth than France. So it is no surprise that the king of

vocabulary
truce an agreement to stop fighting

France made a terrible mistake: He was overconfident. He misjudged England and overlooked some of the strengths of the island nation.

One of the things that England had going for it was the wool trade. The climate of England was bad for growing crops, but it was good for raising sheep. The wool from these sheep provided a good income. It also caused Flanders, a cloth-producing region of northern France, to side with England.

In military terms it looked like France had a big advantage. First, most of the war was fought in France, so the French were fighting on their home territory. Second, it was very expensive to ship armored knights and horses across the English Channel to France. Finally, in most battles, the French had a big advantage because they had many more knights.

But once again, the English were stronger than they appeared. England was the first nation to make use of a new kind of bow called the longbow. With the longbow, archers could shoot arrows a longer distance with greater power. In fact, arrows shot from a longbow could cut through armor.

To make a very long story short, the French misjudged their rivals. That is one of the reasons why a war that the French thought they could win quickly turned into a war that went on for such a long time.

Bloody Battlefields

The Hundred Years' War was a series of bloody, costly wars. Thousands of soldiers died on each side. The use of the longbow took away the great advantage that armored knights had previously enjoyed on the battle-field. English archers, when given the chance, used their weapons to mow down French knights.

One of the most famous battles of the war was fought at the French town of Agincourt (AJ ihn kor). A large, powerful French army cornered a small English army. The French were sure of victory. The English

The blue and red flag carried by the English soldiers on the right displays symbols of both England and France—the English lion and the French lily.

were sure they would be slaughtered by the French forces. But the superior tactics and powerful longbows of the English resulted in a horrible, bloody defeat for France.

The End of the War

The way armies fight at the end of a war is often very different from the way they fight at the beginning of the war. That certainly was the case in the Hundred Years' War. Remember how the longbow gave the English a military advantage?

Well, the French never stopped trying to come up with better weapons of their own. Around 1400 they did. The French developed cannons that were powerful, easy to move around, and accurate. Soon, French artillery gave them a big advantage.

When the fighting stopped, the French had won. England had to give up almost all the territory it had controlled in France.

Effects of the War

But the Hundred Years' War is more important for what happened to England and France than for the military results. Yes, France won the war and took back territory from England. But both countries were changed forever by the fighting.

The use of the cannon changed warfare in the Middle Ages.

France was left in terrible shape from the fighting. English soldiers, far from home, had routinely stolen and looted from French towns and farms. Soldiers also had held entire villages for ransom. They would capture a village, threaten to burn it and kill everyone in it if people in the surrounding villages didn't pay some money. All this looting and ransoming left France much poorer than it had been before the war. It also left a feeling of hatred between the French and the English that lasted for more than 400 years.

A Different World

The real winners of the war were the kings of both France and England. The deaths of so many knights weakened many noble families. The power of the noble barons was reduced, and kings in both countries became stronger.

The war also weakened the rule of feudalism. Towns and cities began to grow in size and power. They owed no loyalty to a feudal baron but to the king from whom they received their charter. So, instead of feeling loyal to their feudal lord, people felt loyal to their king and their country.

This feeling for their country led to another big change that affects us today. During the war the rulers of England and educated and wealthy people stopped speaking French and began speaking English. Books and documents began to be written in English.

History is always clearer when we look back from the present than it is to the people living through it. Although the people didn't know it at the time, a new world was being born.

 **Hero for the Ages** You have read about great kings and warriors. Now you are going to read about a great warrior who was certainly one of the greatest heroes of the entire Middle Ages. Her leadership turned the tide of battle in the Hundred Years' War. Her actions helped the French win a war they seemed certain to lose.

Yes, that's right, this great warrior was a woman, actually a teenager. She was a simple peasant girl, not a well-educated woman of noble birth. She was about the same size as most of you. But Joan of Arc became a giant in the history of the Middle Ages. Her story is still exciting to read more than 500 years after she lived.

Hope Returns

In the last lesson you read about how the English won battle after battle against the French in the Hundred Years' War. Yet, France seemed to have all the advantages in the war. But these advantages were of no use against the English. All the years of fighting and looting had left the French pretty hopeless and dispirited. It seemed as if they had lost the will to fight the English.

In battle after battle, 10 to 15 times as many French soldiers were killed as English soldiers. This was partly because the French had a very old-fashioned way of fighting. They treated war as a tournament, or game. They wanted to play fair, so they waited patiently on their horses until the English had set up their barricades of pointed stakes and had put all their archers into position. Then, when the English were ready, the French would attack. At that point the English would shower arrows on the advancing French horsemen. Shot from powerful longbows, the sharp arrows could pierce the thin sheets of armor of the French knights, most of whom never even got close enough to use their swords on the English.

In the last decades of the war, though, the French regained their courage and their will to fight. They stopped fighting to be fair and started fighting to win. This change came from a most unexpected source: a simple girl named Jeanne. In English we call her Joan. Joan believed that God had given her the mission of driving the English out of France and restoring the French king to the throne.

Visions and Voices

Joan grew up in a small village called Domrémy (dohm REH mee). When she was about 13 years old, she began having visions of God and angels and hearing voices, which she believed to be the voices of God and the saints. At first, they simply told her to live a good life. As the years went by, however, she heard the voices more often. Finally, she understood that she was being told that God had chosen her to rescue the kingdom of France. Joan was 17.

Joan was stunned at this idea. She knew nothing about war or politics. Yet the voices continued. After the village of Domrémy was burned by the English, the voices became urgent and more specific. They told her that she should go to a nearby large town about

12 miles from her home. At this town, Joan was told to ask the help of the governor in reaching the man who was next in line to be king, the **dauphin** (doh FAN). The voices told Joan her mission was to free the city of Orléans (or-lay AHN), which was under siege by the English, and to see the dauphin crowned king of France.

The governor had no interest in meeting with her. So Joan simply stood outside his castle, praying and explaining to people why she had come.

Joan soon had a small group of supporters. One of them, a young soldier, gave her the clothes of a young man to put on. Someone else gave her a horse. Yet another person cut her hair for her. The governor finally agreed to see her. At first he laughed at her; but later, for reasons no one knows for sure, he changed his mind. He gave her a sword and permission to go to the dauphin. He gave her an archer, a royal messenger, and three servants. Her friend, the young soldier, and his squire came as well.

Joan is usually portrayed wearing the clothing and armor of a soldier.

A Victory at Orléans

Joan and her little band traveled through 350 miles of cold, flooded rivers and war-torn countryside. She was admitted into the grand hall of the castle where the dauphin was staying. It was filled with more than 300 knights and many courtiers dressed in fine clothes. The dauphin stood among them.

Legend has it that the dauphin was testing Joan by mingling with the crowd, but Joan surprised everyone by walking right up to him and kneeling before him. It may be that Joan had seen his picture before on coins or banners. Yet, it was impressive that a simple peasant girl could pick him out of such a crowd.

Joan was given a room in the castle, and she began to practice her fighting skills. A group of strong and even famous knights gathered around her. We can't explain how, but Joan soon had these famous warriors willing to do whatever she asked. All we can assume was that Joan's faith and her leadership inspired others to follow her. With an army of some 3,000 to 4,000 soldiers, Joan set off for Orléans.

The city had been under siege for nearly seven months. The English hadn't succeeded in capturing the city, but the French forces were weak and losing ground. As Joan rode through Orléans on the night of her arrival, townspeople carrying torches pressed around her. Rumors had spread through France that a young woman dressed as a boy had been sent by God to save them from the English.

Joan was eager to battle the English, but the French commander urged her to be patient as he assembled his troops. Joan agreed, but a few days later, just as she was settling down for an afternoon nap, she suddenly jumped up. "In God's name," she said, "my counsel [advisor] has told me I must attack the English." Her voices had spoken to her. She rode down to the gates of the city where she found French soldiers, wounded and bleeding, retreating from the English forces. When the French soldiers saw Joan on her horse, waving her white banner, a new spirit filled them. They turned around and headed back toward the English with such a surge of force that the English, who had been winning just a short time before, began to retreat.

She predicted that she would be wounded, but she fought without a helmet so that her soldiers could see her. An arrow pierced her neck. She almost fainted with pain, but a few hours later she returned to the fight. After three days of fighting, the English were finally driven out of Orléans. The war was not over, but for the first time it seemed that the English might be defeated.

This was an important victory, but the sight of the blood and the corpses upset Joan. Though she thought that fighting was necessary to win the freedom of France, she demanded that her soldiers go to church, and she did not allow swearing or looting among her men.

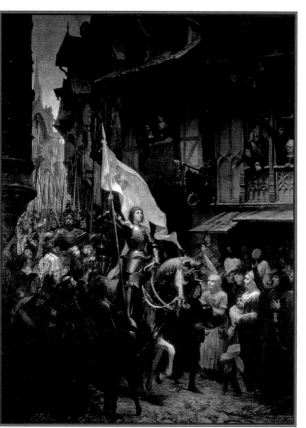

The people of Orléans cheered the victorious Joan and her soldiers.

A Crown for a King

Now Joan devoted herself to the next part of her mission. She returned to the dauphin and convinced him to travel to Reims (reemz). This was the city where French kings had been crowned for hundreds of years. The problem was that Reims was controlled by the Burgundians (bur GUN-dee unz) who were on the side of the English. When Joan arrived, however, the residents of the city had a change of heart. They cheered the dauphin. The Burgundian army quietly slipped out of town, and Charles, the dauphin, walked up the aisle of the great cathedral with Joan at his side. He would be dauphin no longer. He was crowned Charles VII, king of France. Joan was at the peak of her glory.

Politics and Prison

If the story of Joan of Arc were a fairy tale, she and King Charles VII would defeat the English and live happily ever after. In real life, politics entered the story.

Once he was crowned, the king began making deals behind Joan's back. Joan simply wanted to keep fighting until the English were driven out of France. But the king made deals with the Burgundians and the English without telling Joan.

In 1430, Joan was captured by Burgundian soldiers, who then sold her to the English. The English and Burgundians "were more joyous than if they had seized five hundred men-at-arms, for they feared no captain or leader as much as they had . . . feared [Joan]."

Trial and Death

Joan was thrown into prison and prepared for a trial. Because she claimed to hear the voice of God and the voices of saints, she was to be tried for heresy, the crime of going against the teachings of the Church. To prove this crime, they needed to find some people who were willing to repeat gossip or spread rumors, and they did. Finally, some churchmen who did not know Joan but who were either afraid of the bishop or hoped to gain from helping the English were summoned to try her. Day after day they questioned her. They focused most of their questions on the voices that Joan claimed to hear and on the fact that she wore men's clothing. For a woman to wear a man's clothing was a serious crime.

Joan conducted herself so well and answered so simply and truthfully that it was hard to make much of a case against her. But after weeks of questioning and accusations, the court sentenced her to death.

She was burned at the stake, a death she dreaded. "I would rather be beheaded seven times than burned," she said. As the fires licked at her, she gazed at a large cross that one of the spectators held before her. She called to Jesus, and then she was silent. Some people wept as she burned. An English person called out, "We have burned a saint."

Joan's death was a public event at which many people wept. She was nineteen years old.

Victory

Although Joan was dead, the tide of the war had turned. The French succeeded in driving the English out of all of their territories except the city of Calais.

Twenty years after her death, the Church held an investigation of her trial. After a complete review of the evidence, it was decided that the trial had been unfair. It was too late to help Joan, and no one involved in the unfair trial was ever punished, but Joan's reputation as a great hero was secure. For centuries, writers and artists have told her story in poems and plays and statues. In 1920 the Catholic Church declared the simple peasant girl a saint.

**Terrible Way to Die** Imagine that you are a ten-year-old child living in Florence, Italy, in the year 1348. You have been sent by your parents to a nearby market. As you wander about the busy marketplace, you overhear people talking. "It started in Sicily," one man says.

"No, no," says another man, "it started in the East. The Tartars began it."

The first man waves his hand impatiently. "No matter where it started. It's killed most of Sicily, and now it's coming here."

What on earth are these people talking about? You pull on the jacket sleeve of one of the men. "Sir, sir," you ask. "What are you talking about?"

The two men glance at one another. The man in the jacket turns to you and looks at you with stern eyes. "It's the Great Death, child. It's coming. Now, run home and tell your parents to get you and your brothers and sisters out of town."

Before much time had passed, you would learn a great deal more about the Great Death. All around you, people would die. Some would die very quickly, almost as though they were poisoned. Others would linger for three days or even six, most developing ugly growths the size of eggs in their armpits, neck, and lower body. Large red and black spots appeared on their skin. Some would fall into a coma. Others would seem to do a strange dance as their nervous system was attacked by the disease.

Nowhere to Run, Nowhere to Hide

The man who feared the worst would turn out to be right. The Great Death did come to Florence, and it killed more than half the people in the city.

The **plague** seems to have started in Asia in the 1320s. It was carried by ships to cities in Italy and France and to ports in Sicily in 1347. The next year it moved inland and attacked Italy, France, Spain, northern Africa, and Greece. There was still hope that it would stop, but eventually it covered northern Germany, Scotland, and the Scandinavian countries of Norway and Sweden. It reached all the way to Iceland and Greenland.

> **vocabulary**
> **plague** a highly contagious, usually fatal, disease that affects large numbers of people

Today, it is believed that the plague was spread by rats and fleas. Some scholars believe that the Black Death, as it is now called, was really a combination of three or four diseases spreading through Europe at roughly the same time.

Disappearing Villages

The worst outbreak of the Black Death only lasted four years. But when it was over, Europe was a very different place. It is estimated that about one third of the people in Europe, around 25 million people, died of the plague. It wasn't until 1600, about

250 years later, that Europe reached the population level that existed before the plague hit.

Some areas were hit harder than others. In some regions as many as two thirds of the population died. In England alone, about a thousand villages disappeared as a result of the plague. In some places there were not enough people remaining to bury the dead. People who survived moved to larger towns.

The Black Death was so severe that in many places there were not enough coffins and, often, no one to conduct church services.

Long-Term Effects

Once the Black Death had passed, people started to pick up the pieces. One positive result of so much death was the sudden labor shortage. Serfs could bargain for better working conditions. In fact, most serfs were able to buy their land and freedom. Within a hundred years, serfdom disappeared from Europe.

The shortage of workers also inspired people to try to invent labor-saving devices.

New types of water mills and windmills were invented, along with other new inventions like the printing press. Efforts to understand the horrors of the Black Death and to prevent it from happening again encouraged an interest in science and medicine.

The End of the Middle Ages

Remember how the Hundred Years' War helped weaken feudalism? The Black Death also helped weaken feudal ties. It was not easy to keep society going when so many people died so quickly. Strong rulers helped to keep order, and that helped to strengthen kings and city governments.

By about 1500, Europe was changing. Both kings and towns were stronger. Knights and armor were on the way out; cannon and cannon balls were on the way in. Kings and city governments both founded more universities so that more people could study law, medicine, and other subjects. In Italy, learned people had begun to look back to the learning and the art produced by ancient Greeks and Romans thousands of years before them. The movement we call the Renaissance had begun. There were more cities and more trade. Some traders began to look for more ways to trade with more people outside of Europe, going as far as Africa and even to America. With the dawn of these new times, the Middle Ages—the world of feudalism, lords and vassals, serfs, knights, and courtly love—faded into the past.

abbot the leader of a monastery

charter a document given by a government or ruler to a group of people or a company

circuit an area or district through which a judge travels to hold court sessions

Code of Chivalry a set of rules for knights

convent a community of women who devote themselves to religious life

cooper a person who makes barrels

dauphin the title given to the eldest son of the king of France

excommunication the punishment of not allowing someone to continue as a member of the Church

feudalism a system of government in which land is exchanged for loyalty and services

fief a plot of land exchanged for loyalty to a ruler

journeyman an apprentice who is qualified to work in a particular trade

jury a group of people who hear evidence in a trial and then vote on the guilt or innocence of the accused

knight a military servant of a feudal king or other superior

manor the estate over which a lord had control; also the lord's house on an estate

monastery a community of monks

pilgrimage a journey undertaken for a religious purpose

plague a highly contagious, usually fatal, disease that affects large numbers of people

serf a farmworker who was bound to live and labor on his lord's land

smith a person who works with metals, such as a goldsmith, silversmith, tinsmith, or blacksmith

tournament a staged battle fought by knights for money and honor without the intention to wound or kill

troubadour a person who composed poems that were set to music

truce an agreement to stop fighting

vassal a person who receives land from a ruler and in return promises aid

The Spread
❁ of Islam ❁

Contents

 **he Call to Prayer** The white-robed man climbed the stairs that circled the outside of the tower. It was not an easy climb. It was just after noon, and the sun beat without mercy on the tower and the buildings below. The place was Cairo, Egypt, and the year was AD 1082. There were 175 steps in all.

The man—let us call him Khalid ibn Zayd (Khalid, the son of Zayd)—no longer thought to count them.

When he reached the top step of the tower, Khalid ibn Zayd turned, looked down on the courtyard below, and squinted toward the fields beyond. Then he raised his hands beside his head, palms forward, took a deep breath, and called out to the people below in a powerful voice:

> God is most great.
> I bear witness there is no god but Allah.
> I bear witness that Muhammad is the messenger of Allah.
> Come to prayer.
> Come to salvation.
> God is most great.

Below him, worshipers moved steadily through doors cut into the courtyard wall toward a covered area extending from the opposite wall. Before entering the area, each worshiper removed his shoes, covered his head, and carefully took a place facing a small arch cut into the wall. Each, like Khalid ibn Zayd, raised his hands beside his head, palms forward, and prayed in the Arabic language, "*Allahu Akbar*" ("Allah is most great!"). Allah is the Arabic word for "God."

The worshipers then knelt down and bowed their heads to the ground, while praising Allah for his goodness. They sat up and said, "There is no god but Allah, and Muhammad is His messenger." Finally, they turned to the right and then to the left, saying, "Peace be with you and the mercy of God."

The Muslims

Khalid ibn Zayd was proud of his service in calling his people to prayer. He was a *muezzin* (myoo EZ ihn), a special person trained to call others to prayer. The tall tower from which he made his daily calls was a **minaret** (mihn uh RET).

Like Khalid ibn Zayd, the worshipers he summoned were Muslims (MUZ lumz). Their religion is known as Islam (IHS lahm), which means "surrender to God." Muslims, then, are "those who have given themselves to God."

The Muslims' place of prayer is a building called a **mosque** (mahsk). Muslims believe they can pray anywhere and do not need a special building. However, when they are praying, Muslims always must face in the direction of Mecca, an important city located on the Arabian peninsula in the Middle East. Muslims consider Mecca the holiest of cities because Mecca is the birthplace of the prophet Muhammad, the founder of Islam.

vocabulary
minaret a high tower on a mosque
mosque a Muslim house of worship

High on a minaret, a muezzin calls the Muslim faithful to prayer five times a day.

Allah's Messenger

Khalid ibn Zayd felt fortunate that he lived in Cairo, which was a great center of Islamic learning. His son, Yusuf, could attend the mosque school and learn how to live according to the Koran, the Muslims' holy book.

Soon after the noon prayers, young Yusuf ibn Khalid returned to his schoolroom in the mosque.

"Peace be upon you," the teacher greeted the students.

"And on you be peace," responded the students in one voice.

"Yusuf," his teacher called, "why do we Muslims worship Muhammad, praise be upon him?"

Yusuf knew it was a trick question.

"Honorable teacher," he answered, "we do not worship Muhammad, praise be upon him. We honor him as Allah's greatest messenger, but we worship only Allah."

"Well said," replied the teacher, allowing himself a small smile. "Can you tell me about Muhammad. How did he come to be Allah's messenger?"

"Once, when Muhammad was asleep," Yusuf answered with confidence, "the angel Gabriel came to him in a vision and told him to read some words on a piece of cloth Gabriel held up. Muhammad read the words, but did not understand what was happening to him. He was afraid. Then he heard the voice of the angel telling him that he was Allah's messenger."

"And did Muhammad begin immediately to act as Allah's messenger?" asked the teacher.

"No," said Yusuf, "he was still afraid. But the angel came to him again and told him to begin his work and warn the people to change their lives."

"You have listened well, Yusuf," said the teacher. Yusuf bowed slightly and smiled, happy with his teacher's praise.

"Ali," the teacher called to a tall boy seated beside Yusuf, "did the people listen to Muhammad's message?"

"No," replied Ali, "at first only a few people among Muhammad's family and friends believed what he said. Most of the people ignored him or did not like what he said."

"And what did he say that made him unpopular?" prodded the teacher.

"Well," Ali answered thoughtfully, "he told them that only Allah was God and that they should not worship other gods. The people did not like that because they had lots of gods and put statues of them in the Kaaba."

"And what was the Kaaba?" the teacher cut in.

"It was a shrine where various gods were worshiped."

"And what is it today?"

"It is the holiest place in Islam," answered Ali, adding quickly, "and only Allah is worshiped there."

The Five Pillars of Islam

"Excellent," said the teacher.

"The people did not listen to Muhammad because he told them only Allah is God. That is the first pillar, or foundation, of our faith. We believe there is no god but Allah and that Muhammad is the messenger of Allah."

"What are the other pillars of our faith?" the teacher asked.

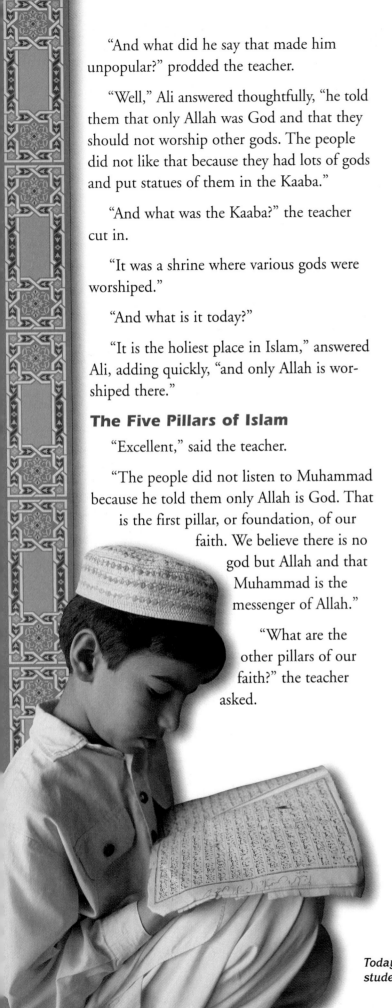

"You first, Hassan," he said.

"The second pillar of our faith," Hassan responded, "is prayer. Five times a day we Muslims pray toward the Kaaba in Mecca. We must first pray early in the morning, then we pray at night, and we must also pray three times during the day."

"The third pillar," Hassan continued, "is sharing wealth with the poor. Muhammad taught that we must help the poor and those in need by giving them money."

"You have answered well," interrupted the teacher. "We shall give someone else a chance to answer now."

"Ishaq," he called, "what is the fourth pillar of our faith?"

"The fourth pillar is fasting," Ishaq said. "We Muslims fast during the month of Ramadan. That means . . . uhm . . . it means we do not eat or drink between sunrise and sunset for the whole month."

"And the fifth pillar, Ishaq?" encouraged the teacher.

"Well, . . . the fifth pillar," said Ishaq slowly, stalling for time. "The fifth pillar," Ishaq finally said slowly, "is to make a pilgrimage to Mecca."

"If we are able," Ishaq continued, "we should visit Mecca at least once in our lives."

"Well done, Ishaq," said the teacher with genuine pleasure. "You all have answered well today." He was very proud of his students and felt that they would become fine faithful Muslims.

Islamic schools much like the one described can be found today in many parts of the world, not only in Islamic countries but also in places like the United States.

Today, a young Muslim studies the Koran, much as the students in the story did almost 1,000 years ago.

ho Was the Prophet? Muhammad was born in the Arabian city of Mecca more than 1,400 years ago, in about AD 570. Muhammad's father died shortly before he was born. His mother died when he was only six years old, and then his uncle raised him. Muhammad is reported to have been thoughtful and honest.

A story is sometimes told about Muhammad that shows how much people respected him.

One year, floodwaters badly damaged the Kaaba, the holy shrine in Mecca that housed a sacred black stone. In the flood the stone was knocked loose from its special place in one of the Kaaba's walls. At that time there were many groups of families called **clans** living in Mecca. These clans argued over which one of them would have the privilege of re-placing the stone. When they could not agree, they decided that the next man who entered the courtyard surrounding the Kaaba would be granted the privilege.

> **vocabulary**
> **clan** a number of families claiming a common ancestor

Muhammad was the next man to enter the courtyard. When he was told of the decision that had been made, he grew uneasy. He did not come from an important clan and he feared that the leaders of more powerful clans would resent the privilege that had been granted to him.

An idea came to him. He took off his cloak, spread it on the ground, and carefully placed the sacred stone in the middle of it. Then he turned to the rival clan leaders and invited all of them to take hold of the ends of the cloak and lift the stone as high as the place in the wall where it belonged. When they had done so, he gently slid the stone into its place. The clan leaders praised him for the way he had given all of them an equal part in returning the stone to its honored place.

Muhammad: The Prophet

Often Muhammad would go off by himself to think about life and how it should be lived. In 610, during meditation, Muhammad had a vision. He believed the angel Gabriel, a messenger from God, appeared to him and

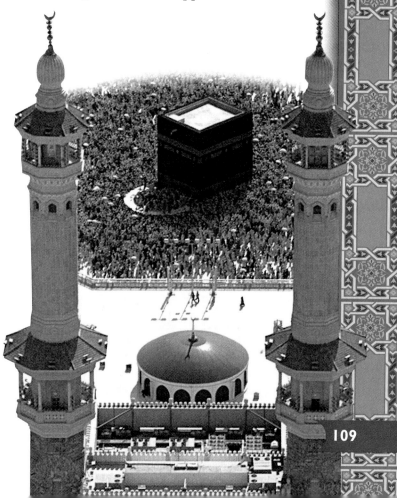

The black building in the center of this picture is the Kaaba, the holiest place in all of Islam. The Kaaba is in the grand mosque in Mecca.

told him he was to be Allah's messenger. At first, he was confused and frightened. Muhammad did not know what he was expected to do. His wife, some family members, and friends reassured him. They told him he was meant to be a **prophet** who spoke on behalf of God.

In 613, after a second vision, Muhammad began teaching in public what he had learned. He taught the people of Mecca that Allah alone was God. To Allah alone, he insisted, should the people pray. Muhammad also taught that in Allah's eyes, all believers were equal. The rich, he said, must share their wealth with the poor. He warned people that they would be judged by their deeds, not by their wealth.

Some people accepted his message, but many opposed it. Some were afraid that doing away with all gods except Allah would reduce the number of pilgrims who came to the Kaaba to honor their gods. The pilgrims spent much money in Mecca and were an important source of income.

Some members of his own clan stopped supporting him. He would not have their protection if he were attacked.

A Narrow Escape: The Hegira

In July 622, Muhammad arranged to have most of his followers move quietly to a town more than 200 miles north of Mecca. The people there had welcomed Muhammad's message. But Muhammad himself remained in Mecca.

Some Meccans, it is said, were so upset by Muhammad's teaching that they planned to kill him. In September 622, when he learned of his enemies' plans, Muhammad and a trusted friend secretly left Mecca. They traveled on little-used routes to the city where his followers were now living. Along the way, they hid in caves. After some days they joined their friends in the city that came to be called Medina. Many people in Medina welcomed Muhammad.

The escape of Muhammad and his followers from Mecca to Medina is very important to Muslims. This event is called the *Hegira* (hih JYE ruh), and Muslims begin their calendar with the year in which it took place.

The escape of the early Muslims from Mecca to Medina in 622 is known as the Hegira.

rom Medina to Mecca Again The Hegira, Muhammad's flight to Medina, marked the beginning of a new period in the history of Islam. Muhammad tried hard to convert all the citizens of Medina. He concentrated on building a community among the Arabs. He began to give Islam its own distinctive features.

Muslim pilgrims flock to Mecca today as in earlier times.

Followers of other religions—Christians and Jews—called people to prayer by using wooden clappers or rams' horns. Muhammad appointed a crier, or muezzin, to call Muslim believers to prayer.

Jews fasted on the Day of Atonement, which came once a year. Muhammad's followers fasted between sunrise and sunset during the entire month of Ramadan, the ninth month of the Islamic calendar. Jews prayed toward Jerusalem, their holy city. Muslims, said Muhammad, must pray toward the Kaaba in Mecca. Jews set aside Saturday as their holy day of the week. Christians chose Sunday. Muslims chose Friday.

Muhammad successfully converted most of the people of Medina to Islam. The merchants of Mecca, however, were not pleased. Muslims from Medina had been raiding their **caravans** for food and supplies. Meccans launched several attacks on Medina but were turned back. Finally, in 630, backed by a large force, Muhammad entered Mecca. Few Meccans fought against him. He destroyed the statues and other symbols of the many gods in the Kaaba and turned it into a holy place

vocabulary
caravan a group of travelers journeying together, often across a desert

dedicated to Allah alone. Mecca was now the center of Islam.

Muhammad's Final Years

Muhammad was to live two more years. During that time, Islam spread throughout the regions surrounding Mecca and Medina, often through the efforts of Islamic warriors.

Muhammad taught that Muslims must spread Allah's rule. Doing so, he warned, might require *jihad* (jee HAHD), that is, extraordinary effort and struggle. Sometimes, he said, that effort might take the form of fighting, even of war.

During his final years, Muslims believe, Muhammad continued to receive **revelations** from Allah. After his death the revelations were collected in a single book, the Koran. Muslims believe the Koran is the final word of God, which does not contain any error.

> **vocabulary**
> **revelation** something that is made known to humans by God

Some of his followers thought Muhammad would never die, but in 632 he became ill. The man known as Allah's messenger could not overcome his illness, and he died.

Muhammad's First Successors

When Muhammad died, he left no instructions for appointing a successor. His followers had considered him the last of the prophets. But Islam was spreading, and the Muslims knew they needed strong leadership if they were to survive.

Muhammad's successors were called *caliphs* (KAY lihfs). The first four caliphs oversaw the spread of Islam throughout Syria, Palestine, Egypt, North Africa, and Persia.

Muslim warriors were fierce soldiers who helped spread Islam throughout Asia and Africa, and into Europe.

They depended often on a combination of jihad, military strategy, and good fortune to accomplish their goals. In one important battle for the city of Damascus in Syria, for example, the Muslim warriors were forced to retreat before a much larger army of 50,000.

The Muslims camped with the desert at their backs, waiting for the enemy forces to follow them. When the two armies met in battle on a hot summer day, a strong wind blew in from behind the Muslims, swirling dust and sand and blinding the enemy forces. The clever Muslim warriors were able to overcome superior numbers and won an important victory. The great Syrian city of Damascus was theirs.

In time, new caliphs came to power and they became more like worldly rulers than religious leaders. They used their powerful armed forces to control their growing empire. They also made Arabic the official language of government.

Within the 100 years after the death of the Prophet Muhammad, Muslim rule had spread from the Arabian Peninsula to the borders of India and China in the east, through North Africa, and into Spain in the west. Muslim armies also advanced as far as Constantinople, the capital of the Byzantine Empire.

slamic Civilization Thrives For the first 130 years, Islam spread mostly through military conquest. Thereafter, the empire became stronger also through trade. In AD 750, new rulers moved the center of Islamic government from Damascus to Baghdad, in what is now Iraq.

Soon, Baghdad changed from a small village into the center of a great empire. Growing international trade meant Muslim traders had to develop ways to determine the worth of products from different regions.

More important than the material goods that traders brought to Baghdad were the ideas, customs, and practices that Muslim traders and travelers brought back from lands near and far. From all over the Islamic empire, the writings of the best minds of many cultures were brought to Baghdad and to other great Islamic cities. Baghdad even boasted a "House of Wisdom," a research library with a

staff that translated manuscripts from all over the known world.

Here, the works of Plato, Aristotle, and many other great philosophers and mathematicians were translated into Arabic. Many works of Greek and Roman thinkers were later available to medieval Europeans only because they were saved by Arab scholars. The Greek works opened up new worlds of understanding for Muslim thinkers, who built upon them. Muslim philosophers, scientists, mathematicians, and doctors were not content just to translate the ancient works. Their studies in astronomy,

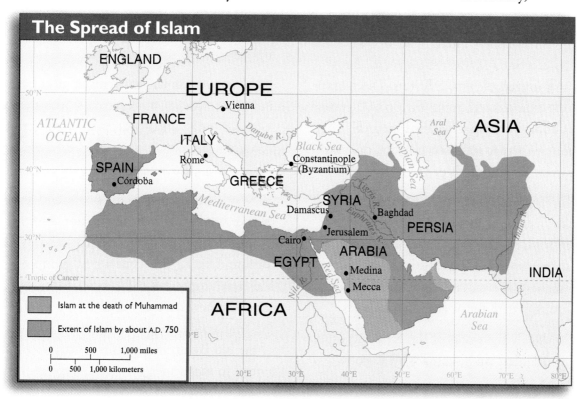

This map shows how far Islam spread from the death of Muhammad in AD 632 to AD 750.

medicine, mathematics, and technology made great advances in many of the fields. Other manuscripts were translated into Arabic from their original languages. The writings brought from India introduced the numerals 0 through 9 and a place-value system based on powers of ten. These numerals have been used since that time throughout the world. The mathematics in your textbooks today is based on these numerals and this place-value system. Ninth-century Muslims called these numerals "Hindi numbers," after the language of northern India. However, since their translation into Arabic, they have been called "Arabic numbers."

Learning and Discovery

In medicine, the Islamic empire was far ahead of western Europe. Muslim doctors were the first to describe measles and smallpox accurately, and they were the first to discover how some diseases spread. One doctor and philosopher, Ibn Sina, became especially famous. In the West, Ibn Sina is known as Avicenna.

Ibn Sina was a wonder child. It is said that by the time he was ten years old, he had memorized the entire Koran. The Koran has 114 chapters and more than 6,000 verses! As an adult he wrote a detailed medical encyclopedia that was used to teach doctors in Europe for hundreds of years afterward.

Ibn Sina described with great accuracy what was known about various diseases and their treatments. He also wrote a famous poem about the art of healing. His interests didn't stop there, however. He also wrote books on philosophy, astronomy, and mathematics.

Eventually the works of Ibn Sina and other Islamic scholars were shared with Europe.

The greatest story collection in Muslim literature is *A Thousand and One Nights*.

When the Muslims conquered southern Spain in the late eighth century, the city of Cordoba became a center of art and learning. Cordoba boasted 3,000 mosques, 700 libraries, and several institutions of higher learning. Indeed, as the Muslims expanded into Spain, their books and knowledge became more available to Europeans. By the year 1100, European doctors were reading translations of Avicenna on medicine, and by 1200, Europeans had been introduced to algebra through an Italian translation of Islamic works on the subject.

Architecture and Art

During this time some of the most beautiful buildings in the world were designed and built by Islamic architects and builders. Muslim artists created complex patterns and designs in bright colors and applied them to all types of surfaces: pottery, tile, glass, wood, plaster, stucco, and even brick. Islamic artists developed calligraphy, the art of elegant writing. Muslims considered writing the words of Allah from the Koran in calligraphy to be the highest form of decorative art.

Muslim poets wrote poems of great beauty, and other Muslim writers told stories that are still read today. The greatest story collection in Muslim literature is *A Thousand and One Nights*, also known as *The Arabian Nights*.

While Muslim scholars, poets, and architects created great treasures, Islam continued to spread, by preaching, by trade, and by warfare. During this time a new group of Muslims, the Seljuk (SEL jook) Turks, became the new leaders within Islam. By 1100, the Seljuk Turks had seized more than half of the old Byzantine Empire. Islam also had spread to eastern Asia.

Call for Help Near the end of the eleventh century, the Byzantine emperor asked Pope Urban II for help in turning back the Muslim Turks who were conquering parts of the Byzantine Empire. Urban II was the religious leader of Christians in western Europe.

The Byzantines were also Christians. The emperor did not stress the dangers the Muslims posed to his empire. Instead, he cleverly stressed the need for all Christians to unite so they could drive the Muslims from Jerusalem and win back the surrounding areas, known to Europeans as the Holy Land.

The Holy Land (Palestine), the place in the Middle East where Jesus once had lived, had been under Muslim control nearly 400 years. During most of that time, many Christian pilgrims to this area usually came and went as they pleased, to pray and to visit the places sacred to Christianity. But when the Turks came to power, their rulers changed their minds about who should and who should not be allowed to visit the Holy Land. Some Turkish rulers

made it difficult for Christians to visit the Holy Land. Christian pilgrims returning from Jerusalem claimed the Turks were destroying places holy to Christians and treating the Christians cruelly.

These reports were often exaggerated, but Pope Urban II responded as the Byzantine emperor had hoped. He delivered a stirring speech in 1095, urging all Christian men to free the shrines of the Holy Land from "the infidel" (someone who did not believe in the teachings of Christianity) and from what he called an "accursed race." The Christians, assembled in a field, listened to Urban's powerful call for war against the Muslims. The crowd grew angry and cried, "God wills it!" Within a month, crusaders from western Europe were marching off to war.

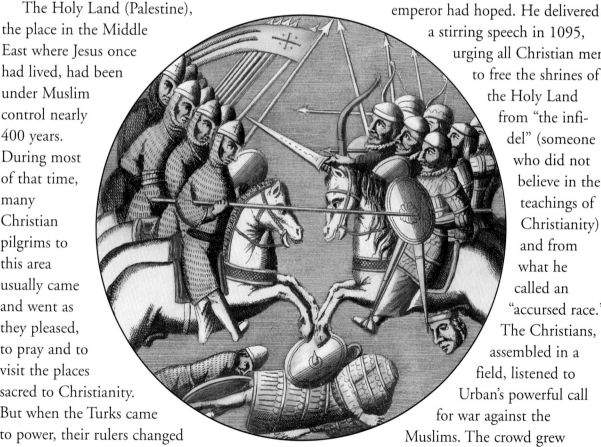

Crusaders from western Europe (left) clashed with Islamic warriors during the Crusades.

Wars Between Muslims and Christians

A series of "holy wars" followed, but these bloody wars turned out to be anything but "holy." Christians from Europe set off to fight Muslims for control of the Holy Land. In Europe, these wars were called the Crusades. The word "crusade" comes from the Latin word *crux* meaning "cross." Many crusaders wore strips of cloth in the shape of a cross sewn onto the backs of their clothes.

Among Muslims, these wars were called "the Frankish invasions." The Arabic word for "Frank" referred to all Europeans in general. Muslims saw the Christian armies as barbarian invaders of their land.

Whether known as Crusades or Frankish invasions, these clashes were a sad chapter in history. From 1095 to 1272, Christians eager to expel nonbelievers sometimes attacked not just Muslims, but also Jews and other Christians they considered **heretics.** Muslims, fighting for the lands they had conquered years before, took up the sword and fought right back. They believed that the crusaders were infidels, so these were holy wars for the Muslims, too. The result was nearly 200 years of gruesome warfare.

Of the eight Crusades fought during this period, only the First Crusade brought the Europeans military success. They gained some territory in Palestine and conquered Jerusalem. Over time, however, the Muslims gained back all the territory they had lost.

> **vocabulary**
> **heretic** one who holds beliefs that are contrary to or different from official religious teaching

Richard and Saladin

The Third Crusade (1189–1192) is perhaps the most famous because the leaders of both sides were heroes to their followers. The crusaders were led by Richard the Lion-Hearted, king of England, and the Muslims were led by Saladin, sultan, or ruler, of Egypt and Syria.

This portrait of Richard the Lion-Hearted is taken from an illustrated book produced around the year 1240.

This portrait of Saladin was made around 1180, when he was Sultan of Egypt and Syria.

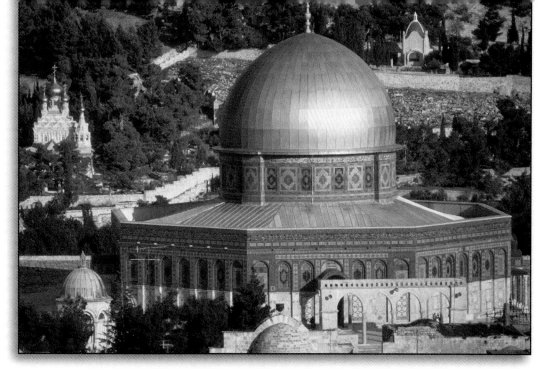

The Dome of the Rock, one of Islam's holiest places, is on Temple Mount in Jerusalem.

Loved by his subjects, Richard was everything a knight in the Middle Ages was supposed to be. He was brave in warfare, a fearless leader whom men were willing to follow into battle. It is said that he put everything he owned up for sale to raise money for the Third Crusade. He was so committed to the cause that he once said, "I would sell London if I could find a buyer."

Saladin was an equally courageous and skillful leader. He was a devout Muslim and believed in the *jihad* he was leading against the invaders from Europe. He insisted he would fight until "by God's help not a Frank is left on this coast!" He talked about pursuing the crusaders "until there shall not remain on the face of this earth one unbeliever in God."

Both Richard and Saladin were men of courage and were willing to fight for their religions. They were both convinced that the religion of the other was wrong. They were both convinced that the Holy Land should be theirs. What they admired about each other was their bravery and skill in battle.

Saladin was to triumph. In 1187, his forces recaptured Jerusalem, which had been in European hands for 88 years. Saladin did not have his Muslim soldiers kill the inhabitants of Jerusalem. He left the Holy City's shrines and churches unharmed.

The crusaders under Richard never did retake Jerusalem, but the two sides came to an agreement. The size of the European-held lands along the Mediterranean Sea would be reduced. For a price, Saladin allowed Christians to leave Jerusalem with their possessions. He also permitted them to make pilgrimages to the Holy Land, provided they came unarmed. Richard agreed to these terms and returned to England.

Some Effects of the Crusades

By the end of the last Crusade, the Muslims had reclaimed all the territories they had lost earlier. The Crusades had some lasting effects, and not all of them were good. The years of brutal warfare left Muslims and Christians suspicious and distrustful of each other.

Yet in the Crusades, for the first time, many European nobles learned about Muslim leaders and were impressed. To their surprise, they discovered Muslims were not, as they had supposed, ignorant "devils." They were intelligent, resourceful people from whom much could be learned. By 1140, Christian countries had schools that taught the Arabic language and Muslim ideas. Arabic works, like those of Avicenna, were being translated into European languages. Trade was on the rise. Distrust, even hatred, remained, but they existed alongside a new curiosity about the other culture.

The Ottoman Turks

By 1453 the Islamic empire was dominated by another group of Muslim Turks, called the Ottoman Turks. They had grown powerful enough to accomplish what had long been a goal of Muslim warriors: the capture of Constantinople. This city had been the center of the Byzantine Empire for more than 1100 years. The Ottomans gathered a large fleet of ships and many warriors for an assault on Constantinople.

On May 29, 1453, the Ottomans captured this prize of the Byzantine Empire. The city—which they began to call Istanbul, from a Greek word meaning "into the city"—would be a major center of Islam for centuries to come.

The Ottomans did not stop at Constantinople, however. Over the next 75 years, they pushed into southeastern Europe. They were halted first in 1529 at Vienna, in present-day Austria. In 1571 the navies of western Europe dealt the Ottomans a decisive defeat, finally stopping the Ottomans' expansion into Europe.

For hundreds of years, then, Islamic armies had successfully defended themselves and conquered new lands. Islamic cultural accomplishments had continued to grow, too. Islam influenced people around the world who benefited from its scientific and mathematical advances and from the riches of its art.

This painting shows the siege of Constantinople, which was finally conquered by the Turks in 1453.

Glossary

caravan a group of travelers journeying together, often across a desert

clan a number of families claiming a common ancestor

heretic one who holds beliefs that are contrary to or different from official religious teaching

minaret a high tower on a mosque

mosque a Muslim house of worship

prophet someone chosen by God to bring a message to people

revelation something that is made known to humans by God

African Kingdoms

Contents

Large Continent At one time Africa was called "the dark continent." It had this name because Europeans and other non-Africans knew little about the continent. Much of Africa was unmapped and unexplored.

For centuries, Europeans and people from western Asia had visited North Africa and parts of eastern Africa, but most of the rest of the continent was *terra incognita*, a Latin term meaning "unknown land."

Africa is a big continent—the second largest in the world. It stretches about 5,000 miles from its northern border to its southern tip, and about 4,600 miles at its widest east-west point. It is a land of vast deserts, huge rain forests, mighty rivers, and wide, grassy plains.

Seas and Oceans

Africa is surrounded by water. The Mediterranean Sea, bordering Africa on the north, provides the continent with an important route to Europe and western Asia. The ancient Greeks and Romans used the Mediterranean Sea to trade with the peoples of North Africa. Later, in the Middle Ages, Islamic merchants and seamen from North Africa traded with Europe and western Asia.

The stormy Atlantic Ocean on the west kept Europeans away from western Africa for centuries. In the late 1400s, better ships were developed by Europeans, and brave explorers began to explore western and southern Africa.

The Indian Ocean borders Africa on the east and is the third largest ocean in the world. It stretches from east to west about 4,500 miles from eastern Africa to Australia, and about 6,000 miles north to south from India to Antarctica. Africa's east coast along the Indian Ocean was better known to non-Africans than the Atlantic coast. Arabic, Indian, and Chinese traders visited the eastern coast of Africa long before Europeans explored western Africa.

The world's fourth largest island, Madagascar, lies in the Indian Ocean about 200 miles east of the African continent. The island is almost as big as Arizona and New Mexico combined. Africans and visitors from Asia explored the island thousands of years ago.

The southern tip of Africa is where the Indian and Atlantic oceans meet. It was—and still is—a dangerous place. On the west coast of the southern part of Africa is an area that receives so many storms that it originally was called the **Cape** of Storms. Its name was later changed to the Cape of Good Hope to make it sound more attractive to explorers.

> **vocabulary**
> **cape** a point or tip of land sticking out from the mainland into a body of water

The Red Sea lies off the northeastern coast of Africa and separates the continent from the Arabian Peninsula. The Red Sea extends northwest for about 1,200 miles from the southern tip of the Arabian Peninsula to the

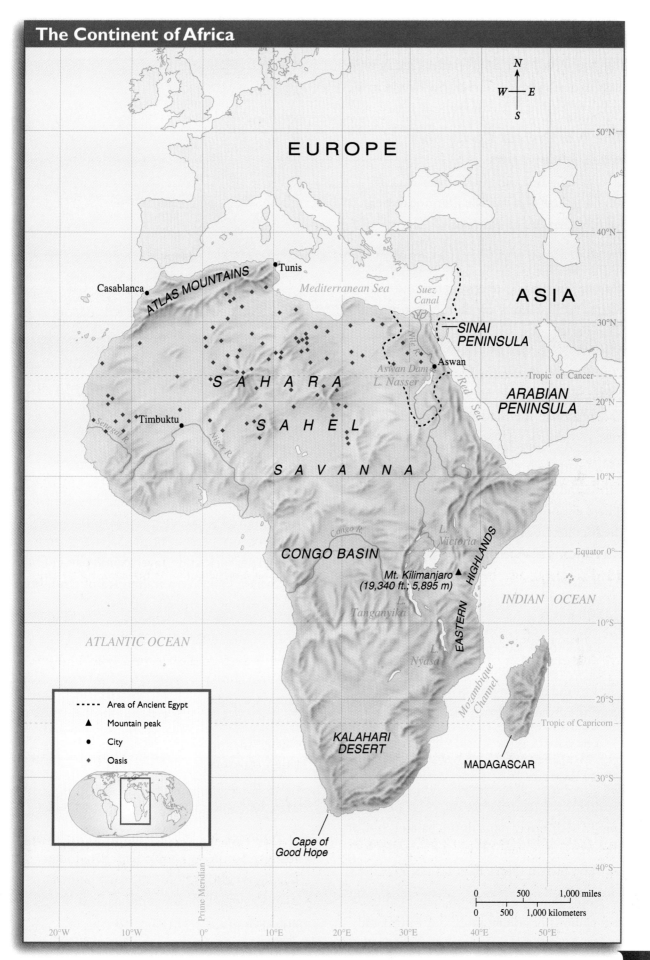

EUROPE

N
W—E
S

Casablanca
Tunis
ATLAS MOUNTAINS
Mediterranean Sea
Suez Canal
ASIA
SINAI PENINSULA
Aswan
Aswan Dam
L. Nasser
Tropic of Cancer
ARABIAN PENINSULA
S A H A R A
Nile R.
Red Sea
Timbuktu
Senegal R.
S A H E L
Niger R.
S A V A N N A
CONGO BASIN
Congo R.
L. Victoria
Mt. Kilimanjaro
(19,340 ft.; 5,895 m)
EASTERN HIGHLANDS
Equator 0°
INDIAN OCEAN
L. Tanganyika
10°S
ATLANTIC OCEAN
L. Nyasa
Mozambique Channel
20°S
Tropic of Capricorn
KALAHARI DESERT
MADAGASCAR
30°S
Cape of Good Hope
Prime Meridian
40°S

- - - - - Area of Ancient Egypt
▲ Mountain peak
● City
◆ Oasis

20°W   10°W   0°   10°E   20°E   30°E   40°E   50°E

0   500   1,000 miles
0   500   1,000 kilometers

50°N
40°N
30°N
20°N
10°N

Africa, the world's second-largest continent, is a land of diverse geographic features, including deserts, capes, and mountains.

Sinai Peninsula in Egypt. For centuries, the Red Sea served as a major trade route between East Africa and Asia. Today, the Suez Canal links the Red and Mediterranean seas.

The Northwest Coast and Atlas Mountains

Working our way south from Africa's northern coast on the Mediterranean Sea, we find that Africa has many different physical features and climates. Along the northwestern part of the continent is a narrow strip of land that is relatively flat and has warm, rainy winters and hot, dry summers. This narrow strip of land lies between the Mediterranean Sea and the Atlas Mountains 200 miles to the south. It stretches east about 1,200 miles from the modern city of Casablanca to the modern city of Tunis.

The Atlas Mountains form a barrier between the narrow strip of land in northwest Africa and a large desert called the Sahara. There are no barriers between the Sahara and the Mediterranean in the eastern part of northern Africa. The desert stretches right to the sea.

The Sahara

The Sahara is the largest desert on Earth. It measures about 3,000 miles from east to west and about 1,000 miles from north to south. It stretches south from the Atlas Mountains to the Sahel region of Africa, and east from the Atlantic Ocean to the Red Sea.

The Sahara is the world's hottest desert. The highest temperature ever recorded on Earth, 136.4°F, was measured in the Sahara. At night, the temperature can drop to a freezing 32°F. It rarely rains in the Sahara, but on the occasions when it does, the rain can be so heavy that it causes flash floods.

Some people imagine the Sahara as endless ribbons of golden sand, but in fact only

The Sahara is dotted with oases where water and some vegetation can be found.

about twenty percent of the Sahara is sand. The rest is rock and gravel. Some parts of the Sahara look like a rolling sea of sand, but other parts are hard, flat plains.

The Sahara is dotted with **oases**. The water at these oases enables people to grow fig, olive, and date trees and other fruits and vegetables. Even today, travelers across the Sahara stop at these green spots to refill their water containers and get food.

> **vocabulary**
> **oasis** a small area in a desert that has water

Although life in the Sahara can be harsh, nearly 2.5 million people live there today. The desert also is home to many animals, including gazelles, antelopes, jackals, foxes, and hyenas.

The Nile River flows through the eastern Sahara from south to north. Separating the western Sahara from the more fertile lands to the south is a strip of land called the Sahel.

The Sahel

The Sahel is a semi-dry rolling plain that stretches eastward across Africa from the Atlantic Ocean to the Indian Ocean. The region is an area of gradual change between the desert to the north and the savanna regions to the south.

Most of the Sahel receives 10 to 20 inches of rain each year. Most rain tends to fall during the summer months of June, July, and August. Various grasses and other types of plants that can survive with very little rain grow in the Sahel. The land is used mainly for grazing animals such as goats, sheep, and cattle. Some crops, such as peanuts, are raised here. To the south and west of the Sahel lies a large grassland known as the savanna.

The Savanna

The savanna is a vast region of tall grasses, scattered trees, and herds of animals. It reaches from the Atlantic Ocean in the west to the highlands of the modern country of Ethiopia in the east.

Sometimes this area is called the Sudan. This name comes from the Arabic term *bilad as-sudan,* which means "land of the black peoples." People have lived in this region for many thousands of years. Some scientists believe that the first humans lived in this region.

In the drier parts of the savanna, broad rocky plains are crossed by deep **ravines**. Farther south, the region becomes wetter, with rolling hilly grasslands good for grazing herds of animals. Many **nomadic** peoples raise their camels, sheep, and cattle on the savanna.

The savanna has two seasons—wet and dry. During half the year, it rains, and rains, and rains. Not surprisingly, this part of the year is called the "rainy season." During the other half of the year, the air is dry and hot. This is called the "dry season."

> **vocabulary**
> **ravine** a narrow, steep valley
> **nomadic** moving from place to place

Animals, such as these Kudus, graze on the plentiful grasses of the Sahel.

Because the temperature is neither too cold nor too hot in the savanna, and because there is enough rain, many crops are grown here. These include grains such as corn, sorghum, and millet. In addition to grains, farmers work the land to produce beans and peas, squash, melons, and okra. In areas with more rainfall, farmers grow rice, oranges, lemons, limes, and yams. Farmers clear their fields by burning the plants and then using the ashes as fertilizer.

At harvest time, farmers in the villages of the savanna rush to gather up the grains before the many birds that live in the region carry off more than their fair share of food. Containers of the grains rest on high shelves, away from mice, rats, termites, and other small, hungry creatures.

The Rain Forest

As you travel south of the savanna, temperatures remain warm but rainfall increases. This combination of warm temperatures and heavy rainfall creates tropical rain forests throughout central Africa. Like the rain forests of Brazil, Indonesia, and other parts of the world, Africa's rain forests are covered with dense vegetation.

There aren't any "seasons" in tropical rain forests. The climate is the same all year. The temperature usually stays between 75 and 80°F year-round. This part of Africa usually gets between 80 and 400 inches of rain a year. Because of this abundant rainfall, the rain forest is home to thousands of different types of plants.

Southern Africa

South and east of its rain forests, Africa has a variety of climates and land features. Much of the land is rolling savannas. Some parts of southern Africa get enough rainfall to raise a variety of crops, but one large section of southern Africa gets hardly any rain at all. This region is the Kalahari Desert.

The Kalahari Desert, in the modern-day countries of Botswana and South Africa, is covered with red soil, dry grasses, and parched brush. It is difficult to grow anything in the Kalahari because there is so little water, yet wild animals such as wildebeests, zebras, giraffes, and elephants live there. The Khoikhoi and San peoples (sometimes called "Bushmen," or people of the bush) survive in the Kalahari Desert by hunting and raising livestock.

Although most of the land east of Africa's rain forests consists of savannas, the highest mountain in Africa is also found here. This mountain, Mount Kilimanjaro, is located in the country of Tanzania.

Africa's highest mountain, Mount Kilimanjaro, towers over the high plateau of east-central Africa.

The Nile River is the longest river in the world and is used for both transportation and irrigation.

African Rivers

Some of the world's mightiest rivers slice through the African continent. The Niger and Senegal rivers flow through the savanna. Some of the great empires of ancient and medieval Africa developed along these rivers. Among these empires were Ghana, Mali, and Songhai. You will learn more about them later.

South of the Niger River, in the hot rain forest regions of Africa, is the powerful Congo River. The Congo is the second longest river in Africa. It is about 2,720 miles long and flows from its headwaters in central Africa to the Atlantic Ocean.

Of all of Africa's rivers, perhaps the most important and certainly the most famous is the Nile River. The Nile is the longest river in the world. Starting at Lake Victoria in east-central Africa, the Nile flows generally north to the Mediterranean Sea, for a total of more than 4,130 miles.

In ancient times, the Nile flooded its banks once a year, depositing rich, black soil nearby. Egyptian farmers planted their crops in this soil, making Egypt a major agricultural country. Grain raised along the Nile was sent to many places, including Rome. Since the 1970s, the flooding of the Nile has been controlled by the gigantic Aswan High Dam near the city of Aswan in Egypt. A large lake, called Lake Nasser, has formed behind the dam. The waters from this lake are used to generate electricity and to irrigate farmlands.

The Egyptian Civilization

The geography of Africa played a big role in the development of early and medieval kingdoms there. The greatest of these kingdoms was Egypt. Egyptian civilization stretches back more than five thousand years, to about 3100 B.C. The Nile River, which runs through Egypt, helped make this ancient civilization prosper. A Greek historian once called Egypt "a gift of the Nile."

Farmers of ancient Egypt produced an abundance of food. This allowed Egyptians who were not farmers the freedom to become craftsmen, soldiers, weavers, and other specialized workers who helped make the civilization grow and prosper. The Nile River also played an important role in the development of the ancient kingdoms of Kush and Aksum, which you'll read about on the next page.

Egypt's Rivals In addition to the great Egyptian civilization, other African civilizations thrived in ancient times. Two of these were Kush and Aksum.

"Kush" was the Egyptian name for the ancient African land of Nubia, the home of a highly advanced ancient black civilization. Historians believe that the Kingdom of Kush began sometime around 2000 B.C. It was located in eastern Africa, south of Egypt. The Kushites were good farmers, metalworkers, and traders. They also had contacts with many of the surrounding areas.

Other than the Nile River, Egypt has few natural resources of its own. The Nile provided the water to make Egypt an important agricultural nation. For centuries, Egyptians traded the food they raised with Kushites to get gold or precious, exotic products that were brought to Kush from western Africa and other parts of the continent. These imported goods included rare ebony wood, creamy white ivory, fragrant incense, and lion and leopard skins. The Egyptians adorned their bodies with Kush's beautiful gold jewelry and decorated their homes with ivory and metalwork purchased in the marketplaces of Kush.

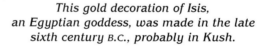

Harvard University.- Museum of Fine Arts Expedition

Courtesy, Museum of Fine Arts, Boston

This gold decoration of Isis, an Egyptian goddess, was made in the late sixth century B.C., probably in Kush.

Around 1500 B.C, the Egyptians invaded Kush. The imaginary story that follows describes a battle between the Kushites and the Egyptians and how it might have taken place.

Attack!

Arrows hissed through the shimmering heat as the invading Egyptians tore into Kerma, the capital of Kush. Egyptian soldiers swarmed into the walled town, burning crops and storehouses in their path.

As they raced from their mud-brick homes and workshops, some of the Kush men grabbed bows and arrows to use against the invaders. Others threw spears tipped with sharpened antelope horns, or swung massive wooden clubs at the Egyptian soldiers, smashing them to the ground.

Within moments, sweat and blood stained the hot earth. Stray arrows shattered magnificent glazed Kush pottery. Heavy gold beads were ground underfoot in the terror. Kush women hid behind palm trees, frantically trying to shelter themselves and their children from the Egyptian attack.

The Kush warriors fought heroically, but they were no match for the Egyptians, who were the most powerful people in the region. The destruction the Egyptians left behind struck terror into the hearts of the Kush people.

Kush Becomes an Egyptian Colony

After the Egyptians took over Kush, the Egyptian pharaoh wore sandals with the images of the Kush people carved into the soles to remind himself—and the Kush people—that he had crushed them. Over the next five centuries, from 1500 to 1000 B.C., the Kush people seemed to become Egyptian. They wore Egyptian-style clothing and worshiped Egyptian gods. Yet underneath their borrowed robes, the Kush people kept their culture and identity. The strength of their spirit would eventually lead Kush to challenge and conquer the Egyptians.

Around 730 B.C., Egypt grew weak, and the Kush struck the Egyptians with all their might. The prophet Isaiah described the Kush army as "whirring wings" because the soldiers tore into Egypt like a plague of starving insects. The Kush defeated the Egyptians. For a few decades, Kushite rulers became the pharaohs of Egypt. The victim had become the conqueror. This was the greatest period in the history of Kush, but it didn't last long. In 591, the Egyptians struck back, defeating Kush and capturing its capital.

The Kush people then moved their capital to the city of Meroë (MUHR oh ee), south of Kerma. Meroë was located on the Nile River and was surrounded by fine grazing land for herds of cattle, goats, and sheep.

Meroë became the greatest Kush city. It was a major trading center and one of Africa's first iron-producing centers. Kush shipped its ironwork across Africa and became the center of trade that may have extended more than 2,000 miles east, or perhaps all the way to China. Incredible rumors of Kush's wealth spread far beyond Africa. The region was called the "Land of Gods."

Land of Wonders

The Greek historian Herodotus recorded some of the rumors that had reached him about Kush and Meroë. Herodotus had heard that the land in Kush brought forth all sorts of food without cultivation. Another report described stone pyramids and a temple covered in some places with thin sheets of gold and shining like beacons in the bright African sun.

In some cases, Herodotus seems to have recorded wild rumors and not solid facts. Except along the Nile, the soil in Kush is not rich. However, dozens of stone pyramids still stand outside Meroë. These pyramids are steeper than Egyptian pyramids and have flat tops, and they were used as burial sites for the Kush kings, just like the Egyptian pyramids.

Archaeologists have found jewelry and other valuable artifacts in these burial sites. These relics tell us that Meroë was once a prosperous place, even if it wasn't as prosperous as Herodotus made it sound.

A Bitter Fate

In the early part of its history, Kush was attacked by its northern neighbor, Egypt. In the later part of its history, Kush was attacked by its southern neighbor, Aksum, (also spelled Axum), a kingdom located in what is now Ethiopia and Eritrea. The war with

> **vocabulary**
> **archaeologist**
> **a scientist who studies remains from past civilizations**

Aksum turned out to be the worst war of all because it destroyed the Kush kingdom.

Early in the fourth century A.D., Aksum's great warrior-king Ezana conquered Kush. Ezana bragged:

> I made war on them. . . . I pursued them . . . killing some and capturing others. . . . I burnt their towns, both those built of bricks and those built of reeds, and my army carried off their food and copper and iron . . . and destroyed the statues in their temples, their granaries, and cotton trees and cast them into the [Nile].

After his victory, Ezana thanked the "Lord of Heaven, who has helped me and . . . has this day conquered for me my enemy."

Unlike the pyramids of Egypt, some of Kush's pyramids had flat tops.

Ezana had converted to Christianity, and Aksum would become a Christian outpost in eastern Africa.

Aksum

After Aksum defeated Kush, the trade routes through Kush were ignored, and traders began to travel to Aksum by sea instead of trekking to Kush on land. At Aksum's bustling port of Adulis on the Red Sea, traders exchanged cloth made by the Egyptians for cloth made by the Berbers, nomadic people living in North Africa and the Sahara. According to one observer, they also traded "double-fringed linen mantles [cloaks]; many articles of flint glass . . . and brass, which is used to make ornaments; sheets of soft copper, used for cooking utensils and cut up for bracelets and anklets for the women; iron, which is made into spears used against the elephants and other wild beasts, and in their wars."

With all this trade, it's not surprising that Aksum became the strongest power in East Africa. The king of Aksum lived in a splendid palace with high corner towers. A traveler to Aksum reported that "the king . . . [wore] a garment of linen embroidered with gold [and] . . . around his neck was a golden collar. He stood on a four-wheeled chariot drawn by four elephants; the body of the chariot was high and covered with gold plates. The king stood on top carrying a small gilded shield and holding in his hands two small golden spears. His council [advisors] stood similarly armed and flutes played."

Aksum prospered for several centuries. Its kings built many churches and monasteries and had the Bible translated into the local language, Ge'ez. It also conquered neighboring lands, including part of the Arabian Peninsula.

Eventually, however, Aksum began to decline. During the 700s, Muslims began to move off the Arabian Peninsula and into Africa. They gained control of much of the land along the shores of the Red Sea and took over many of the trade routes that had made Aksum a mighty kingdom. Eventually, the Muslims took over the seaport of Adulis, and the Aksumite Christians were forced to retreat into the mountains. The descendants of the Aksumites lived on for many years, but in a weakened and isolated condition, surrounded by the Muslim world.

The three great kingdoms of Kush, Aksum, and Egypt were all located in northeastern Africa.

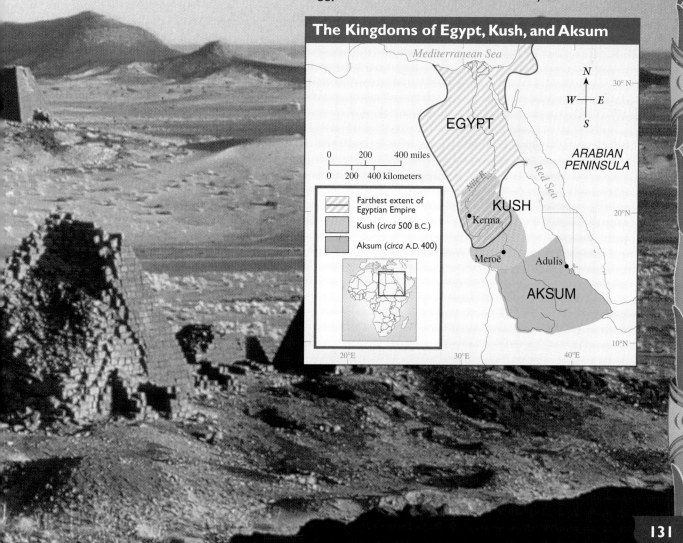

The Kingdoms of Egypt, Kush, and Aksum

Mediterranean Sea

EGYPT

ARABIAN PENINSULA

Red Sea

Nile R.

KUSH

Kerma

Meroë

Adulis

AKSUM

0   200   400 miles
0   200   400 kilometers

Farthest extent of Egyptian Empire
Kush (*circa* 500 B.C.)
Aksum (A.D. 400)

30° N
20°N
10°N
20°E
30°E
40°E

3 Trans-Sahara Trade

Traders of Medieval Africa "I hope we're near the oasis," Yusef the trader sighed as the sweat dripped into his eyes. The sun stood at its highest point, and the air shimmered with heat. Yusef's throat was parched with thirst. His tongue was so dry that it felt like a slab of wood in his mouth.

Yusef felt like sitting down to rest, but he plodded on beside his camels. "It will be worth all this trouble when my salt fetches a great price at market," he whispered to himself. "Then I can buy more camels and become a rich man."

Like the other traders in this camel **caravan**, Yusef was transporting salt mined from the salt regions in the middle of the Sahara to a trading center in the Sahel grasslands, on the southern edge of the Sahara.

At the mines, Yusef had watched the quarry owner's slaves dig out 200-pound cakes of salt and tie two cakes on each camel. "There is so much salt here that we build houses and mosques from it," the salt-quarry

owner had said. Yusef had actually seen a couple of these salt houses, glittering in the sun like gigantic, frosted cakes. Now, Yusef's camels swayed under the 400-pound loads of salt they were hauling 500 miles to the Sahel.

> **vocabulary**
> **caravan** a group of people and pack animals traveling together

Ships of the Desert

Yusef's camels were nasty and smelly, and they often spat at their master. But Yusef was glad to have them. He knew that camels were made for the desert. Broad splayed feet let them walk over hot sand without sinking in. A double row of eyelashes kept out stinging

sand from windstorms. They stored fat in their humps and could live off this fat when there was no food available. Camels could also go without water for days. Yusef was glad his precious cargo was carried on camels, not the horses used for the first desert caravans.

Yusef's last trip had gone smoothly, with nothing more than stinging bites from sand fleas and other pests. But Yusef knew that many traders ran into big problems on their journeys. Yusef had heard stories about traders who got caught in fierce sandstorms or who had gotten lost and had to slaughter their camels for food. Sometimes even this desperate measure was not enough. Yusef's own cousin had marched into the desert as part of a caravan, and neither he nor his fellow travelers were ever heard from again. As Yusef considered what might have happened to his cousin, a shiver ran down his spine.

Yusef tried to forget about his cousin and the dangers of the desert by thinking about the goods he would be able to trade for when he arrived at the markets of the Sahel. He ran over in his mind all the things he would be able to buy with his salt: gold, furs, silks, fruit, cotton cloth, ceramics, tools, horses, and even slaves.

On past trips, the leather pouch Yusef carried had been loaded with cowrie shells from the Indian Ocean and glass beads from Venice, Italy. Yusef had traded these for sweet dates and chewy figs from the oases he passed on the trade route, and for shiny copper from the bronze-manufacturing centers in the kingdoms of western Africa.

Yusef knew that the west African kingdoms in the vast savanna lands also purchased slaves from the interior of Africa and paid for these slaves with horses or gold. These slaves were often prisoners of war. They often came from lands that had been conquered by one African kingdom or another.

West Africans also supplied the cross-Sahara traders with kola nuts, pepper, leather, and cotton. Traders like Yusef would transport these items north and east, where they could trade them for more salt and other things the rulers of the savanna kingdoms wanted. And then the process would start all over again.

Camels are often called "ships of the desert" because they carry goods and people across vast desert wastelands.

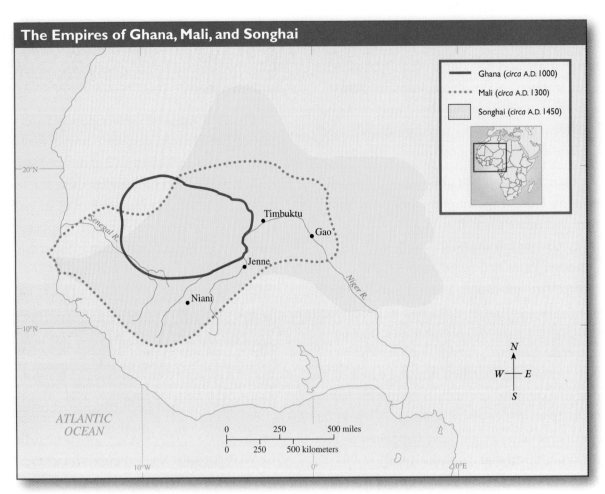

Three great empires—Ghana, Mali, and Songhai—developed in the northwestern part of Africa.

Traders Carry Precious Ideas

Caravans like Yusef's went back and forth across the desert for hundreds of years, and slaves, gold, horses, salt, and other material objects were not the only things they carried with them. The traders also carried things that couldn't be seen, felt, smelled, tasted, or heard, but that had far more impact than all the goods bought and sold.

What invisible items did Yusef and his fellow traders carry? Ideas, art, culture, and religion.

Sometimes scholars, poets, musicians, and artists traveled along with the traders. The scholars and poets on the caravan educated people and stressed the value of learning. The artists and musicians sold their works and

spread their songs. These people also brought their religious ideas with them, and most of them were Muslims. By A.D. 1000, the traders and scholars had spread the Muslim faith so effectively that many people in western Africa knew about the Islamic faith and culture.

In the 700s, Arabs of the eastern-Mediterranean countries conquered North Africa and Spain. They also made a great deal of money from the trans-Sahara trade routes.

The caravans helped the African people of the Sahel prosper and develop large and powerful kingdoms. During the centuries that followed, three great empires developed, expanded, and flourished in western Africa: Ghana, Mali, and Songhai.

An Empire Built on Gold King Tunka of ancient Ghana sat on his throne in a vast, open building called a pavilion. Behind him stood ten servants holding shields and swords decorated with gold. To his right stood Ghana's noblemen and their sons. They wore beautiful robes and had gold threads braided into their hair.

The pavilion was in Ghana's royal capital of Kumbi Saleh. The governor of the capital and other officials of the empire took their places around the king's throne. Even the animals wore gold. King Tunka's dogs, adorned with gold and silver collars, stood guard at his feet. Ten horses, covered with gold-embroidered cloth, pawed the ground outside the pavilion.

An early Arab explorer claimed that the king of Ghana was the "wealthiest of all kings on the face of the earth." Muslim scholars called Ghana the "Land of Gold."

How did Ghana become so rich?

Ancient Ghana was located on a large slice of land between the upper Niger and Senegal rivers. Ghana's wealth grew out of its location—right in the middle of the trade routes that brought salt from the Muslim Arabs of northern Africa and gold from the lands to the south of Ghana. Another trade route extended east to the Nile River valley. Ghana's capital, Kumbi Saleh, was at the center of these trade routes.

Ghana's king and his court reflected the fabulous wealth and power of the kingdom.

Ghana's location helped it become the first of the great western-African trading empires. The empire is said to have begun around A.D. 300 and lasted until the 1200s. At the peak of its power, around 1000, the kingdom of Ghana extended over an area of about 250,000 square miles, making it almost as big as the state of Texas.

Ghana's Great Kings

The kings of Ghana helped their kingdom flourish by making shrewd trade agreements with Arab traders. In addition, each king of Ghana collected taxes from merchants traveling through his empire. Merchants paid taxes on the goods they brought to sell and on the goods they purchased. These taxes went into the king's treasury and helped support his wealthy court.

The king also claimed all gold nuggets found in his kingdom, but he let traders keep the gold dust they brought from the gold fields. The important gold mines lay south of Ghana along the Senegal River. The miners kept their exact location a secret. The gold was sometimes stuffed into feather quilts for safe travel across the Sahara. With their enormous wealth, the kings of Ghana built a strong army that kept the trade route through Ghana safe.

Around 1150, an Arab traveler from Spain, visited Ghana and reported on the great trade of salt for gold that was making Ghana rich:

These gold weights, in the form of lions, were used to weigh gold dust in Ghana.

"In the sands of that country is gold, treasure inexpressible. . . . Merchants trade with salt for it, taking the salt on camels from the salt mines. They . . . travel in the desert as it were upon the sea, having guides to pilot them by the stars or rocks. . . . They take **provisions** for [the long trip], and when they reach Ghana, they weigh their salt and sell it [for] gold . . . according to the market and the supply."

Salt, Vital for Life

You know that gold is valuable for its rarity and great beauty, but do you know why ancient Africans valued salt so highly? Africans prized salt for many important reasons. Salt kept meat and vegetables from spoiling in the hot weather and made bland food tastier. Salt

> **vocabulary**
> **provisions** food, water, and other necessary items

was also used as a medicine to treat many different illnesses. In addition, people in hot climates such as the Sahara needed—and still need—salt to replace the salt the body loses from sweating.

Although salt was abundant in the northern deserts, it was rare in western Africa. By the time a trader like Yusef had hauled his salt to western Africa, its value would have increased greatly. In fact, salt was so valuable in this area that it was traded for an almost equal amount of gold.

Ghana Flourishes

As the country where the gold and salt caravans met and traded, Ghana became very rich and powerful. Ghana's kings used the profits made from this trade to build beautiful cities. Ghana's citizens felt proud of their country's great cities, built of sturdy stone.

Since iron ore was plentiful in Ghana and easy to mine, villagers skilled in iron-working built sturdy iron tools and weapons. As traders passed through Ghana, they brought many new products and interesting foods with them. Some traders paid their taxes in gold or salt, but others paid in copper, cloth, dried fruit, or other goods. As a result, the people of Ghana had many fine things to purchase and enjoy.

Because of Ghana's location and its great wealth, many traders from northern Africa and the Middle East moved to its cities. Most of these traders were Muslims. They believed strongly in Islam and were allowed to practice their religion freely. Many of the people of Ghana adopted this new religion. Those who did not follow Islam followed their traditional beliefs. They worshipped spirits in nature and the spirits of their ancestors.

Ghana's Downfall

Of course, neighbors envied a country as rich as Ghana. Enemies often attacked, hoping to get their hands on the gold.

Beginning in the late 900s Ghana was attacked by various groups of Berbers from North Africa. The people of Ghana fought off the first few attacks, but in 1076, Kumbi Saleh was conquered. The Muslim conquerors killed many people, forced others to convert to Islam, and seized the property of those who refused to convert. This was the beginning of Ghana's decline.

Ghana regained control of Kumbi Saleh in the late 1000s, but the kingdom never recovered its former power, in part because the gold supply to the south of its kingdom ran out. Ghana was further weakened when important trade networks slipped from its control.

In the early 1200s Kumbi Saleh came under attack yet again. This time the attacker was an African king named Sundiata Keita. In 1240 Sundiata Keita and his army captured Kumbi Saleh and absorbed the defeated empire of Ghana into the new empire of Mali.

These modern Berbers of North Africa celebrate a religious feast by galloping their horses across the sand and firing off their rifles.

Mali and Sundiata Keita

**Cruel King** As Ghana's power decreased, many of the areas it had controlled claimed their independence. Among these was the kingdom of Mali. Mali would eventually become the most powerful kingdom in West Africa, but during its early years it was dominated by more powerful kingdoms.

One of Mali's rivals was the Soso people who lived in the coastal regions south of Ghana. In the early 1200s, Sumanguru (su MAN gu ru), king of the Soso people, marched into Mali and conquered it. Cunning and cruel, Sumanguru taxed the people of Mali without mercy. He took their food. He took their gold. He even took their daughters and wives. In order to eliminate any rivals for his throne, Sumanguru decided to slaughter all of the former king's sons.

A Moment of Mercy

Sumanguru eventually did kill all but one of the king's sons. However, he decided to spare the life of a young Mandinka prince named Sundiata (sun DI ah ta).

Little Sundiata was paralyzed. He could not even stand up, much less walk. Perhaps

Sumanguru was being merciful. More likely, though, he decided that a crippled child could not possibly be a threat to him.

Sumanguru was wrong about that. Sundiata eventually grew up to be a great leader, known as "the hungering lion." Although the young boy was crippled, he had a noble pride and a hunger for greatness. He refused to submit to his sickness. After months and months of agonizing pain, Sundiata forced himself to walk. Leaning on an iron cane, he hobbled around his village. Sundiata pushed himself further and harder. His intense effort paid off—years later, he was able to walk without a cane. Sundiata even became a superb horseman and hunter.

Stories of Sundiata's determination, bravery, and accomplishments spread among his people.

The Soso people were powerful warriors.

Soon, the Mandinkas looked to Sundiata to rescue them from Sumanguru's hard rule. Sundiata's people counted on him to get rid of Sumanguru and get their country back.

Sundiata versus Sumanguru

In 1230, the other leaders of Mali rallied around Sundiata and proclaimed him the king of Mali. Sumanguru now realized that Sundiata was a leader who could topple his dictatorship. But Sumanguru did not plan to give up without a fight. He had a large, powerful army, and his people believed that he had special, occult powers that protected him from injuries during battle. This belief made them strong, fearless warriors.

War erupted in 1235, when Sumanguru's army met Sundiata's army in battle. During this battle Sundiata's Mali warriors crushed Sumanguru's army.

According to one Mandinka legend, Sumanguru vanished when he was struck with an arrow. A giant tree sprung up on the very

spot where Sumanguru had stood. Another version of the legend claims that Sumanguru hid in the mountains after his army was smashed. Whichever legend you decide to believe, no one disagrees that Sundiata defeated Sumanguru. Sundiata had shown great bravery in battle, and even today, the Mandinka people celebrate Sundiata as a hero.

Sundiata went on to conquer other lands. In 1240, Sundiata and his generals plundered Kumbi Saleh, Ghana's capital. The kingdom of Mali became the most powerful kingdom in western Africa.

Mali's Power Grows

Mali now controlled all the trade between northern and western Africa. Mali had fair leaders and a strong government.

Ibn Batutta, a scholar from Tangiers on the Mediterranean Sea, spent a year in Mali. He praised the leaders for making the country safe for all. "The traveler has no more reason

This nineteenth-century painting of Timbuktu depicts Mali when it was the most important empire in western Africa.

than the man who stays home to fear **brigands** or thieves [in Mali]," Batutta wrote.

The Mandinkas had Sundiata to thank for this. He proved to be as powerful a leader in peace as he had been in war. Sundiata created a strong central government that brought peace and order to the entire kingdom of Mali. This helped him regain control of the trade routes. Unfortunately, Sundiata died in 1255, before he could see his empire become even more powerful.

> **vocabulary**
> **brigand** a bandit

A Muslim Nation

Islam had been a force in western Africa for many years. However, with the growth of Mali, Islam now became the most powerful religion in the area, and western Africa became a key region in the Islamic world of the Middle Ages. By the time of Sundiata's death in 1255, Mali had a rich culture based on Islam. The Muslim holy book, the Koran, had become the basis of Mali culture. Mali had new laws, a tax system, and a dedication to education, all based on Islam.

Timbuktu, a Center of Learning

In an empire as large and important as Mali, many important cities developed and prospered. One of these was the capital city of Niani (NEE ah nee). Another was Timbuktu.

Timbuktu was (and still is) located at the great bend of the Niger River. The people of the desert and the people of the river traditionally met at this spot to trade their goods. Over the years, Timbuktu grew from a group of tents into a great center for learning and trade. Its fame spread throughout western and northern Africa and beyond.

Timbuktu boasted many mosques, libraries, and stone buildings. The city also had a famous Muslim university, and Muslim scholars throughout Africa traveled to Timbuktu to study at the university and do research in the library.

After Sundiata died, two of his sons took over the throne. The new leaders of Mali took the proud title "Mansa," which means emperor. In 1307, the second most famous ruler in the history of Mali took the throne. His name was Mansa Musa.

Glorious Reign Mansa Musa ruled Mali for twenty-five years, from 1307 to 1332. In that time, Mali's fame spread across the Sahara to the Middle East and across the Mediterranean Sea to Europe.

Mansa Musa extended Mali's borders far and wide. A trader passing through Mali in the 1330s described Mali as "square in shape" and said it took four months to go from corner to corner of the vast kingdom.

Mansa Musa also increased trade. As many as 12,000 camels passed through Mali every year. Mali's oases supplied water, food, and rest for the thirsty and weary travelers. Mansa Musa promoted education and the arts. He was especially interested in collecting books and in constructing new buildings. But above all, Mansa Musa was very religious.

A Golden Pilgrimage

In 1324, after converting to Islam, Mansa Musa decided to make a pilgrimage to Mecca, the holiest city in the Muslim world. Mecca is in Saudi Arabia. Followers of Islam are required to make a pilgrimage to Mecca during their lifetime if they can afford to do so. Muslims call a pilgrimage to Mecca a *hajj*. Making the pilgrimage is one of the five basic observances, or pillars, of Islam.

The fact that Mansa Musa made a pilgrimage to Mecca wasn't unusual; after all, several other rulers of Mali had already made pilgrimages there. It was how Mansa Musa made his pilgrimage that was so amazing.

As the ruler of the richest empire in western Africa, Mansa Musa could afford to travel in grand style. He ordered a huge caravan to take him to Mecca. Family, friends, teachers, and doctors came along. Mansa Musa also brought along the local chiefs of his kingdom. This was

This fourteenth-century Spanish map of northwestern Africa shows King Mansa Musa of Mali seated on a throne.

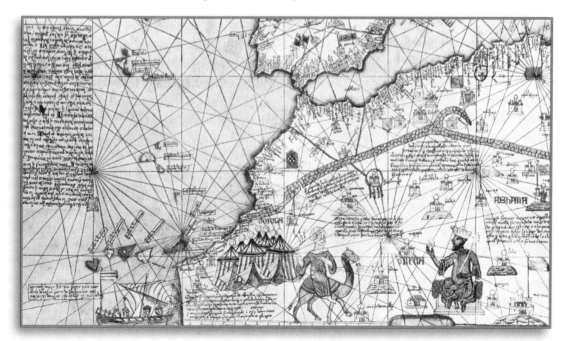

smart, for two reasons. First, being part of Mansa Musa's pilgrimage brought honor to the chiefs. Second, getting the chiefs out of Mali eliminated any competition for Mansa Musa's son, who had been left to rule the kingdom.

By the time the caravan was complete, it included thousands of people. Some history books say more than 60,000 people were part of Mansa Musa's caravan. It was very likely the biggest caravan ever to cross the Sahara. To make sure that he had enough money for his journey, Mansa Musa ordered that gold be packed on his camels. As a result, the caravan supposedly included 80 to 100 camels weighted down with gold. Each camel is said to have carried 300 pounds of gold. These numbers may be somewhat exaggerated, but

This modern illustration shows how Mansa Musa's caravan might have looked.

there is no doubt that Mansa Musa set out with lots of money.

Sharing the Wealth

In 1324, Mansa Musa's extraordinary caravan entered Cairo, Egypt. Mansa Musa himself entered the city in royal style, with 500 slaves, each carrying a golden staff. Everyone in Cairo was impressed by Mansa Musa's wealth.

Mansa Musa's generosity was as impressive as his religious faith. Everywhere he stopped on his pilgrimage, Mansa Musa gave away gold. He gave **lavish** gifts of gold in the Muslim holy cities of Mecca and Medina. He gave gold to everyone who helped him on his trip, too.

On his return trip from Mecca back to Mali, Mansa Musa once more passed through Cairo—and gave away more gold. According to one historical source, Mansa Musa "spread

the waves of generosity all over Cairo. There was no one, officer of the court or holder of any official job, who did not receive a sum of gold from him." Mansa Musa supposedly gave away so much gold that the market for gold was glutted and the value of gold dropped for more than ten years.

"The Century of Musa"

Mansa Musa returned from his pilgrimage to Mecca in 1325. He wanted to pass the leadership of his kingdom to his son so that he, Mansa Musa, could return to Arabia. He wanted to be near the holy city of Mecca and devote his life to religion.

Mansa Musa's son had done a good job ruling Mali during the time Mansa had been on his pilgrimage. His son had even extended the kingdom to the east by conquering the city of Gao, the capital of the neighboring territory of Songhai. To make sure that Songhai would not revolt against Mali, Mansa Musa took two Songhai princes under his protection. The idea was that Mansa Musa would serve as a foster parent. He would help to educate the boys, but he would also keep an eye on them.

Once he had made these arrangements, Mansa Musa thought that he would be able to have his son rule Mali and return to Mecca. But one thing after another kept him in Mali, and Mansa Musa never did return to Mecca.

Mansa Musa died in 1332. He had ruled Mali for twenty-five years. His reign was so successful that some historians describe the history of western Africa in the 1300s as "the century of Musa."

Mansa Musa's fame had spread beyond Africa's borders to Europe, and European mapmakers began to include Mali on their maps. In 1375, after Mansa Musa had been dead for forty-three years, one mapmaker wrote next to the picture of Mansa Musa on a map, "So abundant is the gold which is found in this country that he [Mansa Musa] is the richest and most noble king of all the land."

Mali Declines

After Mansa Musa's death, his son Mansa Maghan (MAH gan) succeeded to the throne. Mansa Maghan ruled only four years, but his reign was a disaster. Under his leadership, Mali suffered serious setbacks. First, Mali lost the valuable city of Timbuktu. Second, Mansa Maghan allowed the two Songhai princes to escape and return to their homeland. There, they established a new government that eventually would become the Songhai Empire.

When Mansa Maghan died, his uncle Mansa Sulayman took the throne. Mansa Sulayman proved to be an able leader, and he greatly strengthened the country. But when he died in 1359, there was no powerful king to take his place. The combination of weak kings and the growing threat of the Songhai Empire eventually proved too much for Mali. By 1500, Mali had lost its hold on the gold and salt trade across the Sahara, which it had controlled for almost 300 years. As a result, in the late 1400s, the Songhai Empire replaced Mali as the richest and most powerful empire in western Africa.

Mansa Musa's fame spread far beyond Mali to Europe and parts of Asia.

**risoners of War** In 1325, Mansa Musa's son captured Gao, the capital of the Songhai people. To make sure that the people of Songhai submitted to Mali's rule, Mansa Musa had taken two of the Songhai king's sons back to Mali with him.

The two Songhai princes were named Ali Kolon and Sulyaman Nar. Ali Kolon was a fierce warrior and a natural leader. As a result, Mansa Musa had big plans for the prince. Since Ali Kolon had shown his skill on the battlefield, Mansa Musa had him lead military expeditions for Mali.

But Ali Kolon had some big plans of his own. According to legend, he cleverly used his military operations to plan his escape from Mali. On each military expedition for Mansa Musa, Ali Kolon got a little closer to his home in Gao. At every stop, he hid weapons and food in secret places that only he knew.

As we have seen, when Mansa Musa died in 1332, his son Mansa Maghan took the throne. Mansa Maghan was a weak leader, which gave Ali Kolon the chance he had been waiting for during his seven years in Mali.

The Great Escape

Along with his brother and a few loyal supporters, Ali Kolon escaped from Niani, Mali's capital. Mansa Maghan then sent warriors after them. The Songhai princes escaped from these warriors and made it safely back to their home in Gao.

Ali Kolon became the new chief of Gao and started the Sonni (soon NEE) **Dynasty**. For most of the 1300s and during the early part of the 1400s, Mali and Songhai tried to overpower each other. Neither side had much luck. However, the deadlock was broken in 1464 when the fierce Songhai king Sonni Ali Ber (soo nee AHL ee bar) came to the throne.

Hard Times for Timbuktu

In the early 1400s, nomads from the desert had invaded Timbuktu. Led by Chief Akil (ah KEEL), the nomads decided not to live in the city they had conquered. Instead, they chose to live in the desert, and they sent a representative to collect the taxes they charged the citizens of Timbuktu. Chief Akil appointed a man named Ammar (am MAR) to be his tax collector.

Akil promised that Ammar could keep one-third of all the tax money he collected. But Chief Akil went back on his word. He really wanted every cent of the money for himself, so he rode into town

> **vocabulary**
> **dynasty** a series of rulers who are related

and took all the tax money before Ammar could collect it. That made Ammar angry, and he decided he had to get even with Akil.

Having lost his share of the taxes, Ammar sent a letter to Sonni Ali Ber, offering to give Timbuktu to the Songhai chief if he would get rid of Akil. Ammar thought that maybe Sonni Ali Ber would give him a reward to delivering Timbuktu into Sonni Ali Ber's hands.

Modern Mali women meet in front of the great Mud Mosque in the city of Jenne.

Sonni Ali Ber knew a good opportunity when he saw one. In 1468, he sent an army marching into Timbuktu. Akil and Ammar saw the army approaching. It was so large and powerful that Akil decided not to try fighting back and instead escaped to the desert. Ammar remained in Timbuktu.

Ready to complete his betrayal, Ammar sent small boats to help Sonni Ali Ber's army cross the Niger River. Then, at the last minute, Ammar panicked and ran away. This turned out to be a wise decision, because Sonni Ali Ber's Songhai troops **sacked** Timbuktu and killed many people who lived there.

The Capture of Jenne

The powerful Songhai empire grew stronger when Sonni Ali Ber sacked Timbuktu. All the scholars, teachers, and students fled from the city. They feared for their lives because, although Sonni Ali Ber said he was a Muslim, he did not follow his religion very closely.

About five years later in 1473, Sonni Ali Ber conquered Jenne, a city about 300 miles southwest of Timbuktu. Like Timbuktu,

Jenne was a great center of learning and trade, but it was also much more beautiful than Timbuktu.

The kings of Mali had tried to capture Jenne nearly a hundred times, but the soldiers couldn't get past the swamps near the city. Sonni Ali Ber and his soldiers tried a new way to defeat the proud residents of Jenne: They starved them. For seven years, Sonni Ali Ber and his men cut off supplies to Jenne. Finally, its citizens gave up. To seal the victory, Sonni Ali Ber married the queen of Jenne. By adding the cities of Timbuktu and Jenne, the Songhai Empire became the main power in west Africa.

> **vocabulary**
> **sack** to plunder, burn, and almost completely destroy a place

Even though Sonni Ali Ber spent most of his reign conquering other lands to expand the Songhai Empire, he kept his huge kingdom firmly under his control by dividing his lands into smaller regions and appointing a governor to rule each one.

Life in the Songhai Empire

Songhai had a strict social system. At the top of the system were the descendants of the original Songhai people. They had special rights and did not live like or with everyday people.

The next level in Songhai was made up of traders, merchants, and soldiers. Unlike other armies in the western Sudan, the Songhai army was made of professional soldiers. In other African kingdoms, any male could be **drafted** into the army. These other armies were made up of men who weren't trained to fight. The Songhai professional army was much more efficient and effective.

Then there were everyday people, whose identities were based on what the family had done for years. People born into a certain group worked with horses; those born into another group made weapons for war. You could not change your group or the job that came along with it. Your position was set in stone for your whole life.

At the bottom of the Songhai social scale were prisoners of war and slaves. For hundreds of years, Africans had been taking prisoners of war and enslaving them. Slaves were often sold to other African kingdoms. Songhai, too, participated in the slave trade.

Religion also played a role in Songhai life. Throughout the 1400s, the Songhai kings followed the teachings of Islam, but not too closely. Some reports even claimed that Sonni Ali Ber refused to say his prayers five times a day, as Islam commanded. Most of the common people of Songhai shared their leader's attitude toward Islam and even continued to worship their own traditional gods.

> **vocabulary**
> **draft** when a government forces people into an army

Askia Muhammad Rules

Sonni Ali Ber died in 1492. He had ruled twenty-eight years. The throne passed to his son, but the Muslims in Songhai refused to accept him as emperor. A revolt against the

Life in Songhai was good for the middle and upper classes of people, but these classes of people were supported by the hard work of many slaves.

new king was led by one of Sonni Ali Ber's soldiers, Askia Muhammad Toure. Unlike the Sonni kings, Askia Muhammad was a very **devout** Muslim.

In 1493, Askia Muhammad's army and the emperor's army battled each other. Askia Muhammad's army smashed the emperor's forces. Askia Muhammad then established the Askia dynasty, which was named after him.

The Muslims of Songhai celebrated their new leader and his deep faith in Islam. They wrote: "He gave much **alms** . . . and undertook special religious devotions. . . . He caused all the bloody cruelties, iniquities [evils], and faulty innovations introduced by the Sonni to disappear. He established religion [Islam] on the most solid basis."

With Askia Muhammad in control of the government, Muslim scholars, teachers, and students once again settled in Timbuktu. They knew they would be safe from religious persecution with the new head of the Songhai empire. Not only did Askia Muhammad protect them, but he also respected their vast learning and asked them for advice.

The Songhai Empire Expands

As other rulers before him had done, Askia Muhammad began to expand his empire. In the west, he took land that had belonged to Mali. He also conquered lands to the south of Songhai and took many prisoners. Many of these prisoners were children who became soldiers in his army. About 1513, Askia Muhammad's soldiers invaded the lands of the Hausa people east of the Niger River.

After a year's battle, the Hausa people fell to the Songhai Empire. From there, Askia Muhammad drove the nomadic tribes deeper into the Sahara. Askia Muhammad's conquests created a huge, tightly-knit empire.

Askia Muhammad's Pilgrimage

As a devout Muslim, Askia Muhammad knew that it was his religious duty to make a pilgrimage to Mecca. So in 1495, he set off to Mecca for a two-year pilgrimage. As you would expect, his caravan was huge and lavish. About five hundred horsemen and one thousand soldiers accompanied the king. He also took a great deal of gold, reported to be 300,000 "pieces." About 100,000 pieces of gold went to charity, 100,000 pieces paid his traveling expenses, and 100,000 pieces went to merchants for wonderful souvenirs.

But Askia Muhammad didn't travel to Mecca just to distribute charity and buy beautiful things. Far from it. As a devout Muslim, he tried to set an example for all Muslims through his faith and worship. Askia Muhammad saw it as his **sacred** duty to spread Islam all through western Africa.

As his empire enlarged, Askia Muhammad appointed Muslim judges in every district. These judges used Muslim justice in place of traditional Songhai laws. His own court followed the same religious guidelines, as well. As a result of these measures, Islam spread throughout western Africa.

> **vocabulary**
> **devout** very religious
> **alms** charity given to the poor
> **sacred** holy

Askia Muhammad's final years were bleak, a bitter contrast to his early glory. One of his own sons overthrew him and exiled Askia Muhammad to a lonely, miserable island. He grew old and went blind. Finally, in his last years, Askia Muhammad was allowed to return home, where he died in 1538.

8 The Travels of Ibn Batutta

See the World Today, many people have the chance to travel near and far. However, this was not always the case. In medieval days, travel was dangerous, difficult, and expensive, so very few people ventured far from their villages. Ibn Batutta was a remarkable exception.

Ibn Batutta traveled far and wide throughout the Muslim world. Fortunately, he wrote all about his journeys, giving countless readers who lived long after him a priceless peek into the world of medieval Islam.

A world traveler, writer, and geographer, Ibn Batutta was born in 1304 in Tangiers, Morocco. By the end of his life in 1368, he had journeyed across Africa, Arabia, Turkey, India, and China. He is the only traveler we know about who visited all the Muslim-ruled countries in the 1300s. Scholars estimate that he traveled up to 75,000 miles.

It All Started With a Pilgrimage

As a child, Ibn Batutta probably never imagined that he would become the most famous traveler of his day. Since he was a very religious Muslim, Ibn Batutta no doubt cherished the dream of visiting Mecca, the Muslim holy city. He was able to make the holy pilgrimage because he came from a wealthy, educated Muslim family. Several of his relatives were well-known Muslim judges, respected members of the Berber community in Morocco. Coming from such a distinguished family, Ibn Batutta would have enjoyed a good, solid education. He would have studied the Koran, and read many classical works of literature.

When he was twenty-one years old, Ibn Batutta set out from Morocco traveling east across northern Africa on his *hajj* to Mecca in Arabia. Later that same year, 1325, Ibn Batutta reached Egypt, the first stop on his pilgrimage to Mecca. However, he did not go in a straight path from Egypt to Arabia. Instead, he traveled first to Damascus in Syria, which is north of Arabia, and trekked across that country before joining some other Muslim pilgrims headed for Mecca. This journey sparked Ibn Batutta's interest in seeing more of the world, and he decided he would visit all the Muslim regions in the world.

Traveling Man

Ibn Batutta spent three years in Mecca. In addition to completing his religious obligations as a Muslim by making his *hajj*, Ibn Batutta also studied Islamic law. When he completed his studies, Ibn Batutta qualified as a Muslim judge.

Then Ibn Batutta began traveling again. Since

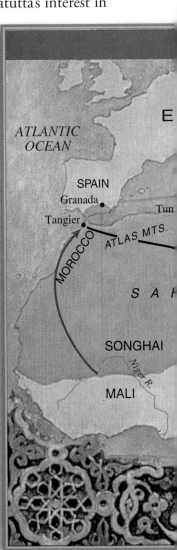

he was a devout Muslim, his fellow Muslims gave him food and places to stay all along his route. He traveled across the Black Sea, stopping first to visit Constantinople, and then took a journey across the **steppe** of central Asia.

Ibn Batutta must have had a warm, friendly personality, because people all along the route admired him greatly. In India, the **sultan** liked Ibn Batutta so much that he gave him a job as a judge in the city of Delhi. Later, the sultan even asked Ibn Batutta to lead a group of Indians on a visit to the emperor of China.

Ibn Batutta's trip was going very well until he suffered a few accidents. He ended up on the coast of Malabar in southeastern India without any money. Fortunately, he was able to sail to the Maldive Islands off the southern coast of India, where he got a job as a judge. But Ibn Batutta once again got "itchy feet" and a yearning to see the world. In 1345, he voyaged to Ceylon. After his visit to Ceylon, he resumed his trip to China. According to his account, he landed in China at the port city of Zaytun (now called Ch'üan-chou) in southeastern China and later traveled as far inland as Beijing.

Ibn Batutta (right) traveled from his native home in Morocco, throughout much of Africa and Asia, using four different routes.

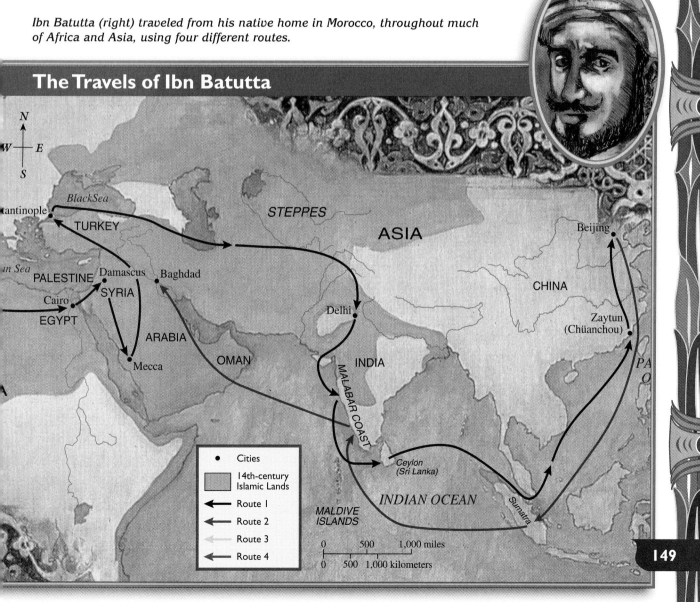

The Travels of Ibn Batutta

N
W — E
S

BlackSea

STEPPES

ASIA

Beijing

CHINA

Zaytun
(Chüanchou)

antinople
TURKEY

in Sea
PALESTINE
Damascus Baghdad
Cairo   SYRIA
EGYPT

ARABIA
Mecca
OMAN

Delhi

INDIA

MALABAR COAST

PA
O

Ceylon
(Sri Lanka)

INDIAN OCEAN

Sumatra

MALDIVE
ISLANDS

- Cities
- 14th-century Islamic Lands
- ← Route 1
- ← Route 2
- ← Route 3
- ← Route 4

0   500   1,000 miles
0   500   1,000 kilometers

149

Later, on his way back to Morocco, he stopped at Sumatra, Malabar, Oman, Baghdad, Cairo, and Tunis. In 1349, Ibn Batutta arrived home in Morocco.

Ibn Batutta thought he wanted to take part in the Crusades, the wars being fought between Muslims and Christians over control of Palestine, the land in the Middle East where Christianity began. He eventually decided that being a soldier was not for him. Instead, he traveled to the city of Granada in Spain. After two years in Spain, he traveled to the western Sudan in 1352.

From 1352 to 1354, Ibn Batutta trekked by camel caravan across the Sahara and then visited the people who lived along the Niger River in western Africa. Ibn Batutta trudged along the ancient caravan trade routes that you read about in previous lessons. He stayed for months at a time with the chiefs of the great kingdoms of Mali and Songhai. He even stayed with the nomads who camped along the Niger River.

Ibn Batutta's Travel Book

Ibn Batutta's extraordinary travels alone would have made him famous in his own day, but by writing down his adventures he ensured himself lasting fame.

Ibn Batutta's travel book contains vivid details and descriptions. Batutta visited Mali at the height of that empire's power. His description of Mali's sultan is especially vivid.

On certain days the sultan holds audiences in the palace yard, where there is a platform under a tree. . . . It [the platform] is carpeted with silk and has cushions placed on it. The sultan comes out of a door in a corner of the palace, carrying a bow in his hand and a

quiver [of arrows] on his back. On his head he has a golden **skullcap**. . . . His usual dress is a velvety red tunic. . . . The sultan is preceded by his musicians, who carry gold and silver *guimbris* [two-stringed guitars]."

Ibn Batutta called his book *Rihlah*, which means "The Journey." A fitting name, indeed. *Rihlah* is still considered a reliable source of information about the medieval Islamic world.

The Traveler of Islam

Ibn Batutta's extensive journeys to Muslim countries earned him the nickname "the Traveler of Islam." He claimed to have met sixty rulers and thousands of people during his travels. Along the way, Ibn Batutta rode in a dog sled, sailed on a Chinese ship called a junk, and crossed the Atlas Mountains in northern Africa in a blizzard. With such wild adventures, it's no wonder some later readers thought his book was filled with lies.

After his last journey across the Sahara and along the Niger River, Ibn Batutta returned home, where he spent his last days. He died around 1368.

In 1829, an English scholar discovered Ibn Batutta's travel book and translated it. Ibn Batutta's name and adventures spread to an entirely new generation of readers.

vocabulary
skullcap a small round cap usually worn on the back of a man's head

People celebrated his bravery, intelligence, and courage. Ibn Batutta, one of the world's most curious travelers, would be thrilled to know that today there is a crater on the moon named after him.

Glossary

alms charity given to the poor

archaeologist a scientist who studies remains from past civilizations

brigand a bandit

cape a point or tip of land sticking out from the mainland into a body of water

caravan a group of people and pack animals traveling together

devout very religious

draft when a government forces people into an army

dynasty a series of rulers who are related

lavish generous

nomadic moving from place to place

oasis a small area in a desert that has water

provisions food, water, and other necessary items

ravine a narrow, steep valley

sack to plunder, burn, and almost completely destroy a place

sacred holy

skullcap a small round cap usually worn on the back of a man's head

steppe grassland plain

sultan a king or sovereign ruler of a Muslim country

Dynasties of China

Contents

The Emperor's Clay Army In the spring of 1974, some villagers in central China needed a new well. The well diggers' muscles ached as they dug deeper and deeper into the reddish soil, looking for water. At 12 feet down they hit something—but not water.

It was a head! Not a human head, but a life-sized head made out of terra cotta, or clay. Its face startled them because it looked so real, but it clearly came from an earlier time. The workers kept digging, and they eventually uncovered the complete figure of a Chinese warrior, buried for over 2,000 years.

Archaeologists rushed to the site of the well. They carefully dug up the whole area. They found more clay soldiers, then still more, and clay horses, too. In all, they found a whole army of life-sized soldiers and horses—about 7,000 of them!

Each warrior had his own per-sonality. Some seemed angry, while others appeared cheerful. The sol-diers wore armor made of clay. They carried real weapons—bows and arrows, swords, spears, and crossbows.

The clay horses, their tails knotted and their ears leaning forward, seemed so real that you could practically hear them neighing and stomping their feet. Some pulled real wooden chariots.

Guardians of the Tomb

The clay army stood in silent formation, guarding the secret underground passageways leading to the tomb of the first emperor of China. Alert and ready for battle, they were to protect the emperor from evil spirits and robbers. If a robber did manage to break in, he might not get out alive—stones and arrows would fly at him from booby-traps set up inside the tomb.

Chinese emperors hated robbers—and with good reason. The emperors had greater wealth than you could possibly imagine. They filled their palaces with treasures of all kinds. And they thought they would live this way even after they died. They believed that they would enter an afterlife that would be like their life on Earth. So they buried their most valuable possessions with them—precious silks, priceless objects of **jade** or bronze, and musical instruments.

Over 700,000 workers built the first emperor's tomb and created his army of clay. And it took them almost 40 years to do it. The emperor did not want anyone to know about the tomb and its contents. So after he died, many workers in the underground tomb found that they could not get out. Walls and doors sealed them inside the tomb forever. They were buried alive just to keep a secret.

> **vocabulary**
> **jade** a greenish mineral used as a gemstone

Uniting the Country

The first emperor frightened everyone. One of his own advisors said that the ruler had "the voice of a jackal and the heart of a tiger or wolf." Named Zheng (jung) at birth, the emperor came from the northwestern Chinese state of Qin (chin).

When Zheng was a young boy, China was not a single unified country, as it is today. Instead, many separate states existed, and they fought one another. Zheng became king of the state of Qin when he was 13—probably not much older than you are now. To keep his power, he had to fight wars with his neighbors. After ruling as king for 25 years, he defeated all the other states.

In 221 B.C. Zheng declared himself emperor of all of China and took the name Shihuangdi (shur hwong dee), meaning "First Supreme Emperor." Shihuangdi established the Qin dynasty, named after his home state.

Shihuangdi had to be very tough to hold the new country together. His old enemies still hated him, so he commanded that all the weapons in the empire be brought to the capital city. He melted them all down and turned them into harmless bells and 12 enormous statues that he placed inside his palace.

Shihuangdi struggled to unite the many different states into one nation. Each of the old states had its own particular kind of writing, money, calendar, and system of weights and measures. This caused great confusion. How could you understand a written command from the emperor if you did not use the same kind of writing as he did? How could you make a date with a friend if he used a different calendar? Even

These life-sized soldiers were part of the vast clay army Shihuangdi ordered made to guard the entrance to his tomb.

the money was different all over China. Some places used coins in the shape of knives, while others used coins shaped like shovels or fish or small scallop shells. Which one was the most valuable? And if you and your neighbors measured out grain differently, who decided which was the right amount?

Shihuangdi eliminated all those differences. He insisted that all people use the same written language so that everyone in the empire could understand each other. Shihuangdi declared that all coins must be round with a square hole in the middle so that coins could be strung together. The emperor established one calendar and one single system of weighing and measuring goods that everyone had to follow.

Shihuangdi wanted to travel easily throughout his empire, so he ordered the building of canals to connect the great waterways of China. He also commanded that roads be built—4,000 miles of them! Trees lining the roads provided shade for travelers. The emperor controlled even the tiniest things. He insisted that the wheels of carriages had to be a precise distance apart from each other so that they would fall exactly into the wheel ruts already worn into the roads.

A Cruel Ruler

Such improvements made life easier for the Chinese people. But the emperor could also be very cruel. He hated crime, and people who broke his laws were punished in horrible ways. They included being boiled alive, having the ribs torn out of one's chest, being cut in two at the waist, and being torn apart by chariots driving in opposite directions. The emperor punished not only the criminal but his entire family as well. He held *all* of them responsible!

Shihuangdi hated any ideas that were different from his own, and he hated it when scholars looked back on the past and said life was better back then. He had every book of history, philosophy, and literature in all of China collected and burned. He commanded that 460 scholars be killed, just because he thought they objected to what he was doing. Even the emperor's own son was upset, and he told his father it was wrong to be so cruel. But you shouldn't talk back to your parents—especially if the parent is a **tyrant**! Shihuangdi became angry at his son and sent him far away, all the way to the northern edge of China.

Shihuangdi, the first Qin emperor, hated ideas different from his own, so he had scholars buried alive, as is shown in this painting.

Construction of the Great Wall of China continued for nearly 2,000 years.

The Wall Builder

Shihuangdi gave his son a job to keep him busy. He told him to supervise the construction of a series of walls in northern China. Some old walls were already standing. Shihuangdi wanted to connect some of these walls and build new ones. The wall building did not end with Shihuangdi.

vocabulary
tyrant a ruler who rules in a harsh, cruel manner

Later dynasties built more walls. The Chinese worked on these walls for almost 2,000 years. The rulers of the Ming dynasty built the last and most elaborate ones. These Ming-dynasty walls are the ones that we usually think of as the Great Wall of China. But the work had begun many years earlier, and the Chinese honor Shihuangdi as the first great wall builder.

The Great Wall snakes through China's mountains and deserts for over one thousand miles. According to legend, the wall was designed by a dragon. You can understand why when you see a photograph like the one above. Put your finger on the wall and follow it. See how it twists and turns like the tail of a dragon?

Why in the world would anyone need such gigantic walls? Well, one thing walls can do is say, "Keep Out!" And that's why Shihuangdi ordered the walls built—to keep out the people who lived beyond the northern border of China.

The Europeans called these northern people the Huns; the Chinese called them the Xiongnu (syoong noo). The Xiongnu were nomads, which means they had no permanent homes and moved from place to place. They moved around on their great herds of horses, riding like the wind. They wandered the open grasslands, called **steppes** (steps), in search of good grass for their horses to eat. When they found a place where they wanted to stay briefly, they would set up a large tent-like house, called a yurt, that they could take down quickly when they were ready to move.

> **vocabulary**
> **steppes** vast treeless plains extending from southwestern Europe into central Asia

In contrast, the Chinese at that time led settled lives. Most of them were farmers who lived in the fertile valleys of the Yellow River in the north and the Yangzi (yang see) River farther south. They rarely left their farms and villages. To the settled Chinese, the nomadic Xiongnu seemed like barbarians.

The Xiongnu were fierce warriors. They would mount their swift horses and swoop down on Chinese villages, raiding and stealing from the people who lived there. Shihuangdi was determined to protect China from these northern raiders, and so he started building walls.

He sent 300,000 soldiers and workers—including criminals who had to march hundreds of miles in chains—to the northern border. Many died on the way. And once they got there, there was no food. Half-starved, the men had to work anyway. The emperor didn't care. He just wanted to get the walls built as soon as possible. So the work never stopped, even during blizzards and sandstorms and freezing rain. Many workers died from hunger and exhaustion.

Dead workers became part of the walls: Their bones were mixed in with the stones. If you complained or tried to run away, you would be caught and buried alive inside one of the walls. For this reason, the walls have been called the world's largest graveyards.

Searching for Immortality

In his later years the emperor himself became more and more worried about dying. Shihuangdi was determined to find a magic potion that would make him live forever. He sent out several sea expeditions in search of islands that were supposed to hold the secret of immortality. Of course the expeditions failed.

In his capital city Shihuangdi had built 270 different palaces and gardens for himself. They were all connected by covered passageways. The emperor became so fearful that he slept in a different palace every night. He moved secretly and no one except his closest advisors knew where he was. Anyone revealing the emperor's whereabouts would be put to death—and the informer's whole family would die as well!

Shihuangdi became completely mysterious during his lifetime—and even his death remained a secret. The emperor died while on his way home from a long trip. Only a few advisors knew about it, and they didn't want anyone else to find out. The only problem was that the emperor's decaying body was beginning to smell! How could they hide that? They came up with a plan to have a cart full of rotten fish follow the emperor's carriage until they got back to the capital. That way people would think it was the fish that stunk, and not the recently deceased emperor!

Shihuangdi had boasted that his descendants would rule for 10,000 generations. But within four years of his death the Qin dynasty collapsed. Another emperor emerged and another ruling family took over China.

The Emperor with 72 Spots What sort of person do you think would be the next emperor after Shihuangdi? Someone from a rich and powerful family? Not necessarily. The new emperor, Liu Bang (lee oh bahng), was a poor, uneducated peasant.

Even as a young man, Liu Bang was unusual. His left thigh had 72 spots on it, and it was said that a woman once saw a dragon over his head while he slept. According to the Chinese, these things indicated that he would achieve greatness one day.

A powerful warrior, Liu Bang took control of all of China and declared himself the emperor of the Han (hahn) dynasty. This dynasty would last for 400 years.

Liu Bang lived in a grand palace in the capital city of Changan (chahng ahn). The emperor wanted his father to come live with him. Forget your old farm, he told his father. Come live like the richest man on Earth, in the most luxurious palace in all of China.

China's geography varies greatly, from the low-lying plains in the east to the deserts, mountains, and plateaus of the west.

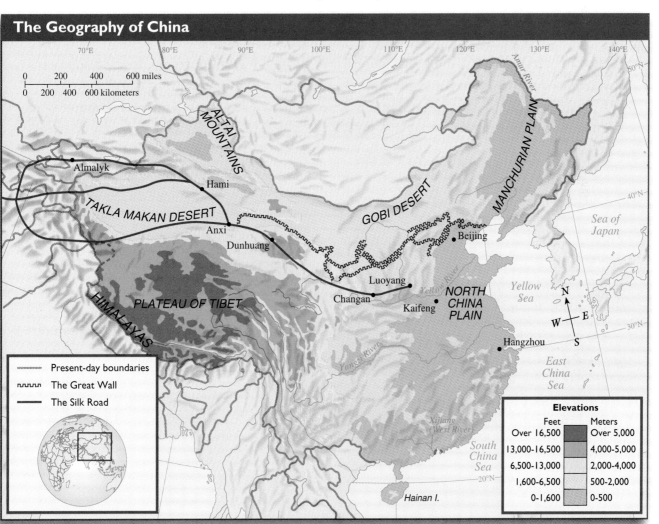

The Geography of China

0   200   400   600 miles
0   200   400   600 kilometers

70°E   80°E   90°E   100°E   110°E   120°E   130°E   140°E

50°N

Amur River

ALTAI MOUNTAINS

Almalyk

Hami

TAKLA MAKAN DESERT

GOBI DESERT

MANCHURIAN PLAIN

40°N

Anxi

Dunhuang

Beijing

Sea of Japan

HIMALAYAS

PLATEAU OF TIBET

Luoyang

Changan

Kaifeng

NORTH CHINA PLAIN

Yellow River

Yellow Sea

N

W   E

S

30°N

Hangzhou

East China Sea

Yangtze River

~~~~~ Present-day boundaries
ᴗᴗᴗᴗ The Great Wall
──── The Silk Road

Xijiang (West River)

South China Sea

20°N

Hainan I.

Elevations

	Feet	Meters
	Over 16,500	Over 5,000
	13,000–16,500	4,000–5,000
	6,500–13,000	2,000–4,000
	1,600–6,500	500–2,000
	0–1,600	0–500

But his father wasn't sure. He thought he'd miss his old home and small village too much. Have you ever had to move? Maybe you felt sad leaving your old home. Well, Liu Bang's father felt the same way.

But Liu Bang was determined to get his father to move, so he had an exact copy of his father's village created near the capital. He moved his father's friends to the new place. He even moved the cows and chickens from the old village so that his father would feel right at home. Only then did Liu Bang's father come.

But all was not peaceful in China. Shihuangdi's walls had not stopped the raiding by the Xiongnu. They continued to pour over the walls and into China. Liu Bang and the emperors who came after him made war against the northern horsemen, but still the raiders came. What could the Chinese do about them?

A later Han emperor, Wudi (woo dee), had an idea. Maybe other countries would be willing to fight the hated Xiongnu. But the Chinese didn't know anything about other lands or other peoples.

China had always been separate from the rest of the world because of its geography. The Pacific Ocean lay to the east of China; to the west lay the Himalayas, with some of the tallest mountains in the world; to the north were vast steppes and the forbidding Gobi (go bee) Desert; and to the south lay more mountains and jungles.

Because the Chinese were so isolated, they believed that they were the center of the world. They called their country the Middle Kingdom or All Under Heaven. They had no interest in exploring other places.

But one day in 138 B.C. Emperor Wudi ordered a court official to go out into the wilderness. Wudi commanded this official to find another country that would help China fight the northern tribesmen. The explorer headed west into central Asia. He discovered amazing things, including the most wonderful horses he'd ever seen.

The official went as far as the country of Bactria (BACK treeyuh), which is now called Afghanistan (af GAN ih stan). He begged the people of Bactria to help the Chinese fight the Xiongnu. But they said no.

Disappointed, the official returned to China. He probably thought he had totally failed in his mission. But his stories about the western land fascinated the Chinese. They listened carefully when they heard about the magnificent horses in central Asia. They realized that these horses would be perfect for fighting the northern nomads.

The Silk Road

To get the horses, the Chinese traded silk, which was then a precious fabric. Have you ever felt silk? It is very soft and beautiful. The Chinese got silk by raising special worms, called silkworms. They'd feed the silkworms mulberry leaves. In the springtime the worms would spin a cocoon made of delicate threads. The Chinese learned how to unwind those threads and weave them into a beautiful fabric.

At that time the Chinese were the only ones in the whole world who knew how to make silk, and they wanted to keep it that way. Silkworm eggs were not allowed out of the country. If you tried to sneak them out, you would be punished with death. But finished Chinese silk could leave the country, and when foreigners saw the gorgeous fabric they immediately wanted to trade for it.

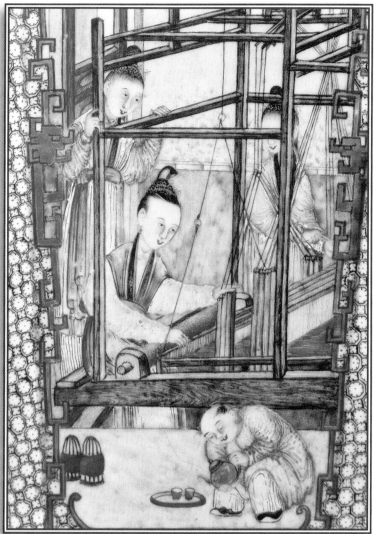

Silk has been made and valued in China for over 3,000 years. This illustration on a Ming dynasty vase portrays a worker weaving silk into cloth.

People were eager to buy China's silk. Cleopatra, the queen of Egypt, wore a silk gown to impress her guests. Silk was so popular in Rome that the emperor had to forbid men from wearing it so that there would be enough for the women.

Making Paper

The Han dynasty founded by Liu Bang lasted from 206 B.C. to A.D. 220, roughly the same period as the mighty Roman Empire. But in many ways the Han culture was far more advanced than that of Rome. The Chinese themselves look upon this dynasty as a kind of golden time. They still call themselves the sons of Han.

One of the great achievements of the Han dynasty was the invention of paper. The Chinese made paper by mashing together a variety of ingredients, including tree bark, hemp, rags, and fish nets.

Can you imagine not having any paper? What would you write on? Before paper the Chinese used the bones of animals or strips of bamboo or even precious silk.

> **vocabulary**
> **oasis** a fertile area in the midst of a desert; most oases have at least some drinkable water

The invention of paper was a huge advance. It would be another 1,000 years before paper would appear in Europe

That was how the Silk Road began. The road was really a system of trails that stretched thousands of miles across the mountains and deserts of central Asia. Traders traveled in groups called caravans. Animals like camels and yaks carried the silk. The route led from one **oasis** to the next. The caravan would stop at the oasis to rest in the shade and get food and water before continuing on in the desert. Following this route, silk traders made it all the way to the countries on the Mediterranean Sea.

3 Wu Zhao

City of Foreigners In the year A.D. 638, an imperial carriage hurried through the countryside on its way to Changan, the capital city of China. The carriage rocked and swayed as it went. In the back of the carriage sat a 13-year-old girl named Wu Zhao (woo jow).

The emperor had commanded that she leave her home and come live in his imperial palace. The emperor at that time was Taizong (tye dzoong) of the Tang (tahng) dynasty. Emperor Taizong had never met Wu Zhao, but he had heard of her great beauty and he wanted her to be near him.

Can you imagine how Wu Zhao must have felt? She had probably never been away from her home and her mother before this. And now she had to leave both of them—forever. Her mother cried and cried when Wu Zhao left, but the young girl tried to be brave. She had no choice. The emperor had to be obeyed.

At that time, young women made almost none of the decisions about their own lives. They could not choose their own husbands; their parents did that. Once married, a new wife lived in a household with her husband's parents, and perhaps even grandparents. All of them ordered the new wife around, making constant demands on her. The Chinese character, or word, for "wife" was a combination of the characters for two different words— "woman" and "broom." That perfectly described the wife's job, because she worked like a broom—she had to clean and work all day serving others. Until she gave birth to a male child, she had almost no power in the family. But the wife could not complain. If she did, she might be sent home in disgrace.

Wu Zhao's New Life

In the back of the carriage, young Wu Zhao must have been excited and scared about her new life. The roads became crowded as they approached the city of Changan, the largest and grandest city in the entire world at that time. Merchants carrying luxury goods from the Silk Road filled the streets leading to the capital. The carriage came to a high wall. It prepared to pass through one of the four great gates that led into the city.

The Chinese characters representing "woman" and "broom" were combined to form the character for "wife."

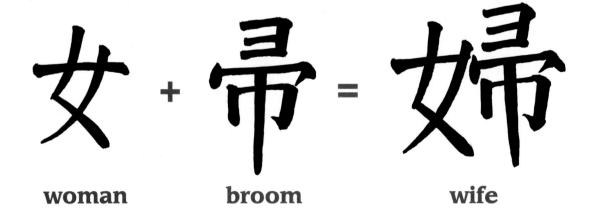

woman   broom   wife

Wu Zhao saw amazing things. Roughly one million people lived in Changan. Many of them were foreigners—Koreans, Arabs, Persians, Turks, and Indians. Wu Zhao had never seen so many different kinds of people. They looked strange to her. Many had dark complexions. They spoke languages she couldn't understand. Everyone on the streets, even the Chinese themselves, dressed like foreigners. Women wore tightly-fitted dresses that followed the fashions of Persia and Turkey. Rich Chinese men wore hats made of leopard skin. The music that rose up in the streets was unlike anything she had ever heard. In the two great city marketplaces, merchants sold exotic goods—foods, plants, perfumes, medicines, fabrics, and jewels from foreign lands.

As her carriage drove through the streets, Wu Zhao saw many monasteries, temples, and shrines for the Buddhist religion that had come to China from India. She saw houses topped with yellow roofs that were curved to guard against evil spirits, which were believed to move only in a straight path.

Wu Zhao was empress of China and later became the only woman emperor of China.

The Imperial City

Wu Zhao's carriage went up the Street of the Red Bird, a very wide street that stretched 480 feet from one side of the road to the other. At the end of the street lay the walled Imperial City. The emperor lived and worked within these walls, and only certain people could enter this city within a city. All others were forbidden to do so. Even touching the wall was a serious crime. If you dared to put your hand on the wall, you could be hit 70 times with a rod.

The guards at the wall allowed Wu Zhao's carriage to pass through the gate. They could tell immediately that the carriage belonged to the emperor because it was painted a brilliant red, the same color as the emperor's court.

Inside the official court, seated on his throne, Emperor Taizong issued commands that affected a large portion of Asia. He ruled over a vast empire that included 60 million people. Thousands of government officials scurried about the huge rooms with marble floors, carrying out his orders and meeting his every desire.

But Wu Zhao went to an even more secret part of the Imperial City, the place where Taizong lived. Only the emperor and members of his household could enter what was called the Palace City. The emperor was the only grown man allowed inside the Palace City; even the emperor's sons had to leave when they grew up.

Life in the Palace City

The emperor had many wives and concubines, all of whom lived in the Palace City. A concubine is a woman who lives with a man without being married to him. Wu Zhao would be one of them. This would be her new home. She had no idea of what to expect.

Wu Zhao found a world full of strange and wonderful sights. Exotic and magnificent birds—peacocks from India and hunting hawks from Korea and Mongolia—lived in the imperial gardens. Buildings filled with ice kept the emperor's delicacies—peaches, melons and figs imported from the far reaches of the Chinese empire—fresh.

Wu Zhao spent her days learning how to please the emperor. She studied music and literature and learned to write beautifully. She dressed in gorgeous silk robes and precious jewels. She and the other women in the palace arranged and rearranged their hair and used makeup. At that time fashionable women painted eyebrows on their faces. The eyebrows were drawn in different ways to create different moods. One style was named "Distant Mountains," and another was called "Sorrow Brows." "Sorrow Brows" was Wu Zhao's style.

The emperor's wives and concubines walked in the gardens and played games together, including the exciting game of polo, a popular game on horseback that had recently come to China from Persia. While riding at high speed, polo players had to hit a ball with a long stick or mallet. It sounds like fun, doesn't it?

Though the women enjoyed the games and luxuries of the Palace City, their lives were not free of worry. If any one of the women displeased the emperor, she could lose her privileges or even be sent away from the palace forever. Every woman wanted to be the emperor's favorite, so they could be very jealous of and mean to one another. Emperor Taizong had a special name for Wu Zhao. He called her "Beauty Wu," which must have made the other woman envious.

But in 649 it didn't matter how well Wu Zhao pleased Taizong. The emperor died that year, and according to tradition, Wu Zhao and the other women in the palace had to shave their heads and move to a Buddhist temple. They would have to live there as nuns for the rest of their lives. Wu Zhao did not want to leave the luxury of the palace. She swore she would find some way to return.

Changan was the world's largest and grandest city when Wu Zhao entered its gates in A.D. 638.

A year after Taizong's death, his son Gaozong (gow dzoong), the new emperor, went to the temple where Wu Zhao was living to offer sacrifices for his dead father. While there, he saw the beautiful Wu Zhao dressed in nun's clothing. When Gaozong looked at her, she burst into tears. She looked so pathetic that the emperor burst into tears as well. Shortly afterwards, Emperor Gaozong commanded that Wu Zhao be returned to the palace. She grew her hair back and would never again leave the imperial court.

Wu Zhao Turns Ruthless

Once Wu Zhao returned to the Palace City, she began to change. She gradually became more and more ruthless. She decided to get rid of all of her enemies, including the emperor's wife and his favorite concubine. She secretly killed Gaozong's infant daughter and then tricked him into believing that his wife, the empress, had done it. She then became Gaozong's favorite concubine. Later she became his wife and empress of China.

A month after Wu Zhao became the new official empress of China, she took revenge against both the former empress and a former concubine. She had them brutally murdered. She ordered her servants to cut off their arms and legs and leave them to die in a huge vat of wine.

Empress Wu grew very powerful. She even attended government meetings with Gaozong, which a woman had no right to do in China. Many at court hated her, but they could say nothing. The empress sat behind a screen and whispered to the emperor what he should do. An ancient Chinese historian described how she decided everything, even matters of life and death, while "the emperor sat with folded hands."

After Gaozong died, one of their sons and then another took over as emperor, but the real power belonged to Empress Wu. Superstitious and nervous about enemies, Empress Wu planted spies everywhere. But the ghosts of her murdered rivals haunted her. In time, she could no longer stand living in the palace in Changan, so she moved the capital to a new location.

Empress Wu was all-powerful. She had everything except the official title of emperor. But she wanted that, too. In 690 a flock of bright red birds flew through the room that held the emperor's throne. A phoenix, a bird very special to the empress, was also rumored to have flown over the palace. To the empress it was clear: Heaven had sent these birds to show that she should be the official ruler of China. She made her son resign. Wu Zhao declared herself the Holy and Divine Emperor, and the founder of a brand-new dynasty. For the next 15 years, Wu Zhao ruled as emperor—the first and only time a woman would do so in Chinese history.

Buddhism became increasingly popular around the time of Empress Wu. These images of Buddha were carved into caves in the countryside.

The Woman Emperor

Though a cruel tyrant who ruled by fear, Emperor Wu ran the empire skillfully. During her reign, China prospered.

Wu Zhao believed very deeply in Buddhism. She had many temples built, and she ordered the creation of enormous rock sculptures. Caves were hollowed out of rock walls; inside, artists carved giant statues of Buddha out of stone. Some of the largest cave figures rise as high as a 15-story building.

At 80 years of age, Emperor Wu grew weak and sick. Some of her old enemies saw a chance to get rid of her at last. They killed her closest advisors and put Wu Zhao under arrest. She died later that year, and the Tang dynasty once again took control in China.

The Tang Dynasty 4

Before and After "Beauty Wu" Except for the 15 years when Wu Zhao ruled as emperor, the Tang dynasty ruled China for almost 300 consecutive years, from A.D. 618 to 907.

During the Tang dynasty, China was the biggest and richest country in the entire world. It conquered other lands, including Korea, Iran, and a large part of Vietnam. The Japanese were so impressed with China and its culture that they copied most of it, even the written language.

Poetry and the Arts

The Tang emperors loved the arts, especially poetry. Twenty-seven-year-old Xuanzong (soo ahn dzoong) became emperor in 712. He was skilled in music, poetry, and the art of beautiful writing known as calligraphy (kuh LIHG ruh fee). The new emperor surrounded himself with poets, including two of the most famous poets in Chinese history: Li Bo (lee boh) and Du Fu (doo foo).

Du Fu was a very serious and hard-working young man who always

Li Bo, one of the most famous poets in Chinese history, was greatly admired by Emperor Xuanzong.

wanted to be a government official. Li Bo, on the other hand, took life easier. He wrote:

Life in the World is but a big dream;
I will not spoil it by any labor or care.

Li Bo often got himself into trouble by fighting and drinking too much alcohol. Once, while he was drunk, he tried to read a poem to Emperor Xuanzong. Instead, Li Bo threw up all over the ruler of China. Eventually, Li Bo left the emperor's court and became a wanderer. According to legend, he died after a night of drinking. While crossing a river in a boat, Li Bo saw the moon's reflection in the water and reached for it, trying to hug it. He fell out of the boat and drowned while reaching for the moon.

An Era of Glory

Many people regard the Tang dynasty as the most glorious period in Chinese history. The country was bursting with creative energy. Foreigners were more welcome than ever before, and the mix of cultures and ideas made China an exciting place.

Tea became incredibly popular during the Tang dynasty. Everyone loved to drink it. Tea was grown in China, and the merchants who sold it became extremely rich. There was only one problem: So much money passed hands that China began to run out of coins. What do you think the Chinese did? Stop selling tea? No, they would never do that. Instead, the merchants invented a kind of paper money that they called "flying money," perhaps because the money flew so fast from one person to the next. This was the first type of paper money used in the world. Just think of how convenient it is to have money made out of paper. Imagine if we had no dollar bills but only nickels, dimes, and quarters to pay for everything. Our pockets would be overflowing with coins. We'd be so weighed down it would be hard to walk.

A number of other innovations took hold. At the end of the Tang dynasty, the invention of wood-block printing led to the creation of printed books. A worker would carve words and drawings onto a wooden block, cover the block with ink, then press it onto a piece of paper. Presto—a printed page! One worker could produce a thousand pages a day using this technique. The oldest existing book in the world, the *Diamond Sutra*, is a Buddhist text that was printed in China in 868. Once again the Chinese outpaced the Europeans: Hundreds of years would pass before printing was invented in Europe.

An Explosive Discovery

An even more explosive discovery took place in China during the Tang dynasty. For many centuries, Chinese scientists called alchemists had tried to create gold and find the secret to living forever. Their experiments eventually led them to mix charcoal, nitrate and saltpeter together. The results surprised them—the mixture exploded! The Chinese scientists had discovered gunpowder. A warning appears in a Tang chemistry book: Beware when mixing these ingredients because the mixture might explode right in your face and burn off your beard.

Under the Tang dynasty the Chinese used the gunpowder not for warfare but for creating spectacular fireworks. It seems fitting that the brilliant Tang dynasty should be remembered for giving to the world the magnificent gift of fireworks.

The Chinese invented wood-block printing. Here, a printer presses an inked woodcut against a piece of rice paper.

The Pancake Prophecy One day in the year 1125 a very strange thing happened to the Song (soong) dynasty emperor Hui Zong (hway dzoong). He came upon a poor fish-peddler sitting in a doorway, eating a pancake.

The peddler offered to share his humble food with the emperor. "Have a bite!" the peddler said to Hui Zong. But Hui Zong was disgusted by the very idea that he, the great emperor, would share a bite of such miserable food. He would not touch it.

Hui Zong's refusal hurt the peddler's feelings, and the peddler spoke a frightening prophecy. "A day will come," he said to Hui Zong, "when you will be glad to have even a pancake like this."

The emperor went on his way. But the fish-peddler's words hung over him like a mysterious curse. Hui Zong was rich and powerful beyond imagination. How could he be happy with just a pancake for a meal? What a ridiculous idea!

Hui Zong decided to forget all about his meeting with the peddler. He called for his paints, his brushes, and some paper. Of all the Chinese emperors, Hui Zong stood out as the one who loved art the most. Hui Zong filled his palace with beautiful works of art. He collected 6,000 paintings. He learned to paint and write poetry himself. Whenever the business of governing got too boring or too tiring, he sent his officials away so that he could paint a picture or write a poem. He developed new ways to paint birds and flowers, and new styles of calligraphy. He set up an academy of painting, and artists from all over the country flocked to it.

"Mountains-Water" Painting

The painters during the Song dynasty (960–1279) did not use oil paints, and they did not work on canvas. Instead, these artists used water-based paints on paper and silk. Paint spreads rapidly on those surfaces, so the brush strokes had to be done very quickly and lightly. There could be no hesitation whatsoever.

Emperor Hui Zong painted scenes of nature such as The Five-Colored Parakeet.

To the Chinese, paintings of nature were the highest form of art, and the landscapes created by the Song artists have never been equaled. The artists loved to paint rugged scenes with mountains, waterfalls, and rivers. (Indeed, the Chinese word for "landscape" means "mountains-water.") The Chinese considered mountains sacred places where spirits lived. Vertical scrolls with mountain landscapes might reach as high as 7 feet. Small round or square paintings were sometimes made to cover a fan or to be placed in albums. Artists also loved to make panoramic rolls, enormous paintings that were kept rolled up in a box. You would unroll the painting slowly, as if following the artist in a journey across the vast landscape or scene.

Hui Zong insisted that everyone in the government be a skilled artist. The palace even had an artist on call all night long, just in case the emperor wanted something painted in the middle of the night.

Military Problems

Some officials in Hui Zong's palace thought he spent too much time with his paintings and not enough time worrying about China's military problems. Several foreign tribes had moved across the northern border and were fighting for control of North China. Hui Zong made a deal with one of the tribes, the Jurchen (jur chuhn), to fight on China's side. Hui Zong thought he had solved the problem and went back to his paintings. But when the Jurchen defeated China's enemies, they turned against the Chinese.

In 1126 the Jurchen attacked Hui Zong's capital at Kaifeng (ky fung). Forty-eight thousand soldiers defended Kaifeng with crossbows and flamethrowers. But the Jurchen had even more powerful weapons. They brought in siege machines with moveable towers that were so high they reached above the city walls. The attackers propelled firebombs over the walls into the city.

The "Duke of Confused Virtues"

The siege of Kaifeng lasted for more than a month. The Jurchen destroyed the city and captured Hui Zong. They took off his fine clothes and made him put on a servant's robes. Then the captors made fun of him by calling him the Duke of Confused Virtues.

The Jurchen sent Hui Zong to the far northeast as their prisoner. The peddler's curse had come true. The emperor's power and wealth had vanished like smoke. He had no pride left. How Hui Zong yearned to see a simple Chinese pancake again. After nine hard years, Hui Zong died, still a prisoner of the Jurchen.

The Jurchen thought they had captured all of Hui Zong's family, but one of his sons escaped from them. He fled to the south, set up his own capital at Hangzhou (hahng joh), and proclaimed himself emperor. He made a deal with the Jurchen: The invaders would control all of North China, the area that had been the center of all the previous dynasties, while the Song would be left with the south. It was humiliating for the glorious Song dynasty, but the new emperor had no choice.

The Rice-Growing South The southern part of China, controlled by the Song dynasty, was very different from the northern part, controlled by the Jurchen. The south was hotter, wetter, and more humid. It was a perfect place for rice, which grows best in standing water.

Peasants did all the work of planting and harvesting the rice. They had no fancy equipment. Simple plows and hoes were all that they used. The plows had to be pulled by the men themselves or, if they were lucky, by water buffalo. The peasants labored hard in the fields, especially from June to September. At dawn a drum sounded to call the workers to the fields. The drum beat continued all day long to supply a rhythm for the peasants to work by and to prevent any talking among the workers. They ate their midday meal in the fields and then went back to work until it got dark.

Rice became the most important part of the Chinese diet during the Song dynasty. The residents in the capital city of Hangzhou, a city numbering over one million people, ate about 220 tons of rice every single day. In Hangzhou you could buy many different kinds of rice. Some of the varieties included first-quality white rice, rice with lotus-pink grains, yellow-eared rice, rice on the stalk, pink rice, yellow rice, and old rice. All these different kinds of rice had to be harvested. It's no wonder the poor peasants had to work so hard.

City Pleasures

Many peasants left their fields and villages and moved into the city. The city amazed them. Peasant life was **monotonous** and difficult and offered few pleasures. Hangzhou, by contrast, throbbed with constant activity and gaiety. One foreign visitor called it "the greatest city . . . in the world, where so many pleasures may be found that one fancies himself to be in Paradise."

> **vocabulary**
> **monotonous**
> tiresome or uninteresting because of a lack of variety

Entertainers performed on street corners and in areas of the city called "pleasure grounds" that were set aside near the markets and bridges. Here, performers of all sorts captivated audiences. You could stop to watch puppet shows and shadow plays; listen to music and storytellers; delight in jugglers, acrobats, tightrope walkers, and animal acts; and gasp as strongmen lifted huge blocks of stone to the sound of a drum roll.

This is a model of an acrobat, one of the street entertainers in the city of Hangzhou.

Royal Ontario Museum, Canada

City Streets

In the marketplaces and fancy shops, you could buy anything you wanted—pet cats, crickets in cages, even false hair. All of Hangzhou echoed with the noise of street vendors. They beat on pieces of wood or metal or cried out to attract customers. Their wares included tea, toys, food, hot water for washing the face, horoscopes, honeycombs, and sugar-cane. Some vendors sold "mosquito smoke," a powder for getting rid of the mosquitoes that loved the humid air of Hangzhou.

The Chinese word for "bath" also meant a ten-day period of time.

Porters rushed through the streets carrying goods that hung from long poles balanced on their shoulders. Enclosed chairs were also suspended from the poles, and wealthy women, dressed elegantly in silks and gold brocade, rode inside them.

People in Hangzhou loved to eat and drink. Teahouses, bars, and restaurants crowded the streets, and pleasure boats serving food floated on a lake in Hangzhou. Do you think you would like to eat a silkworm pie? That was one of the dishes that the Chinese of the time enjoyed. Isn't it interesting how different cultures like entirely different kinds of food? Silkworm pie sounds disgusting to us, but the ancient Chinese could not even imagine eating a hamburger.

Chinese cities teemed with people and excitement in the 1100s.

Chinese scholars studied the works of Confucius and others; this picture shows scholars taking an examination.

Some people drank too much rice wine and got themselves into trouble. They'd fall into the canals that ran through the city. Eventually, railings were put up around the waterways.

Water was everywhere in Hangzhou. The city lay between a large artificial lake on the west and a river on the east; 20 or more canals crisscrossed the city. North China was very dry, and the people who lived there rarely took baths. But South China could not have been more different. The inhabitants of Hangzhou loved to bathe. Government officials got a day off every ten days just so they could take a bath. (Because of that, the Chinese word for "bath" also meant "a ten-day period of time.") The rich had their own rooms for bathing, but ordinary people flocked to public bathhouses. There may have been as many as 3,000 of them in the city. Though the Chinese did not have toothbrushes at that time, they did wipe their gums with a handkerchief after eating. And they were the first people in the world to use toilet paper.

The Scholars

Amid the crowds strolling on the bustling streets of Hangzhou were men wearing special caps with long "ears." Only scholars had the right to wear these caps, and the only way to become a scholar was to pass a very difficult exam given by the government. The exam tested students' knowledge of the teachings of Confucius, as well as other subjects. It even included a poetry exam. Generally, no more than ten students out of a hundred would pass this exam; sometimes only one or two would.

The scholars were the most honored and respected people in China; they formed an **elite** group and had many privileges. Over the years

> **vocabulary**
> **elite** the best or finest members, as of a society or social group

more and more young men wanted to become scholars, and the demand for education increased. The Song emperors opened many new schools. Country children usually had no time for school because they had to work in the fields. If you had a choice, would you rather go to school or work all day in a muddy rice field?

City kids went to school and learned how to write and how to use the abacus, a primitive type of calculator that makes use of beads on wires to do addition, subtraction, multiplication, and division. Schoolchildren in China still use the abacus today.

Flammable City

Hangzhou was a crowded city. Its houses, made of wood and bamboo, rose up to five stories high. They were built one right next to the other. A resident reported that the houses were so close together that "their porches are continuous. There is not an inch of unoccupied ground anywhere." Lamps and lanterns with live flames provided light, but if you dropped one, it could mean disaster. From time to time, fires swept through huge sections of the city. In 1208 a fire raged for four days and nights, destroying over 58,000 houses and killing many people. The city had no fire department; when fire broke out, soldiers had to fight the blaze. Watchtowers were built in the most crowded sections of the city. Soldiers posted in the towers looked for smoke; if fire broke out, they signaled one another with flags during the daytime and with lanterns at night.

The people of Hangzhou thought they were safe behind their walls. But far to the north, beyond the land of the Jurchen, fresh trouble was brewing. For 20 years a nomadic leader from the Mongolian steppe had been fighting with the other northern tribes to unite them all under his rule. By the year 1206 this powerful and ruthless warrior had succeeded. He was feared by all and was given the title Chinggis Khan (CHIN giss kahn), which meant "universal ruler." (You may have seen his name also spelled Genghis Khan.) He now looked south to China and saw a divided country: the north under the Jurchen, and the south under the Song. Divided meant weak, and Chinggis Khan would soon pounce on China.

This is a model of a watchtower. Watchtowers played an important role in scouting and fighting fires such as the one that engulfed Hangzhou in 1208.

Frightening Trip In the year 1207, Jurchen ambassadors from North China traveled a long distance north to the land of the Mongols. The ambassadors came to announce to the Mongols and their leader, Chinggis Khan, the name of the new emperor of North China.

The ambassadors must have been terrified. They had heard about the fierce Mongols. Chinggis Khan had boasted that nothing made him happier than massacring his enemies, stealing their property, riding their horses, and taking women captive. The Mongols lived on the vast open grassland of Mongolia in tents called yurts. They raised cattle, sheep, and horses. They looked down on the northern Chinese farmers and city dwellers as being soft and weak.

Chinggis Khan lived in a splendid tent decorated with rich fabrics and golden plaques. He sat on a throne made of the skins of pure white horses, animals considered sacred by the Mongols.

When the ambassadors told Chinggis Khan about their new emperor, they hoped that he would offer respectful words and congratulations. Instead, he spat on the ground, jumped on his horse, and rode away. The ambassadors went home

Chinggis Khan made China the center of the great Mongol Empire during his rule.

shocked at this terrible sign of disrespect. Worse was to come, however. Chinggis Khan was planning for war against the Jurchen.

The world had never seen such fearsome warriors as the Mongols. Their children learned how to ride a horse before they could even walk. Then they were taught to shoot with a bow and arrow. The Mongols designed a powerful bow that could shoot arrows hundreds of feet. Because the Mongols rode so well, they could shoot an arrow with great accuracy while galloping at top speed.

The Mongols trained themselves to endure great hardships. They could go without food for a long time. If they ran out of water, they wouldn't panic. They'd just make a small cut in their horse's leg and drink its blood.

The sight of the Mongol attackers must have been terrifying. One ancient historian wrote that the Mongols appeared "more

numerous than ants or locusts."
And now they were headed
toward China.

Terror from the North

The northern Chinese under the
Jurchen thought they were safe because their towns had walls around
them. But they were wrong. The
Mongols thought up a cruel plan.
They rounded up farmers and anybody else they caught outside the
walls of a town. They forced these
captives to march in front of the
army, so when the defenders fired
at the Mongols, they'd hit their
own people first.

The Mongols destroyed 90 towns
in North China, including what is
now Beijing. A foreign ambassador
saw the terrible destruction of the
city. He reported that a huge pile
of bones lay outside the walls of
the city. Almost every single person
was slaughtered, 60,000 all told,
and every building was burnt to
the ground. The ruins of the city
burned for over a month.

*The battles fought by Chinggis Khan and his armies were legendary.
Many, like this one, were chronicled by illustrators of the day.*

It took the Mongols about 20 years to
defeat the Jurchen and conquer all of North
China. Chinggis Khan did not live to see the
end of this war. He died in 1227. The Mongols
did not want anyone to know that he had
died. They took his body to a secret place and
buried him with a huge treasure. A thousand
horsemen rode over the gravesite repeatedly
to wipe out any trace of digging. People have
looked and looked, but to this day no one
has found the tomb of Chinggis Khan.

The sons and grandsons of Chinggis
Khan spread terror through Asia and Europe.

They created the largest empire the world
has ever seen. It stretched all the way from
the Pacific Ocean to eastern Europe. For over
100 years a group of Mongols, called the
Golden Horde, ruled over Russia. The Mongol
conquest of Russia was ruthless. In one town,
a monk wrote, "no eye remained open to
weep for the dead."

The Song Dynasty Falls

It had been Chinggis Khan's dream to
conquer all of China; now his grandson
Khubilai Khan (KOO bee lye kahn) set out
to realize that dream. He unleashed his

powerful army against the southern Song dynasty and its people.

The Mongols ran into all sorts of problems in southern China. First of all, it was just too hot for them. The northern men, as well as their horses, were used to colder weather, and they found it difficult to fight in the heat and humidity. Mosquitoes bit them—mosquitoes carrying diseases that the Mongols had no resistance to. Many of the Mongol warriors got sick.

The Song had a strong navy and amazing weapons such as flamethrowers, rockets, and catapults that could hurl bombs. But the Mongols proved what determined warriors they were. They built a navy of their own and developed artillery that could fire enormous 100-pound rocks. The Mongols defeated one city after another, until they finally captured the capital city of Hangzhou and the five-year-old child emperor of the Song.

The mighty Khubilai Khan had the young emperor brought to him.

Everyone trembled at the thought of what the great emperor, or khan, might do to the helpless boy. The Mongols could be extremely cruel to their prisoners. When the Mongols captured three Russian princes, they sealed them inside a big crate to suffocate, while two Mongol generals ate a victory dinner on top of the crate.

But Khubilai Khan was not as cruel as his uncles and his grandfather. He had studied Chinese customs and admired many things about the Chinese. When the young emperor was brought before him, Khubilai Khan took pity on him. He ordered that he not be harmed and sent him away to live the quiet life of a Buddhist priest.

The Mongol Empire was the largest the world has ever known. This map shows the area it covered, in and around what is now China, at its height in the late 1200s.

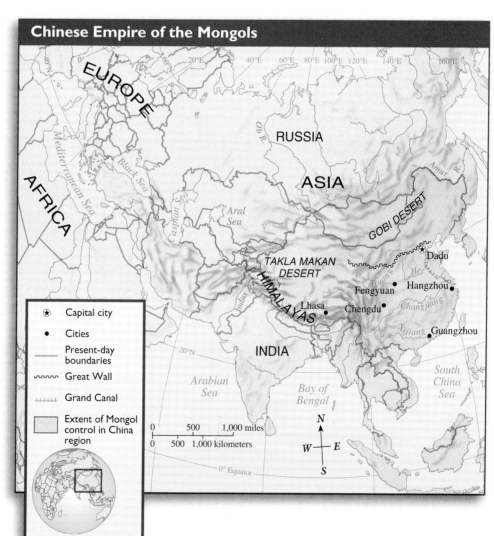

Chinese Empire of the Mongols

- ✪ Capital city
- • Cities
- --- Present-day boundaries
- ∿∿∿ Great Wall
- ⊥⊥⊥ Grand Canal
- ☐ Extent of Mongol control in China region

The Great Capital Once Khubilai Khan conquered China, he decided to build a new capital city for himself. On the site of Beijing, he built a city and called it Dadu (dah doo), or "great capital."

A bodyguard of 12,000 horsemen protected his family day and night. If any visitors thought they could attack the emperor, they got a surprise when they walked into the grand hall where he met guests. There seemed to be tigers on a platform near the emperor. If you were brave enough to walk up to these tigers, you would see that they were actually mechanical models. The emperor had very clever inventors and builders working for him.

Some of the Mongols missed their old way of life and the grasslands of Mongolia. To make the Mongols happy, Khubilai Khan ordered that huge yurts be put up in the gardens of the Imperial City. These new yurts were different from those their families and ancestors had lived in—they had magnificent furniture in them. Khubilai Khan even sent men up north to collect grass from Mongolia. They planted the grass on an altar in the emperor's palace.

This map is one artist's rendition of what Dadu, also called Cambaluc, looked like.

Khubilai Khan was very interested in science. He built a tall building in the Imperial City as an observatory. He also invited a famous astronomer from Persia to Dadu. The astronomer brought instruments for observing the sun, moon, stars, and planets. He also brought a very

Marco Polo, shown with the tall pointed hat, became friendly with Khubilai Khan, shown sitting on the throne. Polo spent many years in China.

special gift to Khubilai Khan. For a long time the astronomer had made careful observations of the movements of the heavenly bodies. He used these observations to calculate a new accurate calendar, which he gave to Khubilai Khan. The Chinese called it the Calendar of Ten Thousand Years.

The Postal System

One of Khubilai Khan's greatest achievements was the creation of a postal system. Khubilai Khan wanted to keep tight control of the country, so he needed to be able to send and receive information quickly. He ordered that new roads and more than 1,400 postal stations be built throughout China. From one station to the next, horsemen galloped at top speed, carrying mail pouches. They had strands of bells wrapped around their bodies, so they made a loud noise as they sped down the roads. Other travelers had to get out of their way. As the rider approached a postal stop, the men inside the station would hear the bells and quickly get a fresh horse ready. The mail carrier would then jump onto the new horse and head for the next station. On a good day

a message might travel 250 miles. Fifty thousand horses were used in this postal system.

Marco Polo

The government allowed foreign travelers and merchants to stay at the postal stations, which were a little like hotels. One foreigner from Europe who became famous for his visit to China was an Italian named Marco Polo. Around 1300 he wrote a very popular book that described the wonders of China in Khubilai Khan's time.

Polo said that Khubilai Khan's palace was "the greatest & most wonderful that ever was seen." He claimed it had 400 rooms, with a dining hall where 6,000 people could sit down for a banquet. Polo was amazed at the decorations. He wrote that gold and silver covered all the walls, along with gorgeous carvings of lions and dragons. Paintings of war scenes also hung on the walls. Near the palace stood the khan's treasure houses, holding gold, silver, precious stones, and pearls.

The khan's beautiful gardens, full of exotic trees and "many kinds of strange beasts," astonished Polo. The khan had built a tall hill, one mile around, which he had had covered with grass and trees. Even in winter the grass remained green and the trees were heavy with fruit. If a traveler told the khan of a beautiful tree in a distant part of the world, the khan would send men with an elephant to dig up the tree by the roots and bring it to his hill. On top he built a palace that was entirely green—both inside and outside.

Khubilai Khan lived a life of luxury. When he went hunting, he traveled in a room that was so large it had to be carried by four elephants. The inside of the room was decorated with cloth woven from silver and gold threads. The outside was wrapped with lion skins. The khan liked to watch his pet hawks hunt for cranes. When a flock of cranes flew overhead, his knights would cry out, "Sir, cranes are passing!" Immediately the khan's servants would roll back the roof of his traveling room so the khan could see the hawks pursuing the cranes.

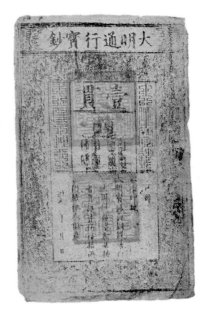
One way to raise money is to issue bank notes. Khubilai Khan issued notes like this beginning in 1260.

Taxing Times

As time went on, the government needed more and more money. Khubilai Khan hired foreign officials to think of new ways to tax the people. The Chinese hated these taxes. It made them especially angry to have foreigners in charge of the taxes. One of these foreign tax ministers was particularly evil. Some people believed that Khubilai Khan had been bewitched by this man's spells. Chinese officials working in the palace plotted against him. One night they lured him out of his house and killed him. But what would they tell Khubilai Khan? Advisors convinced the khan that the tax minister had been stealing from him. Angry, Khubilai Khan ordered the foreigner's body to be hung in the marketplace for all to see. Then the emperor's dogs were allowed to tear it to pieces.

Though the Chinese didn't like it, Khubilai Khan kept raising taxes anyway. He had to. He needed money to pay for his palace, his officials, and his luxurious way of life. He was also fighting wars in far-off places, and these wars cost a lot of money. In earlier times the Mongols had won almost every war, but now they began to lose battles. They tried to conquer the Vietnamese people, who fought back so bravely that the Mongols had to give up.

The Mongols also tried to invade Japan. Their invasion became one of the most famous events in all of history. Khubilai Khan sent a huge fleet of ships to land troops on Japan. A powerful storm called a **typhoon** suddenly started when the ships were at sea. The high winds and waves completely destroyed the Mongol fleet. The Japanese believed that the typhoon had been sent on purpose by their god to destroy the Mongols and

> **vocabulary**
> **typhoon** a windy storm with heavy rain

save Japan. They called the typhoon *kamikaze* (kah mih kah zee), "the divine wind," because they thought it came from heaven.

These defeats made the Chinese realize that the Mongols were not unbeatable. Some Chinese took up arms and revolted against Khubilai Khan. When Khubilai Khan's army put down these revolts, the Chinese people grew even more resentful.

A Famous Name

As he grew older, Khubilai Khan grew very sad. His wife died, and then his favorite son, who was next in line to become emperor, died as well. Khubilai Khan started to drink too much wine and eat too much food. He grew enormously fat—so fat that he became ill. The finest doctors in Asia could not help him because he would not stop drinking. Still, he did not die until he was 80 years old. Like his grandfather, Chinggis Khan, he was buried in a secret place. Even today, no one knows where Khubilai Khan is buried.

When he was old and ill, Khubilai Khan said farewell to his friend Marco Polo. Polo missed Italy and wished to go back. Khubilai Khan granted permission for Polo to leave if Polo promised to return. But Polo never came back.

In Italy, Marco Polo wrote a book about China that made Khubilai Khan famous all over Europe. Khubilai Khan was so famous that 500 years after he died, an English writer, Samuel Taylor Coleridge, composed a poem about him and his beautiful summer palace, which Coleridge called Xanadu (ZAN ah doo). Anything was possible in Xanadu: The khan's sunny paradise somehow had mysterious caves of ice. The poem remains one of the most popular in the English language. Khubilai Khan would have been glad. In his lifetime he had encouraged writers, so it seems only fair that he was **immortalized** by a poet. To this day the very name Khubilai Khan conjures up images of luxury, power, and great mystery.

> **vocabulary**
> **immortalized** made into someone or something that will be remembered forever

Xanadu's beauty has been immortalized by poets as well as artists. This is an eighteenth-century image of what the summer palace might have looked like.

The Ugly Emperor There is probably only one man in all of Chinese history who is famous for being ugly. His name was Zhu Yuanzhang (joo yoo ahn jahng) and he was born in the year 1328. After he reached adulthood, many artists painted portraits of him.

He had a dark, angry, pockmarked face and a huge jaw that stuck out like the bow of a ship. Perhaps when he was a boy, people made fun of him. But when he was an adult, no one dared to do that. The ugly little boy grew up to become the emperor of China.

Zhu Yuanzhang came from a very poor family of farmers. His parents owed money to their landlords and had to move a lot when they couldn't pay the rent. Zhu Yuanzhang never knew a real home. His parents were so poor that they had to give away some of Zhu Yuanzhang's brothers and sisters because they did not have enough money to support them.

When Zhu Yuanzhang was a teenager, the Yellow River changed its course and overflowed. Waters flooded all the fields and destroyed the crops. People starved to death. Disease broke out and killed many others. Both of Zhu Yuanzhang's parents died. At 16 years of age, Zhu Yuanzhang was

This picture of Zhu Yuanzhang, with his pockmarked face, was painted before he became emperor.

an orphan left with nothing. He could not even afford to buy coffins to bury his parents. Desperate, he went to a Buddhist monastery to ask for food and a place to live. But the monks there were very poor themselves. Many people had come to them, asking for help. The monks felt they had no choice but to send such people out to beg for food and money.

For years, Zhu Yuanzhang traveled around the country, begging for money. He saw scenes of terrible poverty and suffering. People blamed the Mongol government for their troubles. The poor got so angry that they formed bands of rebel fighters. They stole food and attacked government troops.

Zhu Yuanzhang returned to the monastery where he thought he would be safe, but Mongol troops came and burned it to the ground. The government accused the monks of helping the rebels.

Ugly and Angry

Zhu Yuanzhang had no place to live. He left the ruined monastery and joined a rebel group. He became well known as a fighter, and the rebels eventually made him one of their leaders. When the commander of the rebels died, Zhu Yuanzhang became the new commander. In 1368, Zhu Yuanzhang sent a huge army to attack the Mongol emperor. The emperor was so frightened that he fled back to Mongolia instead of trying to fight. Zhu Yuanzhang proclaimed the beginning of a new dynasty, the Ming, which meant "brilliant."

Zhu Yuanzhang could be very cruel. One time when some officials made mistakes on government documents, Zhu Yuanzhang had them put to death. Many people refused to work for him because they feared his bad temper. Would you work for someone if you could be killed for making a mistake?

Zhu Yuanzhang knew that he had a bad temper and that people were afraid to tell him the truth. He gave an order saying that he would let people write letters telling him what they did not like about the government. Zhu Yuanzhang promised not to get mad. But when he read some of the letters, he forgot his promise. One letter made him so angry that he ordered the author to be brought to the palace in chains and thrown into prison. This made people even more afraid to trust Zhu Yuanzhang.

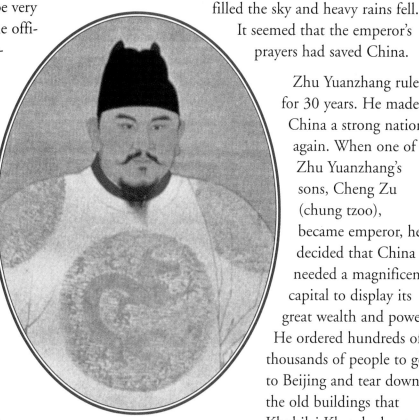

Zhu Yuanzhang, first Ming emperor: Note that his pockmarked face has been "cleaned up" for this royal portrait.

Because he had been poor himself, the emperor worried about China's poor people. He made laws to protect poor farmers from rich and powerful nobles. Zhu Yuanzhang made it a crime to take land from poor people. If you did, the emperor would have your nose cut off.

During this time a drought struck China. No rain fell and the fields dried up. People had nothing to eat. The emperor decided to do something. He sat outside in the hot sun saying prayers for rain. He prayed for three days. When he finished his prayers, clouds filled the sky and heavy rains fell. It seemed that the emperor's prayers had saved China.

Zhu Yuanzhang ruled for 30 years. He made China a strong nation again. When one of Zhu Yuanzhang's sons, Cheng Zu (chung tzoo), became emperor, he decided that China needed a magnificent capital to display its great wealth and power. He ordered hundreds of thousands of people to go to Beijing and tear down the old buildings that Khubilai Khan had put up. In their place he ordered a new Imperial City to be built. At the center of the Imperial City, Cheng Zu wanted a splendid residence for himself and the imperial family. The emperor gave this residence a frightening name: the Forbidden City.

The Forbidden City

Amazingly, the Forbidden City survives today. If you have the chance to travel to China, you can visit it. You can walk through the same rooms where the emperors walked. You can stand in the places where the emperors' officials made their reports. If they had bad news to give the emperor, they trembled. Before they could speak to the emperor, officials had to kow-tow, which means they had to kneel down nine times and touch their forehead to the floor each time. It showed that they had complete respect for the emperor.

The Forbidden City includes 75 buildings. Many of them are palaces where the emperor lived with his family. If the emperor's family got bored with living in one building, they'd close it up and move into another. One time an empress walking in the Forbidden City came upon an empty house with weeds growing all around it. Everyone had forgotten about this house, and no one even knew when it had last been lived in. It's hard to imagine how you could forget about a house, but this part of the Forbidden City was shaped like a maze, with small courtyards, lovely gardens, and narrow walkways.

Other buildings in the Forbidden City contain large reception halls where the emperor met with his officials and with important

The Forbidden City was surrounded by waterways and guarded by bronze lions and other icons that were supposed to protect the imperial family.

foreign visitors. To enter the Forbidden City for a meeting or ceremony, officials had to walk between two lines of elephants guarding the outer gate. After all the officials had passed, the lines of elephants would take a step forward and link their trunks to prevent anyone else from entering.

Many of the buildings in the Forbidden City have yellow roofs. Yellow was a color that only the emperor could use because it was the color of the sun. Each building also has a statue of a magical dragon to protect it. The Chinese believed that these dragons loved water and would guard the buildings from fire.

Unfortunately, there was a great fire in the Forbidden City. One of the emperors loved lanterns. To please the emperor, an official hung up some beautiful lanterns for the New Year's festival. The lanterns caught fire and destroyed many of the buildings, but the emperor ordered them to be rebuilt.

Cheng Zu's architects designed a place of great beauty. They created beautiful patterns with colors and with precious materials like gold, silver, and jade. The architects made a special effort to design a beautiful room for the emperor's throne. The Chinese believed that the emperor's throne was the center of the universe. They called it the place "where the earth and sky meet."

The Admiral of the Western Seas

The Chinese always thought that their country was the most important one in the world. Cheng Zu believed that, too, but he also wanted to find out about other countries. He called for one of his most trusted soldiers, Zheng He (jung huh), and named him Admiral of the Western Seas. He told Zheng He to build a fleet of ships to explore the world. Zheng He's fleet included over 300 ships and a crew of almost 28,000 men. It was like a floating city. The biggest ships had nine masts and measured 444 feet long and 186 feet wide. One Chinese historian described the ships as being like houses and the sails as looking like "great clouds in the sky." The ships carried food for the whole voyage, and they even brought big tubs of earth to grow vegetables on the decks of the ships.

The Chinese had invented the **compass** many centuries earlier, so they were able to navigate great distances on the open sea. On one voyage, Zheng He went all the way to the eastern coast of Africa, which was halfway around the world from China. The rulers of eastern Africa heard that Cheng Zu was fascinated by exotic animals, so they gave Zheng He gifts of animals for the emperor. Zheng He returned with lions, leopards, camels, zebras, rhinoceroses, and giraffes. The emperor's officials were so amazed when they saw the giraffe that they bowed down before it.

> **vocabulary**
> **compass** device for showing direction, made up of a magnetized needle that is free to point to the north magnetic pole

When Cheng Zu died, the explorations stopped. Officials persuaded the new emperor that the voyages cost too much money. And besides, they asked, why should we go to the trouble of exploring other nations if China is the most important country in the world?

To make sure that no one else could follow Zheng He's routes to Africa, the officials took his log books, or detailed records of his voyages, and burned them. Zheng He became famous for his voyages anyway. He is considered one of the greatest explorers in history.

A God Too Old and Tired

The other Ming emperors did not accomplish as much as Zhu Yuanzhang and Cheng Zu. But they excelled at spending money. Some emperors had banquets for 10,000 to 15,000 people in the Forbidden City every day. To feed all those people, the emperors employed over 6,000 cooks. Another Ming emperor decided to start work on his tomb when he was only 22 years old. He wanted to be buried in great splendor. He ordered that a magnificent underground complex, with five enormous halls,

be built. When the workers finished the tomb, the emperor had a party inside it. Archaeologists opened the tomb in 1956 and found the emperor's coffin and 26 chests full of treasure.

The Ming emperors refused to save money by cutting back on luxuries, but one of them had an idea: He would save money by ending the national postal service that Khubilai Khan had started. But when the postal service closed, the emperors in Beijing had no idea what was happening in other parts of the country, because there were so few messages going back and forth. The postmen who lost their jobs grew poor and hungry. They needed to feed their families. Many of them became robbers.

This is a model of one of Zheng He's ships. The battle flags represent his rank and title—battle commander and admiral.

The situation got much worse in the 1620s, when the climate changed. The weather got colder for a while. Lakes that never had ice before suddenly froze solid. The summer growing season shrank. People starved. Rebellions broke out. One group of rebels broke the walls holding back the Yellow River. Floods then killed hundreds of thousands of people. The Chinese thought that their god was getting too old and tired to take care of them. He could no longer hear their prayers or see their suffering. The people sang a sad song about it:

> Old Skymaster,
> You're getting on, your ears are deaf,
>   your eyes are gone.
> Can't see people, can't hear words.

The Coming of the Manchus

Eventually, a large rebellion broke out in northern China. The rebels surrounded and captured Beijing. A Ming general was marching to attack the rebels when he heard that they had already taken the capital. He also heard that his own father and girlfriend were prisoners of the rebels. This made him very angry. He sent a message to China's enemies, the Manchus, who were tough fighters from north of China. The general asked the Manchus to enter China and defeat the rebels. The Manchus were happy to help. They defeated the rebels and then took over China. They set up a new dynasty, called the Qing (ching) dynasty.

The Manchus had lived close to China and had become like the Chinese. The Manchus did not wish to destroy China. They had modeled their own government on the way the Chinese ruled. Many Chinese leaders thought that the Manchus offered the best hope for peace in China.

The Manchus turned out to be very strict rulers. They made it illegal for any Chinese

During the Qing dynasty, men, such as these engravers, were forced to grow pigtails.

person to own a weapon. They insisted that all the Chinese be loyal to them. They thought of a way for Chinese men to prove their loyalty.

For a long time it had been fashionable for Manchu men to braid their hair in a pigtail. Chinese men, however, did not like that style. The Manchu emperor issued an order, in ten days all Chinese men had to start growing a pigtail. If you didn't grow one, that meant you were disloyal to the new government and you would be killed. Being forced to wear pigtails made the Chinese furious. Would you like it if someone made you wear your hair a certain way, even if you hated that style? The Chinese felt that they had lost all control of their own lives. One high official from the old government was so angry at the Manchus that, as a protest, he refused to speak for the rest of his life.

The Emperor Who Possessed All Things The Qing dynasty began in 1644 and stretched all the way to 1912. During much of this time, China enjoyed peace and prosperity. The Manchus encouraged learning but also supported the farmers.

One of the finest Chinese emperors was Qianlong (chee yen loong). Even as a child, Qianlong showed great talent. His family gave him a strict education because they knew that one day great responsibility would be his. He had to start his lessons at five o'clock in the morning and study until the sun went down. He had breaks to practice archery and horse riding. The habits which he formed in childhood helped Qianlong when he became emperor at the age of 24. He rose early every morning and finished a lot of government business before breakfast, which he ate at seven o'clock. He had free time in the afternoon for the activities he really loved. He enjoyed painting pictures and writing poetry. In his lifetime he wrote more than 42,000 poems. He also loved walking in his gardens. He had a beautiful garden, called the Paradise of Countless Trees, where delicate willows bent over fish ponds and fruit trees flourished.

In Qianlong's time, China became very rich and powerful. European nations eagerly paid high prices for China's silk, porcelain, tea, art works, and other objects. The Chinese would not accept foreign money. They demanded to be paid in silver.

Porcelains, such as these Ming-dynasty vases, were traded by the Chinese to Europeans for silver during the Qing dynasty.

China was willing to sell its products to the Europeans, but it was not interested in buying European products in return. Many Chinese believed that China made the best of everything and did not need anything that Westerners produced. Only a few Europeans were allowed to enter China—and only then during certain times of year. The emperor made it illegal to teach the Chinese language to foreigners or to send Chinese books outside the country.

Great Britain became the biggest customer for China's tea and porcelain. It annoyed the British that the Chinese refused to buy their goods, when the British were spending so much money in China. In 1793 a British ambassador, Lord Macartney, traveled to China with 84 assistants

In this picture, Chinese dealers are testing and weighing opium purchased from the British.

and advisors to meet with the emperor. They brought 600 crates of British goods to show the emperor what marvelous products they made.

Qianlong received Lord Macartney politely. He invited the Englishman to a lavish banquet and took him on a tour of the private imperial garden. But whenever Macartney tried to discuss business, Qianlong changed the subject.

Finally, the Chinese hinted to the British that it was time to leave. The British told Qianlong's officials that they had not yet completed their business. The officials handed over a letter from the emperor. The emperor wrote, "We possess all things. . . . I set no value on objects strange or ingenious, and have no use for your country's manufactures."

The British were stunned. They could not believe that they had failed. But you could not argue with the emperor of China. They had to leave.

The Opium Wars

China thought it could remain isolated from Europe and the Western world. But the world was changing. The nations of Europe were growing richer and more powerful. They wanted to have influence over China, and they wanted to sell their goods in China. China would not remain isolated for long.

The British eventually began selling a few goods to the Chinese, including a drug called opium. Opium is a very powerful painkiller. If you use it, you can become addicted to it. That is exactly what happened to many people in China. One Chinese official wrote that opium was "worse than an invasion of wild beasts." It destroyed Chinese lives and families.

The Chinese government tried to stop the drug trade, but the British got angry. They were making too much money from opium. They refused to stop selling it. The British sent warships to force the Chinese to buy opium and other goods. This led to a series of bitter defeats for the Chinese. Whether they wanted to or not, the Chinese now had to open their doors to foreign traders.

In 1860, British and French soldiers burned the emperor's summer palace to the ground and stole many of its treasures: precious furniture, jewels, porcelain, and silk robes. They even stole the emperor's dogs— "very pretty little dogs" of a kind only the emperor and his family were allowed to own. They were Pekingese dogs, and one of them was given to Queen Victoria of England.

The Empty Throne

The great days of the Chinese empire were gone. Life became more difficult in China in the 1800s. The population got so big that the Chinese ran out of land for farming. There wasn't enough food to feed the growing population, and there weren't enough jobs either. Many people left the country to find work in other parts of Asia, in South America, and in the United States.

Some Chinese settled in Hawaii to work in the sugarcane fields. When gold was discovered in California in 1848, thousands of Chinese men sailed to America to work in the mines. They also helped build railroads in the American West.

China's ancient way of government barely lasted into the twentieth century. A series of rebellions changed the country forever. Finally, in 1912 the last emperor of China stepped down from the throne. China became a republic, with an elected government. After more than 2,000 years of rule by emperors, the throne of China was empty.

Many Chinese miners worked in California's gold mines during the 1850s. They lived together in camps.

Glossary

compass device for showing direction, made up of a magnetized needle that is free to point to the north magnetic pole

elite the best or finest members, as of a society or social group

immortalized made into someone or something that will be remembered forever

jade a greenish mineral used as a gemstone

monotonous tiresome or uninteresting because of a lack of variety

oasis a fertile area in the midst of a desert; most oases have at least some drinkable water

steppes vast treeless plains extending from southwestern Europe into central Asia

typhoon a windy storm with heavy rain

tyrant a ruler who rules in a harsh, cruel manner

Courtesy of, The Valley Forge Historical Society

The

American
Revolution

Contents

Coming to America On a pleasant summer day in 1750, a ship carrying 400 Germans arrived at the docks in Philadelphia. These newcomers were about to begin new lives in America.

Now if this had been a hundred years earlier, the arrival of 400 **immigrants** would have been big news. Back then, 400 new immigrants would have been a big addition to any colony. In fact, back then there were only five English colonies in North America. Some colonies didn't "struggle." Colonists struggled just to keep their tiny settlements going.

Not in 1750, though. By this time there were 13 colonies, and all of them were strong and growing. Almost every week a ship arrived with another boatload of new Americans. The population of the colonies had already passed 1 million, and was fast climbing toward 2 million. Settlements had spread from the Atlantic Ocean as far west as the Appalachian Mountains.

Why had so many people come to the British colonies in America? Why were so many still coming in 1750? The answer lies in one word: opportunity. Opportunity to own land of their own. Opportunity to work in America's growing towns and cities. Opportunity to worship as they pleased. Opportunity to start a new life.

And who were these colonists, these new Americans? Where were they from? They were ordinary people, mainly—farmers and people from small towns. Most were from England. But a large number—perhaps a third of them—came from other countries. One of the largest groups was Germans.

> **vocabulary**
> **immigrant** a person from one country who comes into another country to live there

Another large group was the Scots-Irish, who were Scottish people living in the northern part of Ireland. There were Swedes and Finns, Scots and Welsh, Dutch and Swiss, French and Irish.

Not all Americans of 1750 had come to the colonies willingly. About one in every five Americans were slaves who were dragged here from Africa. Most lived in the South, but there were slaves in the North, too. Only a small number of blacks were free. Even freedom, though, did not lead to much opportunity for black people in colonial America.

More than nine out of ten colonial families lived on farms. They farmed their land by themselves. With each member of the family pitching in, they produced nearly everything they needed, plus a little bit more for sale. They raised their own food. They cut and sewed their own clothes from animal hides and wool. They made their own furniture. Most of them even built the houses they lived in.

There were still only four or five cities in all of the colonies, and just a handful of towns. But the cities were growing quickly. In just a few more years, Philadelphia would become the second largest city in the whole British Empire. (London, England, was the largest.)

What sparked this growth of towns and cities? Trade, mainly trade with other countries. From the docks of the cities on the coast, merchants sent lumber, fur, salted fish, flour, and tobacco to many parts of the world. To those docks, ships returned with glass, paint, tea, wine, and other goods the colonists wanted.

Trade meant jobs. Men loaded and unloaded ships. They built boats. They made sails, rope, and barrels for shipping goods. But cities and towns offered other kinds of work also. Men, and some women, ran stores and shops. Skilled workers baked bread and made pots and pans. They printed newspapers. They made fine shoes and clothes for other city dwellers.

As you see, Americans were a busy, hardworking people. They believed that hard work would pay off in a better life. Except for the slaves, it did. It is true that compared to Europe there were few really rich people in America. But there were few really poor people either. It was a good land to live in.

A log cabin could make a snug home for a frontier family.

Staying Apart and Coming Together

When people arrived in the American colonies, they tried to settle near others from the same homeland. This made them feel more comfortable in a strange, new land. They could speak their own language and follow their own ways of life. They wore the same kind of clothing they had worn in their homeland and built the same kind of houses.

In time, however, something interesting and important happened. Immigrant groups began to borrow ideas and customs from each other. For example, consider the log cabin. Swedes had built log cabins in their homeland. Here in America, they found plenty of trees for doing the same. A log cabin was easy to put up. Two strong men with axes could build one in a couple of weeks. Other groups came to America with their own ideas of how a house should look. But then they saw these log cabins. They realized that these buildings were perfect for life on the **frontier.** Soon it made no difference what group the frontier settlers were part of. They all built log cabins.

All this borrowing among immigrant groups even changed

> **vocabulary**
> **frontier** the newly settled area on the edge of the unsettled area or wilderness

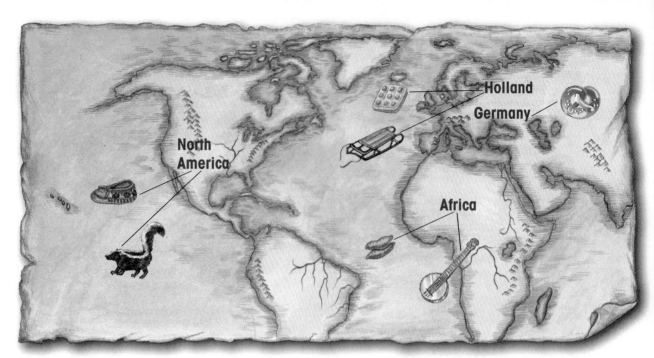

English, as it is spoken in the United States, has borrowed words from many cultures.

the way Americans talked. Most colonists spoke English, but English began to borrow words from the other languages in the colonies. From German came *noodle, pretzel,* and *kindergarten.* From Dutch came *waffle, cookie,* and *sleigh. Pecan, moccasin, skunk,* and *squash* came from Native American languages. And African languages contributed lots of words, including *yams, banjo,* and *tote.*

The result of all this borrowing became a new kind of English—American English. And little by little, this new American English became the language of the children and grandchildren of immigrants from other lands. Borrowings like these helped to bring the different groups of colonists closer together.

Better Roads

By the 1750s, the colonists were also being brought together by improved roads. You would not think of these roads as very good compared to our own. They were narrow, often muddy, and filled with tree stumps. Still, they were better than the roads of 50 or 100 years earlier. These roads made it possible for more Americans to travel and led to increased trade among the colonies.

Better roads also improved communications, by speeding up the exchange of information. By the 1750s, mail was being delivered between Philadelphia and Boston in just three days. That meant that newspapers printed in the cities could be quickly delivered to colonists in the countryside. Everyone in a colony could read the same news and stay informed about the same things. In all these ways, then, colonists of many different backgrounds were starting to come together. They were beginning—just beginning, of course—to have more things in common.

As you will see, that soon became very important in what was about to happen in the American colonies.

rowing Up What would it have been like to grow up in colonial America? Let's spend a little time finding out. We'll begin with your family. It's probably a farm family. Nine out of ten colonial families are.

Chances are that your house is pretty crowded. That's because colonists have large families. Nearly all women marry, and most have seven or eight children.

There might be another reason your house is so crowded, though. You see, in the world of the 1700s, lots of people die young. It's not unusual for a parent to die. When that happens, the remaining parent usually remarries—often to another person who also has many children. So you're pretty sure to have lots of brothers and sisters. And there's a good chance you have some stepbrothers and stepsisters, too.

With a crowd like that, what do you think are the chances that you have your own bedroom? Just about zero. You

not only don't have your own bedroom; you don't even have your own bed. You share a bed with two or three other children in the family, and you hope they all sleep without kicking about.

Actually, you're probably grateful to have so many kids in the family because they are your "built-in" playmates. You don't have neighborhood friends, because you don't have a neighborhood. Only people in the villages and towns have neighborhoods. Farmhouses are far apart. So the children in the family depend on each other for lots of things, including play.

Of course everyone has regular chores to do. That includes you. Everyone's day begins at dawn, if not before.

Nature provided a playground for colonial farm children.

If you are a boy, your first job is to bring in firewood and build the fire. Matches don't exist yet, so you hope there is still a burning coal in the fireplace from the night before. If not, you'll have to start a new fire or run to the next farmhouse in the cold morning air, carrying a metal box or tongs for bringing back a "live" coal.

After breakfast and morning prayers, it's out to the fields with your father. You'll plant and hoe and clear away brush from new land that's to be planted next year. Maybe you'll help repair a fence or two.

If you are a girl, you'll be helping your mother make candles and preserve foods, starting right after breakfast. You'll probably also have to feed the animals. Then you'll spend the rest of the morning helping to cook the noon meal. That's the main meal of the day. In the afternoon you'll sew, knit, weave, or spin yarn.

Did you notice there was no time in your day's schedule for school? That's because you probably don't go to school. Perhaps you did last year and the year before. But you can

Slave children had to grow up quickly and work like adults.

read and write now. Most parents feel that once you can do that, you don't need any more school.

In fact, you may not have gone to school at all. Chances are that you learned to read and write at home. An older brother or sister or maybe a parent started teaching you when you were five or six. If no one in your home could read, then you might have been sent to learn at another farmhouse where someone could.

It's amazing, though. Even though only a small number of colonial children went to school, nearly all of them learned to read. Parents believed it was important. Children were told it was important. And that was that. They learned.

Children of Slaves

If you were a child in a slave family on a southern plantation, your life would be very different. When you were much younger—say five or six—there had been plenty of time for play. In fact, some of your playmates were probably the children of your owner. You fished and picked berries with them, and you and they wandered over the plantation together, moving about freely.

Then, when you reached seven or eight years old, you started to take care of younger brothers and sisters. Also, your owner began to give you some regular tasks, like sweeping the yard and feeding the chickens, the same kinds of jobs that free white children did on family farms. Even at that age, however, you were already starting to understand that you were not the same as those free white children. Your parents taught you to be careful how you talked to members of the owner's family. You began to see some grown-ups, maybe even members of your own family, being badly treated or even whipped.

The big change in your life, though, is coming just as you reach your present age. Now is when you begin life as a grown-up slave. You work in the fields, doing the same hard work as adults. You plant, you plow, and you pick cotton, from sunup to sundown. You can be punished for not working hard enough or for not showing enough politeness to the master's family or for anything at all.

Even if your parents know that reading is important, you will probably never learn to read. The laws actually forbid anyone to teach you to read. Reading, you see, is dangerous to the slave system. You might get "dangerous" ideas about freedom from reading.

Sickness and Cures

Sickness is a serious problem in every colonial home. Many children die from disease before they reach your age. Little is really known about why people get sick or how they can get well and stay well.

A lot of people think they know, though. They make their own medicines

Herbs were an important source of medicine for the colonists.

from plants called herbs and also from the roots and bark of trees. Do you have a cut that isn't healing? A swelling that won't go down? A bad cold, perhaps? There's sure to be an herb or a root that will cure you.

Actually, some of these herbs have been used for hundreds of years and really do seem to do some good. Others, though—well . . .

There are also some special tricks that are supposed to help you get better. For example, to bring down a fever, your parents might cut your toenails and put them into a small linen bag. Then they would tie the bag around the neck of an eel and put the eel in a tub of water. When the eel died, your fever was supposed to go down. One of the best-educated men in the Massachusetts colony has recommended that cure.

Even if you are just feeling tired and need pepping up, there's a special recipe to help. You roast a toad, grind it up, and add boiling water to make a kind of tea. Drink it and

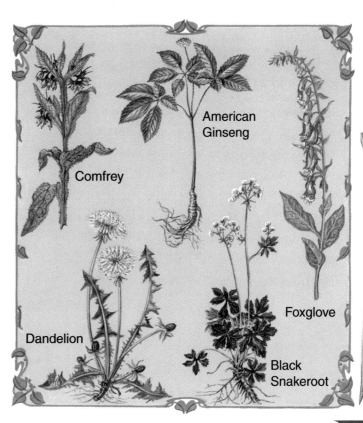

American Ginseng

Comfrey

Dandelion

Foxglove

Black Snakeroot

Colonial doctors often relied on remedies we wouldn't recognize today.

1. Feed your children only plain foods and not much sugar, spice, or salt. No eating between meals, except for dry bread.

2. Keep them away from candy.

3. See that they sleep on a hard bed. No soft feathers.

4. Bathe them in cold water, even in the winter.

5. Give them very thin shoes that will leak and let in water. (A famous man got this idea by noting that poor people often went barefoot and didn't seem to get sick from that.)

6. Strawberries, cherries, and gooseberries are good for children. Melons, peaches, plums, and grapes are not, even though they are tasty. Don't give them any.

you'll be feeling lively in no time. For a cold or a sore throat, sprinkle pepper on a piece of meat and wrap it around your throat.

Of course, you could go to a doctor. There are a few doctors in the colonies. But it probably won't do much good. There are no special schools for training doctors in the colonies, so doctors don't know much more than most others about making people well. Doctors do have a favorite cure for almost any illness, though. They cut open a vein in your arm and let about a cup of blood run out before stopping the wound. This is called "bleeding the patient."

Of course the best thing to do is to stay well. Your parents have been told to do quite a few things to keep you from getting sick. See the list above for a few of them.

Many of our great American leaders grew up following rules like these. But our history books don't tell us whether they enjoyed it! As you see, growing up in colonial times was quite different from what it is today. Based on what you've read so far, do you think you might have liked it?

art of the Empire If bumper stickers had existed in colonial days, one of them surely would have said, "Proud to Be British." For that's how American colonists felt in the middle of the 1700s.

The English Parliament has two houses, the House of Lords and the House of Commons. This is a House of Commons meeting during the eighteenth century.

British navy, the greatest navy in the world. Most important, as members of the British Empire, American colonists enjoyed a great deal of self-government. That is, colonists had a say in choosing their own leaders and making their own laws. Here's how that came about. Self-government started in England several hundred years earlier. At that time, certain wealthy and important English landowners elected people to represent them in the English Parliament. Parliament is a law-making body, much like our Congress.

They were members of the greatest empire in the world—the British Empire, which had colonies all over the world. They could trade with any part of the empire, while other peoples, for the most part, could not. On the oceans, their ships were protected by the

At first, Parliament didn't have much power. The king had most of it. But over time, members of Parliament insisted that only they, not the king, should make decisions where taxes and spending were concerned. They said that Parliament should have a say in making other laws, too.

English kings did not agree. For a couple of hundred years, Parliament and the king struggled over this issue. Parliament finally won.

When the English began to settle in America, they brought along their ideas of self-government. Pretty soon, colonists were voting for representatives to their own law-making bodies. These were usually called **assemblies.** That doesn't mean that everyone in the colonies could vote. Women could not. Blacks could not. Native Americans could not. Only white males who owned land or other property could vote. But most white males did own land, so a large part of the colonial population could vote.

> **vocabulary**
>
> **assembly** a group of representatives who gather to make laws

Soon colonists were insisting that only their elected assemblies could make laws for their colonies. Of course, they knew that it was Parliament's job to run the whole British Empire. It was up to Parliament to pass laws about trade between different parts of the empire. Only Parliament could decide the rules for trade between the empire and other parts of the world. The American colonists didn't argue about that.

When it came to everyday life in their own colony, though, what could a Parliament 3,000 miles away know about such things? Only their own elected representatives could understand what kinds of laws were needed and what kinds were foolish. Therefore, they said, only its own elected assembly could make laws for a colony.

That was especially true about tax laws. You'll want to remember that point, because it's going to become very important. As the colonists saw it, *they could be taxed only by their own elected representatives*. Anything else would be "taxation without representation." Englishmen had long ago fought and won the battle against that.

Americans Claim British Rights

The people of Great Britain—the English, but also the Scots and the Welsh—enjoyed other rights and liberties, too. As members of the British Empire, American colonists felt they had these same rights.

Most of these rights and liberties were meant to protect the people against unfair actions by their own government. Here's one example: The government could not just take away a person's house or land or ship or other property. If the government said it really needed that property for some very important purpose, it would have to prove that to a judge. Even if the judge agreed with the government, the government still had to pay the owner for it.

Here's another: Government officers could not just show up and search your home or business whenever they felt like it. They first had to explain to a judge why they believed you were hiding something illegal. The judge then had to give permission for the officers to conduct a search. Otherwise, no search was allowed.

Here are two more important rights that English people had. They could not be put in jail unless they were accused of breaking a law. And if they were accused, they couldn't just be kept in jail indefinitely. They had the right to a trial before a jury of fellow citizens. A jury is a group of people who hear the facts of the case and then decide whether the person is guilty or innocent. Also, no secret accusations or secret evidence are permitted. Everything has to be out in the open, so that accused persons can defend themselves.

Trial by jury is a very important right, both in English courts, shown here, and American courts. In this picture, the judge sits under the windows on the left and the jury sits under the windows on the right.

There were other rights, too. If citizens wanted to get together peaceably to talk about a problem or to protest something, the government could not interfere. And if they wanted to petition their government—that is, to ask the government to change a law or do something, or stop doing something— well, they had that right, too.

Do these rights seem very special to you? Maybe not. That's because we have them today, and we tend to take them for granted. But the sad truth is that, even today, most people in the world do not enjoy these rights. In the middle of the 1700s, very few people outside the British Empire did. British people were proud to have "the rights of Englishmen," and so were the American colonists.

No wonder American colonists felt they were among the most fortunate people on earth. They lived in a land blessed by nature. They enjoyed rights and liberties equal to anyone, anywhere in the world. They were proud and happy to be a part of the empire of Great Britain. Probably the idea of separating from Great Britain never entered a colonist's head. Thinking back to that time, Benjamin Franklin many years later recalled, "I never heard in any conversation from any person . . . the least [desire] for separation from England."

Ben Franklin was remembering how the colonists felt around 1763. But 13 years later the American colonies separated from England and declared their independence. You are about to learn what happened to make the colonists change their minds.

4 Learning Hard Lessons

hose Land Is It? Traveling 500 miles through the wilderness was a long way to go to deliver a message. That's 500 miles there and 500 miles back. It must have seemed especially long to the 21-year-old military officer from Virginia who delivered the messages because all he got for his troubles was a big No.

The young officer and his party of six were from the British colony of Virginia. They were members of the Virginia **militia,** a sort of volunteer citizen's army. At that time—the year was 1753—France had built a string of forts along the Ohio River, in what is now western Pennsylvania. The young officer's mission was to carry a message from the governor of Virginia to the French general in charge of those forts.

> **vocabulary**
> **militia** a body of armed citizens prepared for military service at any time

For weeks the Virginians traveled by horseback and canoe until they finally met up with the French general. The young officer handed him the message. This is what it said: Your forts are on Virginia's land. Get out!

The French general was polite but firm. No, he replied, my troops will not get out. This land belongs to France. French fur trappers have lived on this land for a hundred years. French colonists have started settlements here. The forts will stay right where they are.

On the return journey the group's horses gave out, and the officer and his men had to walk much of the way. Along the way an Indian fired at the officer, just barely missing him. Then, while crossing an ice-filled river on a raft, the officer was accidentally knocked overboard. He nearly drowned before his men finally fished him out.

The men finally returned to Virginia, and the officer gave the governor the bad news. The French were determined to stay.

The young officer's unsuccessful journey would soon lead to war. That war in turn led to events that brought about the birth of the United States of America.

And the 21-year-old officer from the Virginia colony? He would have a lot to do with the birth of the United States of America, too. His name was George Washington.

Washington's Mistakes

The governor of the Virginia colony was determined to make the French leave the land near the Ohio River. The next year, 1754, he sent George Washington to the west again. This time Washington led a force of 150 men.

The British had built a small fort at the point where two rivers come together to form the Ohio River. Washington was to join forces with the British soldiers at the fort. However, before he got there, Washington learned that the French had already captured the fort and renamed it Fort Duquesne (doo KAYN).

George Washington, on the white horse, was proud to be an officer in the Virginia militia.

In time, George Washington would become a great general. But just then, he was young and inexperienced. He proceeded to make a number of mistakes. Since Washington did not have enough men to drive the French out of the fort, the wisest thing to do would have been to return to Virginia. Instead, he continued on with his small force.

Along the way his troops surprised and defeated a group of 30 French soldiers, killing ten of them. The French at Fort Duquesne had many more men than Washington did, and they had Indian **allies** as well. They were now sure to send out a larger force from the fort to deal with Washington's Virginians.

When he realized this, Washington built a makeshift camp his men called Fort Necessity. The spot Washington chose for Fort Necessity was a low piece of ground. Soon after the French attacked Fort Necessity, it began to rain heavily. Before long, Washington's men, their guns, and their gunpowder were soaked with the rain that collected in their low area. The Virginians fought bravely, but after nine hours, Washington had to surrender.

The French commander then instructed an assistant to prepare a statement about why the fighting had taken place. We, the Virginians, said the statement, are the ones who started the fighting. It was all our fault. The French commander read the statement and then handed it to Washington. "Sign," he said. "Sign, or I will not allow the prisoners to return to Virginia." Washington signed, and the men were released.

> **vocabulary**
> **ally** a nation that has promised to help another nation in wartime

When the men returned to Virginia, British officials were very angry—not just at the French but at Washington. They blamed him for his unwise decisions. They also blamed him for signing the statement. Washington resigned from the Virginia militia. That could have been the end of his military career. If it had been, perhaps we would all be saluting the British flag today instead of the Stars and Stripes.

5 The French and Indian War

War in the Colonies Washington's small battle against the French was the start of the French and Indian War. On one side were France, the French colonists in America, and their Indian allies. On the other side were Great Britain, the British colonists in America, and their Indian allies.

Great Britain and France had been fighting each other on and off for nearly a hundred years. No one was surprised that they were doing it again. Each of these European countries had colonies in other parts of the world. Each wanted to grab the other's colonies. So it was also no surprise when the war that began in the woods of North America was soon being fought on two other continents and on the Atlantic, Pacific, and Indian oceans as well. In Europe and Asia the war came to be called the Seven Years' War.

Fighting in the Woods

The British were determined to take Fort Duquesne and drive the French out of the Ohio River valley. In 1755 they sent General Edward Braddock with 2,200 troops from their regular full-time army to do the job. Eager to join Braddock's army and return to Fort Duquesne, George Washington wrote the British general and offered his services. Braddock appointed the eager young Virginian a colonel (KER null), in charge of 450 colonial soldiers.

Braddock was an experienced general. He knew a lot about fighting wars in Europe, where armies battled on great open fields. But he knew nothing about fighting a war in the woods of North America. Worse, he was too stubborn to listen to anyone who did.

The first thing Braddock did was order his men to cut a hundred-mile-long road through the woods toward Fort Duquesne so that his army could march over it—almost as if they were on parade.

Colonel Washington knew that was unwise. He and his colonists knew something about the woods. They warned Braddock that his troops should advance with great caution. They warned that an attack could come at any time and from any quarter. But Braddock ignored their advice. After all, they were mere colonists. What did they know about the art of war? A few miles from Fort Duquesne, French soldiers and their Indian allies attacked Braddock's army suddenly and without warning. They fired from hiding places in the thick woods. The British didn't know what had hit them. Their bright red coats made them easy targets. They panicked and ran, and General Braddock was killed.

It was fortunate for the British that George Washington had gone along. Courageously exposing himself to danger, Washington managed to lead what was left of the British army to safety. During the fighting, Washington had two horses shot from under him. He later also found that four bullets had passed through his clothing. A few more inches one way or the other, and the history of our country might have turned out differently.

Victory for the British

For a time the war went badly for the British elsewhere, too. Then William Pitt took charge of Great Britain's foreign affairs. This included foreign wars and dealing with the colonies.

It was true that the war was being fought in several different parts of the world and that North America was only one of them. But Pitt knew how valuable the American colonies were to Great Britain. He was determined that Great Britain must win this war and keep control of its North American lands. If it took more troops, Pitt would send them. If it took more ships, Pitt would get those, too. All this cost a lot of money, but Pitt was ready to spend whatever was necessary to win.

Pitt also saw that the key to victory in North America was to win control of two rivers—the St. Lawrence River and the Niagara River. These were the rivers the French used to send supplies to their troops near the Great Lakes and in the Ohio River valley, including those at Fort Duquesne. If the British could prevent the French from using these rivers—well, you can see what would happen to the French armies. They would soon run out of supplies. And without supplies, all their bravery and fighting skills would do them no good.

That's why Pitt sent these instructions to the British armies in America: Get control of the St. Lawrence and the Niagara rivers, no matter what it takes. Aided by their Indian allies and by the American colonists, the British did just that. In addition, British and American troops captured Fort Duquesne. They renamed it Fort Pitt, which is how the city of Pittsburgh got its name.

The dying General Braddock was carried from the battlefield.

Painting: Braddock's Retreat, July 9th 1755; (n.p.); 1865, Creator—Alonzo Chappel. Courtesy, Chicago Historical Society.

A great British victory at the Battle of Quebec in Canada finished off the French. The city of Quebec sits atop steep cliffs alongside the St. Lawrence River. The cliffs secured the city from attack—or so it was thought until one night in 1759. That night, British troops led by General James Wolfe climbed those cliffs and reached the top. When dawn broke, the French found the British assembled on a flat area at the top called the Plains of Abraham, ready to do battle. The British defeated the French troops and took the city of Quebec. Both Wolfe and the French general, Louis Montcalm, lost their lives in this famous battle.

The British now controlled the St. Lawrence River, and the French knew they had lost. In 1763, Great Britain and France made peace. In the peace treaty, France gave all of Canada to Great Britain. France also gave up all the land between the Appalachian Mountains and the Mississippi River to Great Britain. The land west of the Mississippi River was given to Spain, one of France's partners in the war.

How complete was Great Britain's victory? This is how complete: Before the war, France claimed four or five times as much land in North America as did Great Britain. After the war, France had next to none. Britain was now the main European colonial power in North America.

Notice how much territory France lost in North America as a result of the French and Indian War.

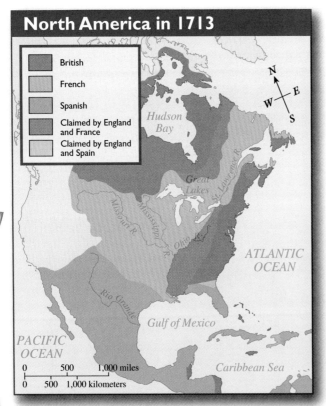

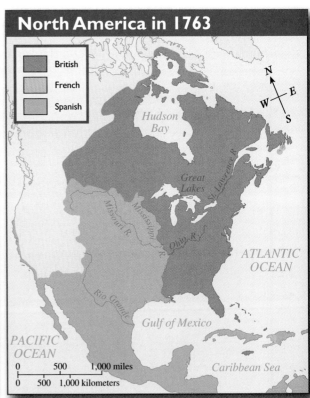

olonists Claim New Land What's the point of winning a lot of land in a war if you're not allowed to use it? Even before the French and Indian War, some colonists had moved onto the land between the Appalachian Mountains and the Mississippi River.

Now that France had given up any claim to this land, many more colonists looked forward to having it all for themselves. To the British government, however, the matter looked rather different. True, France was gone from this land. But the area was hardly empty. It was the homeland of many groups of Native Americans. Some of them had been allies of the British and fought in the war against the French.

Those Indians did not want white settlers taking their lands. Some Indian tribes had united behind a chief of the Ottawa tribe named Pontiac to drive out white settlers who were already there and to keep any more from coming. Indian warriors captured British forts and killed hundreds of settlers before British troops were finally able to end the uprising.

Now that they had finished one war with France, the British did not want a new one with the Indians. They would surely have one, though, if their American colonists kept pushing onto Indian lands.

Great Britain believed that, for the time being at least, it would be best to keep the settlers out of the Indians' homelands. On a map of North America, the new British king, George III, drew a line running along the top of the Appalachian Mountains from New York all the way south to Georgia. Then he issued a proclamation: until further notice,

Native Americans attacked forts like this one to keep settlers out of their homeland.

no more colonists were allowed to settle west of that line.

This Proclamation of 1763 angered the colonists. They had not fought the French to win this land for the Indians. They expected to get it for themselves. Now their own king was telling them they couldn't move there. Not only that, the king also announced that thousands of British troops would be stationed along the frontier to keep peace between the colonists and the Indians. To the colonists that meant stopping them from building houses and farms west of George III's line.

The Quarrel Grows

Soon the colonies had an even bigger quarrel with Great Britain. Like the quarrel over the Proclamation of 1763, this one grew out of the war with France.

To win that war, Britain had poured money into ships and men and supplies—more money than the British government had. So the government borrowed what it needed. Now it had to pay this money back. Also, the government would need money to pay for the troops who were to be stationed in forts on the American frontier.

Where was all this money to come from? To Parliament, the answer was clear. From the colonists of course. Not all of it, maybe, but certainly their fair share. The colonists gained a great benefit from Britain's victory over France, didn't they? Let them help pay for it.

First, said Parliament, let's make the colonists start paying the taxes they *should* have been paying all along but haven't. For example, colonists were supposed to pay taxes on certain goods brought in from elsewhere, or imported. Instead, they had been smuggling—bringing in the goods secretly—to avoid the eyes of the tax collectors.

So the British government sent more officials to America to make sure the

colonists paid the taxes, especially those on sugar and molasses. Even worse, these officials were allowed to enter and search colonists' homes and businesses *without the owner's permission*. They could search for smuggled goods or for any other evidence to show that colonists had broken the law.

Trees were the most available building material for frontier forts.

Do you remember the "rights of Englishmen?" Didn't one of those rights say that government officials could not just show up and search your home or business whenever they felt like it? How could their own British government take away this right from the colonists? Parliament came up with still another way to squeeze money from the colonies. When the French and Indian War ended, there were thousands of British troops in the colonies. The British government wanted to keep them there. So to help pay for them, Parliament passed the Quartering Act. This law required the colonial governments to furnish quarters—that is, places to live—for all these troops.

Americans had a big problem with that. Why does the British government want to keep troops in our colonies, they asked? For our protection? Protection against whom? Could it be that there is another reason for keeping troops here—like, to make us obey British laws we think are unfair? And on top of that, they expect us to pay for these troops?

Tax on Paper There was still another way to collect money from the colonists: new taxes. In 1765, Parliament passed the Stamp Act. This law made the colonists pay a tax on just about every imaginable kind of printed paper—about 50 items in all.

Under this law you would have to buy special tax stamps from a tax collector. Then you would stick one on each of the taxed items you used. So every time you bought a newspaper, you'd pay a tax. Every time you bought a copy of your minister's sermon, you'd pay a tax. Every time you bought a calendar, a marriage license, or any kind of legal or business paper, you'd pay a tax. You'd even be taxed on playing cards.

The colonists had been upset by the Proclamation of 1763. They had been angered by the officials searching their homes and businesses. Now they were outraged! No way, said the colonists, are we going to pay that tax on paper. No way.

Do you see why the colonists were so outraged? Was it their own colonial assemblies that had passed this tax law? No, it wasn't. It was the British Parliament in faraway London, England. Colonists did not elect the members of Parliament. Colonists were not represented in Parliament. Then what right did Parliament have to pass a law taxing them? None. Absolutely none. This was "taxation without representation," said the colonists. Here was the British government trampling on yet another right the colonists believed was theirs.

One colonist who strongly protested the Stamp Act was a 29-year-old Virginian named Patrick Henry. Patrick Henry was a member of the Virginia assembly, known as the Virginia House of Burgesses. He made a fiery speech denouncing this new tax. He warned that the Stamp Act would take away the colonists' liberty. Henry's speech was printed in newspapers throughout the colonies. The speech gave people a lot to think about.

Colonists did more than just talk and complain about the Stamp Act. In New York, Boston, Newport, and other places throughout the colonies, they formed groups called the Sons of Liberty. These groups threatened the stamp tax collectors. They even beat up some

Stamps such as this one attached to a document showed that a tax had been paid, in this case five shillings.

of them. Many a stamp tax collector decided that the wisest thing to do was get out of town and just forget about selling the tax stamps.

That wasn't all the Sons of Liberty did. They organized a **boycott** of British goods. That is, they got people to agree not to buy goods from Great Britain. And they said they would not buy them again while the Stamp Act was law.

There were Daughters of Liberty, too. These women helped make the boycott work by making homemade cloth. That way the colonists could get the cloth they needed without buying it from British merchants.

Sons of Liberty, Daughters of Liberty, and the many other people who supported the colonists' cause gave themselves another name. They called themselves Patriots.

The actions didn't stop there. Some leaders called for a special meeting of all the colonies to decide what else to do. Nine colonies sent delegates, or representatives, to the meeting, which was held in New York. The delegates agreed on a number of statements about the rights of colonists. They also asked Parliament to **repeal** the hated law. This meeting of delegates came to be called the Stamp Act Congress.

All these actions by the colonists shocked the leaders of the British government. They were especially worried by the meeting of the Stamp Act Congress. Never before had the American colonies acted together against the British government. British leaders did not want this to become a habit. British merchants weren't

happy either. The boycott was causing them to lose a lot of money.

In 1766, after only one year, Parliament did repeal the Stamp Act.

When the news reached America, colonists lit great bonfires in celebration. Through their resistance they had brought an end to the hated Stamp Act. Of course they still loved their king. And no one was talking about leaving the British Empire. It had all been just a family quarrel. Hadn't it?

Bostonians protested the Stamp Act by burning the tax stamps.

Who Is in Charge? You might think Parliament would get the message: No taxation without representation. The colonists had drawn the line there. But the British government still needed money. And now it also needed to show the colonists who was boss.

So in 1767—just one year after repealing the Stamp Act—Parliament tried again. This time it placed taxes on glass, paint, tea, lead, paper, and a number of other goods that colonists imported. This was Parliament's thinking: The colonists need these goods, so when ships deliver them to colonial harbors, our officials will be there to collect the tax. Parliament made things worse by saying that whoever was arrested for not paying the tax would be tried *without a jury*.

Clearly, Parliament didn't understand how determined the colonists were. Once again, taxation without representation? And trial without a jury? So much for the "rights of Englishmen!"

Once again the Sons of Liberty swung into action. They organized another boycott of all British goods. This boycott was as successful as the first one. Meanwhile, the colonists began to make their own paint, lead, glass, and paper. Maybe the quality wasn't as good as what they used to get from Great Britain. And maybe it cost a little more to make. But it would do. It would do.

The new boycott lasted for nearly three years. Once again the Americans succeeded. British merchants and manufacturers were losing so much money because of the boycott

that they demanded that Parliament repeal the new taxes.

It was one thing for the colonists to demand that Parliament repeal a tax. Parliament could ignore them if it wished. But Parliament could hardly ignore the powerful businessmen of their own country.

So in 1770, Parliament did repeal the new taxes—all but one of them. They kept the tax on tea. In reply the colonists ended their boycott of all goods from England—all but one of them. You can guess which one. Tea.

Parliament had left the tax on tea to show that it *had* the right to tax the colonists. And the colonists left the boycott on tea to show that Parliament *did not have* the right to tax them. Each side was willing to leave it at that for the time being. By the way, the colonists, who were big tea drinkers, didn't really do without tea. They simply bought it from Dutch merchants who smuggled it into the colonies.

Colonists showed their dislike of the Stamp Act in many ways.

British troops drill on Boston Common.

The Boston Massacre

Meanwhile, more British troops arrived to join those already in the colonies. Colonists were suspicious. The British said the soldiers were needed to defend the colonists against Indian attacks. If that were really so, asked the colonists, then why weren't they on the frontier, where the Indians were? Why were so many in eastern cities, like Philadelphia, New York, and Boston? The troops seemed to be everywhere—on the street corners, in front of buildings, in the parks.

Colonists were angered by the sight of soldiers on their streets day and night. "What can be worse to a people who have tasted the sweets of liberty!" wrote an important Boston minister. As long as the troops remain, he continued, "there will never be harmony between Great Britain and her colonies." And what if a fight should break out between the citizens and the troops? In that case, said this minister, "the moment any blood is shed, all affection will cease." In other words, any good feelings that remained between the colonists and their mother country would end.

The citizens of Boston jeered at the soldiers. They made fun of them. They tried to make their lives miserable. In several cities, fights broke out between colonists and soldiers.

Those fights were not nearly as bad, though, as what happened in Boston on the evening of March 5, 1770. There, a crowd of men and boys gathered around a lone British soldier on guard duty. They shouted insults at him. They threw snowballs at him, some with rocks inside them.

The frightened soldier called for help. More British soldiers arrived. The crowd grew larger. The shouts, the dares, and the insults grew louder and angrier.

Suddenly someone—to this day, no one knows who—called out "Fire!" The soldiers turned their guns on the rioting crowd and shot. When the smoke cleared, five colonists lay dead or wounded, their blood staining the snow-covered street. One of them was Crispus Attucks, a runaway slave who worked as a sailor. Crispus Attucks was the first black American to die for the cause of American liberty, but not the last.

A few days later, more than half the population of Boston turned out for a funeral march for the dead men. Shops were closed. Church bells rang. Angry Bostonians called the killing a *massacre*—a needless killing of defenseless people. The event became known as the Boston Massacre.

A Boston silversmith named Paul Revere made a copper engraving that showed soldiers firing on a group of perfectly peaceful, innocent citizens. You can print many paper copies from a single engraving, and Revere did.

No one knows for sure whether he really saw the shooting. And some of the things shown in the engraving are not true. But Paul Revere was a Son of Liberty. The reason he made that engraving was that he wanted to make people angry at the British. Never mind that the citizens who were shot had been asking for trouble all night. They certainly did not deserve to die for that.

So that is what comes of having all these troops around, said the colonists. Where will this all end?

The colonists and the British reacted differently to this picture by Paul Revere. Can you tell why?

9 A Change in Thinking

Calm Before the Storm In time, the anger following the Boston Massacre died down, as anger often does. The British government didn't do any new things to upset the American colonists. The American colonists didn't do any new things to upset the British government. The next three years were mostly a period of calm.

But important changes were starting to occur in the way many colonists thought about England. Countries that set up colonies in other lands are often called "mother countries." That's what most colonists had always called England. Even those who had never set foot in England called that country "home."

The British used the same words to describe their relationship with the colonies. Even William Pitt, who was a great friend of the American colonies, said, "This is the mother country, they are the children. They must obey, and we prescribe [give the orders]."

But children grow up. They develop their own abilities. They discover they can do many things for themselves. They gain confidence. They feel they need to do things their own way. And eventually, they leave home to live their own lives. Independently.

In the years after the Boston Massacre, some American colonists wondered out loud whether that time had now arrived for them. This

This portrait of Sam Adams shows him with documents that symbolize his work with the Committees of Correspondence.

change in thinking came slowly. At first only a few felt that way. And even most of those people still wanted to remain in the British Empire. They were still loyal to their king. They just thought it was time for Parliament and the whole British government to stop making rules for them.

A small number of colonists, though, talked about going much further. They believed that Americans could only keep their liberties by breaking away from the British Empire completely. The colonies, they said, must become independent.

Sam Adams

Sam Adams of Boston felt that way. Adams came from an important Boston family. He lost most of his family's money because he was not very good at business. Maybe it's more correct to say that he just wasn't very interested in business. He had other things on his mind. Back in 1765, at the time of the Stamp Act, Sam Adams had organized the Sons of Liberty. He had been a leader in the boycott against British goods during the Stamp Act crisis. He had led another boycott when the British government tried to tax goods the colonies imported.

Ever since that time, Adams had been trying to convince colonists that the time had arrived to separate from Great Britain. In newspaper articles he urged his fellow colonists to stand up against Britain for their rights. "The liberties of our country . . . are worth defending at all risks," he wrote. It would be a "disgrace" to allow our freedoms to be taken away "from us by violence, without a struggle, or be cheated out of them by tricks. . . ."

After the Boston Massacre, Adams and several other Bostonians came up with an idea for alerting others if—Adams would say "when"—the British government threatened the liberties of Bostonians again. They set up a Committee of Correspondence.

Correspondence means "an exchange of letters." If the British again took away any

"rights of Englishmen," committee members would immediately send letters to other towns in the Massachusetts colony with the news.

This idea quickly spread to other colonies. Soon there was a great network of Committees of Correspondence. They would get news out quickly within each colony and also from one colony to another.

Of course these Patriot letter-writers didn't leave their quill pens and paper in their desk drawers while waiting for the next incident. They wrote to each other often, exchanging thoughts. Some of these thoughts would have been unthinkable just a few years earlier. Like independence. Little by little, that idea spread throughout the colonies.

Those who wanted independence were still in the minority. But who could say what would happen if the British government threatened their liberties once again?

Relations became strained between Great Britain and the colonies.

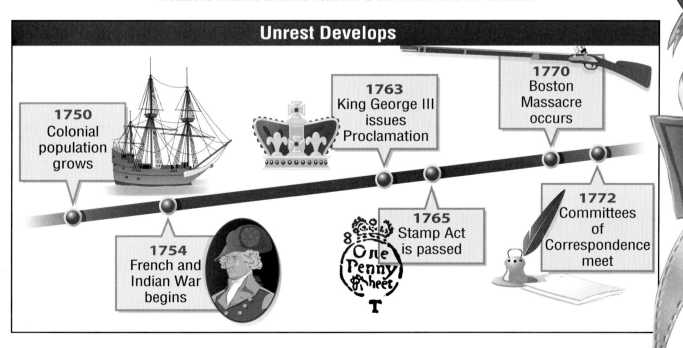

Unrest Develops

1750 Colonial population grows

1754 French and Indian War begins

1763 King George III issues Proclamation

1765 Stamp Act is passed

1770 Boston Massacre occurs

1772 Committees of Correspondence meet

10 A Tea Party in Boston

Parliament Makes Another Mistake Did you ever hear the expression, "He was too clever for his own good"? It means that sometimes a person thinks he has a clever solution to a problem, when in fact all he does is make things worse.

You couldn't get a better description for what the British government did next. You'll remember that Parliament had left the tax on tea just to show the colonists that it had the right to tax them. And the colonists had left the boycott on tea just to show Parliament that it didn't.

Clearly, Parliament decided, that plan had not worked. British tea merchants had lost all their colonial customers. The Americans were buying tea smuggled in by Dutch merchants. And the government still hadn't collected more than a few pennies in taxes. So in 1773, Parliament came up with another plan. It passed the Tea Act.

Parliament's new plan was so "clever" that it's a little tricky to follow, but not impossible. What Parliament did was *lower* the price of the tea itself. At the same time *it kept the tax on the tea.* When you added the new, lower price of the tea and the tax together, the total was cheaper than the tea colonists were buying from the Dutch.

Parliament figured the colonists would know a bargain when they saw it. They would buy tea again from the British merchants. And when they did, they would be paying the tax to Great Britain! Soon 2,000 chests of tea were loaded aboard British ships bound for the American colonies. It was an idea that couldn't miss.

But it did. Parliament "was too clever for its own good." The Tea Act of 1773 just showed how poorly Parliament understood the colonists. This was a matter of principle for the colonists, not money. The principle was "no taxation without representation." They were not going to pay that tea tax, no matter what the price of British tea.

News Travels Fast

As British tea ships headed for the colonies, Committees of Correspondence swung into action. Soon the news spread through the colonies. In several ports, including New York and Philadelphia, the Sons of Liberty prevented the British ships from docking. In Philadelphia, for example, the Sons of Liberty sent a letter to the captain of a ship waiting in the harbor to unload its chests of tea. I wouldn't try to land that tea if I were you, said the letter. Your ship may just happen to be set on fire, and you yourself will be in for some rough treatment. We Pennsylvanians will never pay your tax on tea, for "no power on the face of the earth has a right to tax [us] without our consent." We are "passionately fond of freedom . . . and are determined to enjoy it." The British captain got the idea pretty quickly. He decided not to land.

No one was fooled by the Indian costumes worn by the colonists when they tossed the tea into Boston Harbor.

Similar happenings occurred in other colonial port cities. Some ship captains had their ships wait in the harbor, hoping for a change of heart. Others turned their ships around and headed home.

Not in Boston, however. Early in December three tea ships entered the harbor of that city. Citizens of the town gathered at a town meeting. They demanded that the governor of the colony order the ships to leave. The governor had no sympathy for Sam Adams and his bunch of trouble-makers. He refused.

At that point the colonists took matters into their own hands. On the night of December 16, 1773, a group of them dressed as Indians. They rowed out to the tea ships lying at anchor in the harbor and boarded them. They dumped every chest of tea aboard—342 of them—into the cold waters of the harbor. All of this was done in a quiet, businesslike fashion. When they were through, the "Indians" even swept the deck and put everything back in its proper place before leaving the ships. This was no secret operation. Many people in town knew it was going to happen. Carrying torches and lamps, they showed up at the shore to watch in silence as the chests of tea were thrown overboard. This event became known as the Boston Tea Party.

The Intolerable Acts

You can imagine the reaction of Parliament and the king when they got news of the Tea Party. They were outraged. That does it, they said. We are going to teach these colonists once and for all who makes the rules in this empire.

Parliament passed several laws to punish the people of Boston and the whole Massachusetts colony. One law closed the port of Boston until the colonists paid for the dumped tea. That meant no ships could go in and none could go out. For a city that depended on trade and fishing, this was a severe punishment. Parliament hoped that Boston's merchants and sea captains would be pressured into turning in the guilty persons or perhaps pay for the tea themselves. They did neither. Another law took away most of the Massachusetts colony's rights to self-government. The British also appointed an army general to be the governor of Massachusetts. They sent several thousand more troops to Boston—as if there weren't already more than enough. They ordered the colonists to put these troops up in their homes and even to feed them.

Making Enemies

Can you imagine how that must have felt to the colonists? Even a family that was loyal to Great Britain, even a family that opposed the actions of the Sons of Liberty, even a family that wanted to buy the British tea and pay the tea tax would feel humiliated and angry. The British government thought it was just punishing the colonies. In reality, it was losing friends and making enemies. Once again, Committees of Correspondence spread the news. American colonists everywhere were angry. These acts of Parliament were trampling on the "rights of Englishmen." Colonists called the new laws the Intolerable Acts because they could not tolerate or endure them. And they decided to stand together with the people of Boston to resist them.

This tax collector has been painted with melted tar and covered with feathers. He is also being forced to drink hot tea.

elp from the Other Colonies Parliament was right about one thing: the Intolerable Acts did make the people of Boston and the rest of Massachusetts suffer. But Parliament didn't figure on the other colonies coming to their aid.

Pennsylvania sent barrels of flour to the people of Massachusetts. New York sent them sheep. From South Carolina came sacks of rice; from Connecticut, money; from Virginia, corn and wheat.

Virginia's leaders went further. They set aside a day of fasting and prayer for the people of Boston. They also declared that the Intolerable Acts were a threat to liberty in all the colonies. If the king and Parliament could do these things to Massachusetts, what would stop them from doing the same to other colonies?

Then the Virginians took a bold step. They called for delegates from all the colonies to meet and discuss what to do next. This would be the second time delegates met to resist an act of Parliament. The first time was the Stamp Act Congress, and it had been successful. This time, though, the British government seemed determined not to back down.

The First Continental Congress

With Committees of Correspondence spreading the word, 56 colonial leaders assembled in Philadelphia in September 1774. They represented 12 of the 13 British colonies in North America. You can tell how important the colonists thought this meeting was by the people they chose to represent them. George Washington, Patrick Henry, and young Thomas Jefferson were there from Virginia. Sam Adams and his cousin John came from Massachusetts. New York sent John Jay, who later would serve on the Supreme Court of the United States. John Adams wrote in his diary, "There is in the Congress a collection of the greatest men upon this continent."

This meeting later became known as the First Continental Congress. The delegates talked together about their common problems. They expressed their anger at the British government. They issued a Declaration of Rights, saying that American colonists were entitled to all the "rights of Englishmen." They pointed out all the acts of Parliament since the French and Indian War that had been taking these rights away. They also told King George III that the colonists were still loyal to him and asked him to consider their complaints.

The members of the First Continental Congress did two more things. They voted to stop all trade with the British—buy nothing from them and sell nothing to them—until Parliament repealed the Intolerable Acts. And they agreed to meet again in May 1775 if

Who wasn't there? Only Georgia didn't send a delegation to the First Continental Congress.

George Washington represented Virginia at the Continental Congress.

Parliament had still done nothing to restore their rights.

Talk about defiance! This was the most defiant act of the colonies yet. They had really thrown down a challenge to Great Britain.

But something else had happened, too—something that was hard to put your finger on. This "something" had no exact name. You couldn't put an exact date on when it started. But it was as important as any of the resolutions passed by the Continental Congress. Maybe those shipments of flour and rice and money to Boston from the other colonies were the start of it. Maybe it began with the Stamp Act Congress. Or maybe it had slowly been happening all along, before anyone was even aware of it. That "something" was that the colonies were coming together as never before.

Before this, each colony had thought of itself as separate from the others. Their inhabitants thought of themselves as Virginians or New Yorkers or Georgians. When they thought of an attachment to any other place, it was to Great Britain. Partly that was because each colony had more to do with the mother country than it did with the other colonies. And partly it was because colonists thought of themselves as British citizens, with all "the rights of Englishmen."

By the end of the First Continental Congress, many colonists were thinking of themselves as part of one country, rather than as people living in 13 different colonies. They were becoming more aware of the things they had in common. They were becoming more aware that they needed each other. Patrick Henry, that shrewd Virginian, captured this new mood perfectly. Speaking to the Continental Congress, he said, "The distinctions [differences] between Virginians, Pennsylvanians, New Yorkers, and New Englanders, are no more. I am not a Virginian but an American."

Maybes That Didn't Happen Maybe if King George III had been willing to pay attention to the colonists' pleas . . . maybe if Parliament had repealed the Intolerable Acts and promised to respect the colonists' "rights of Englishmen" . . .

maybe if the British government had taken all its troops out of the colonies . . . maybe if all those things had happened, or even some of them, war might still have been prevented.

Or maybe not. Maybe by that time the colonists had gone too far down the road toward independence to turn back. No one can say for sure what *might* have happened.

But we do know what *did* happen. We know that by the start of 1775, more and more colonists expected the quarrels with the mother country to end up in fighting. By spring, the militias in many colonies were preparing for war. The militia was made up of citizens who volunteered to be part-time soldiers.

In March, members of the Virginia state assembly debated whether their colony should prepare for war. Some opposed the idea. But Patrick Henry believed the time had come for action. Everyone present knew what a great speaker Henry was. As he rose to address the members, a hush fell over the room. Some of the earlier speakers had said that maybe Britain could still be persuaded to change its course. Here is Patrick Henry's answer:

> Shall we try argument? Sir, we have been trying that for the last ten years. . . . We must fight!

Virginians respond to Patrick Henry's "give me liberty or give me death!" speech.

Gentlemen may cry peace, peace—but there is no peace. The war is actually begun! The next gale that sweeps from the north will bring to our ears the clash of resounding arms! Our brethren are already in the field. Why stand we here idle? What is it the gentlemen wish? What would they have: Is life so dear, or peace so sweet, as to be purchased at the price of chains and slavery? Forbid it, almighty God!

And then Patrick Henry, standing tall, arms raised high, his voice clear as a bell, finished with the words that have stirred lovers of liberty ever since:

I know not what course others may take; but as for me, give me liberty, or give me death!

Patrick Henry was mistaken when he said that the war had actually begun. But three weeks after his stirring speech, the fighting did start. For several months, members of the militias throughout Massachusetts had been training to fight. These farmers and towns-people called themselves Minutemen, because, they said, they could be ready to fight on a minute's notice. To prepare for battle, the Minutemen had been collecting guns, gunpowder, and other supplies. They hid these supplies in the village of Concord, about 15 miles northwest of the city of Boston.

Do you remember that the British government had sent an army general to serve as the governor of Massachusetts? That new governor was General Thomas Gage. Somehow General Gage learned about those hidden supplies in Concord. He also learned that two Sons of Liberty who were the chief troublemakers in Boston, Sam Adams and John Hancock, were hiding out in the town of Lexington.

Lexington was on the way to Concord. General Gage figured he could kill two birds with one stone. He would send his troops to Lexington first and capture Adams and Hancock. The soldiers would then continue on to Concord and seize the Minutemen's hidden supplies.

General Gage's plan was to have his troops leave Boston in the dead of night. That way no one would notice, and they would take Lexington by surprise. Gage didn't know that the Sons of Liberty had gotten wind of his plan. Two Sons of Liberty, Paul Revere and William Dawes, got ready to ride ahead of the British soldiers and alert citizens along the way.

But there were two routes to Lexington. Which one would the redcoats take? One was longer, but it was entirely over land. The shorter route required that the troops first cross the Charles River by rowboat before starting the overland march.

The Minuteman is a symbol of Americans' willingness to defend their country.

Billy Dawes started out along the long route to Lexington. He galloped along in the dark of night, calling out to Patriot homes along the way that the redcoats were coming.

Paul Revere hung back, in case the British were taking the other route. He had already arranged for a signal to be sent to the waiting Sons of Liberty on the other shore. A young man would climb to the tower of the Old North Church in Boston and then signal with lanterns. He would hang one lantern in the tower if the British were taking the all-land route. If the troops were taking boats first to get to the shorter route, he would hang two. One if by land, two if by sea. When Paul Revere realized the British were planning to row across the river, he passed along the information to the signaler. That night, two lanterns burned brightly in the church tower. By sea! Now Paul Revere

and two friends hurried to a rowboat he had hidden. The three men rowed across the water ahead of the British troops. Once on shore, Revere borrowed a horse from one of the Sons of Liberty. Then he galloped off to carry the warning to Lexington and Concord. Stopping at every village and farm, he pounded on doors and sounded the alarm: "The redcoats are coming." In Lexington he was able to warn Sam Adams and John Hancock. The two men got away.

The Battle at Lexington

British troops arrived in Lexington at dawn, expecting to see no one. Imagine their surprise when they saw 70 Minutemen facing them on the village green. The leader of the Minutemen, Captain John Parker, told his men, "Stand your ground. Don't fire unless fired upon." Then he added, "But if they mean to have war, let it begin here."

Minutemen responded to the warning of the British plan and were waiting for the troops at Lexington.

E.B. Wollen/National Army Museum

There they stood—on the one side, 600 to 700 well-trained, well-armed men in handsome uniforms; on the other, a much smaller group in rough dress and with fewer weapons. The British officer ordered the Minutemen to leave.

Suddenly someone opened fire, and then both sides began shooting. Minutes later, eight Minutemen were dead, and another ten lay wounded.

The British caught both Billy Dawes and Paul Revere before they could get to Concord. However, another Patriot named Dr. Samuel Prescott rode off to Concord with the warning of a British attack.

The British troops next pushed on to Concord, where they destroyed some of the hidden supplies. Once again they were surprised to find Minutemen waiting for them. This time there were nearly 400 of them gathered at North Bridge, near the Concord village green.

Soldiers at the bridge opened fire. Minutemen fired back. After five minutes of fighting, the British decided to return to their base in Boston.

That long march back to Boston became a nightmare for the British soldiers. All those people who lived along the route had earlier been alerted by Paul Revere. They had seen the British as they marched toward Lexington in the early morning hours. Now they waited for their return—waited behind stone fences, behind barns, behind trees. When the soldiers, wearing their bright red uniforms, appeared, they were easy targets. All the way back to Boston, the shots rang out. Before the British troops got back to Boston that night, the Minutemen killed 73 of them and wounded another 200. That was nearly half the number who had started out. The colonists had losses too—nearly 50 men dead. Americans did not know it at the time, but the War for Independence had begun.

Concord Hymn

By the rude bridge that arched the flood,

Their flag to April's breeze unfurled,

Here once the embattled farmers stood,

And fired the shot heard round the world.

Many years later, Ralph Waldo Emerson wrote a poem to be read at a memorial ceremony celebrating the Battle of Concord. This is the first stanza.

May 10, 1775 Once again the leading men from every American colony gathered in Philadelphia for a Continental Congress. This time, though, was different. This time there had been fighting. This time men had died.

Most of the delegates to this Second Continental Congress weren't sure what to do next. They dreaded the thought of separating from Great Britain and their king. Couldn't Congress try again to patch up the quarrel with the mother country? At the same time, they could not ignore the fact that fighting had started. Shouldn't they take steps to prepare for more fighting, if it should come?

In the end the Second Continental Congress did both. Delegates wrote a **petition** to King George III. A petition is like a request. They told the king they were still loyal to him. There was no talk of

independence. They said they didn't want to break up the British Empire. They only asked the king to make his government change its bad policies and restore their rights.

At the same time the Congress took steps to prepare for more fighting. John Adams of Massachusetts took the lead. Local militias are fine for fighting here and there, he

> **vocabulary**
> **petition** a formal written request signed by several people

This handbook, shown below, was printed in 1776 and describes how the militia should be trained. A farmer, right, prepares to join the other members of his local militia.

said. But we need to create a real American army—an "Army of the United Colonies."

At that moment, members of the Massachusetts militia were camped outside Boston, near the British troops. Those militiamen, said Adams, were ready to be the first soldiers in the new army.

And to lead it? How fortunate the Congress was, Adams continued, to have the right man for the job in that very room! He was a man of "great talents and excellent character." He was an experienced military leader from Virginia. As Adams continued to speak, all eyes turned to the tall man in military uniform standing in the back of the room. The man quickly turned and left the room. He wanted the delegates to be free to discuss him without his being present. The man was George Washington.

Adams was right. Washington was the perfect man to lead the Continental army, as it came to be called. He had gained his military experience in the French and Indian War. After that he returned to Mount Vernon, Virginia, to run his plantation. He was a member of the Virginia House of Burgesses and a supporter of the Patriot cause. And he was among the best-known men in the colonies. Everyone admired him for his devotion to duty, his cool head, and his strong will.

It was settled. Washington was to command the army. And the first members of that army would be the Massachusetts militiamen camped around Boston. They might be needed soon, for the news was that more soldiers were arriving from Great Britain.

Washington traveled to Massachusetts to take charge. Before he arrived, though, the militia fought an important battle near Boston.

There are two hills that overlook Boston. One was called Bunker Hill. The other Breed's Hill. Every general knows that it's a great advantage to control hills. From their tops you can fire down at the enemy below—especially if you have cannons. And the enemy has to fight its way uphill to defeat you. The British understood that, too, of course. But they were not very worried about those untrained Massachusetts militiamen nearby, and they did not bother to guard the hills. On the night of June 16, 1775,

On July 3, 1775, George Washington took command of the Continental army.

the militia suddenly marched to Breed's Hill and climbed it. All night they dug trenches, piling the earth into walls six feet high for their protection. When morning came, the British were surprised to see the colonial militia in control of the hill.

General Gage—remember him?—now worried that the militia would be able to fire on his troops below. They would even be able to use cannons to fire upon the British ships in the harbor. Gage decided he must drive the militia off the hill. What Gage didn't know was that the Massachusetts militia didn't even have cannons!

The next day, British soldiers marched up Breed's Hill. The colonists had only a small amount of ammunition. They couldn't afford to waste any.

They stood shoulder to shoulder behind the earthen walls they had built the night before. Their commander gave the order, "Don't fire until you see the whites of their eyes!" When the British got close, the militiamen opened fire. Hundreds of redcoats fell. The rest retreated down the hill.

Once more the British marched up the hill. Once more they were met with a hail of

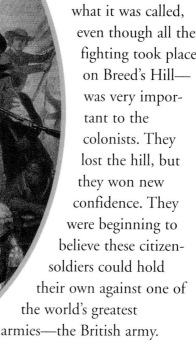

Bunker Hill proved to be a very costly victory for the British.

bullets and driven back. But the colonists were now running out of ammunition. When the British marched up the hill a third time, the militia retreated.

The British won the hill but at a terrible cost. More than 1,000 soldiers were killed or wounded. Just as during that disastrous march back from Concord, the British lost about half their men. A British officer remarked that his army couldn't stand many more "victories" like this. The battle of Bunker Hill—that's what it was called, even though all the fighting took place on Breed's Hill— was very important to the colonists. They lost the hill, but they won new confidence. They were beginning to believe these citizen-soldiers could hold their own against one of the world's greatest armies—the British army.

Soon after, the colonists learned King George III's answer to their petition. Loyal to the king? Hah! Those colonists were nothing but traitors. Give back their "rights?" They have no rights except those I tell them they have. Withdraw my troops? I will show them. I will send 20,000 more men. I will crush them!

Coming to a Decision By the start of 1776, the argument with Great Britain had gone on for more than ten years. The fighting had gone on for almost one. And still, many colonists weren't sure they really wanted to strike out on the path of independence.

This gives you some idea about how difficult that decision was for many. A colony breaking away from a mother country—it had never been done before. Giving up a place in the world's greatest empire and all the advantages of being part of it—was that wise? Still, should the colonists do nothing to defend their rights and liberties? It was a very tough decision.

Tough, that is, until a 29-year-old-English immigrant wrote a pamphlet. After that the decision became very clear.

The immigrant's name was Thomas Paine, and he called his pamphlet *Common Sense*. Tom Paine had a great and rare skill. He could write about important ideas in the everyday language of the farmer, the worker, and the townsperson. If you could read at all, you could understand *Common Sense*. Probably half of all American colonists did read it. And after they did, they talked about it in their homes, on street corners, and in taverns and inns.

A lot of what Paine wrote was, just as he said, plain common sense. He got readers to think about his ideas not just by telling them what he thought but also by asking what *they* thought. Did it make any sense, Paine asked, for a huge continent like America to be ruled by a small island 3,000 miles away? Did it make sense for a people to be ruled by one man, just because he was born into a certain family? Wouldn't it be better to choose our rulers, rather than have one handed to us—someone who might be all wrong for the job but who got it only because his father had it before?

Americans should stop fooling themselves that monarchy—government headed by a king—would ever bring fair government to the people. It had never happened, and it never would. It was monarchy that was reducing the world to blood and ashes. Americans should abandon that form of government once and for all.

Thomas Paine's words rallied undecided colonists to the Patriot cause.

Independence National Historic Park

In Congress, July 4, 1776.

The unanimous Declaration of the thirteen united States of America.

It was an act of courage to sign the Declaration of Independence.

Paine said that it was just common sense for Americans to cut off all ties to Great Britain, to be independent and create a government of their own. Americans didn't need a king, he said. They could live in a land where "the law is king," not some person wearing a crown in a faraway land. The more they thought about it, the more Americans agreed. They didn't need the British Parliament and king to rule them. They had plenty of experience in choosing their own leaders and ruling themselves. Perhaps it really was time, then, to separate and go their own way.

The Declaration of Independence

In June 1776, the Second Continental Congress took up the question of independence. They agreed that the time had come to separate from Great Britain. The Congress chose a committee to write a declaration,

or statement. The purpose of such a declaration was to explain to the world why the colonies were breaking away from Great Britain.

The committee chosen to write the declaration included John Adams, Benjamin Franklin, and a young, tall, redheaded Virginian, Thomas Jefferson. Which one should do the main writing? Benjamin Franklin and George Washington were probably two most famous Americans alive. John Adams was one of the first leaders to speak out in favor of independence. But Thomas Jefferson already had a reputation as a fine writer and was chosen by Franklin and Adams to write the document.

What Jefferson produced became the most famous document in American history, and one of the most famous in the history of the entire world. Of course Jefferson wanted the world to know all the bad things this king had done, all the rights he had taken away. So he listed each of them.

But Jefferson did more, much more. He explained why these acts of the king made it right for the colonists to break with Britain.

> We hold these truths to be self-evident, that all men are created equal, that they are endowed by their Creator with certain unalienable rights, that among these are life, liberty, and the pursuit of happiness.

Jefferson continued by stating, "That to secure these rights, governments are instituted [created] . . ." In other words, the reason we have governments is to protect our rights.

What if a government doesn't protect those rights but actually takes them away? Then, said Jefferson, people have the right to create new governments for themselves. That's what the people of the 13 colonies were now doing.

On July 4, 1776, Congress adopted this Declaration of Independence. On that day the American colonies became independent states. Together, they made up the United States of America.

During the next month, in towns and cities across the land, crowds gathered to hear

Colonists celebrated the signing of the Declaration of Independence by raising Liberty Poles.

the Declaration of Independence read aloud. Everywhere in the new United States of America, church bells rang out. Soldiers fired cannons and shot off guns. Citizens lit great bonfires in celebration.

Meanwhile back in Philadelphia the mood among some of the delegates to the Second Continental Congress was a little more serious. The 56 men who signed the Declaration knew that if the revolution failed, the king would probably put them to death. Benjamin Franklin summed up the need for all the new states to work together. "Gentlemen," he said, "we must all hang together, [or] else we shall all hang separately."

atriot Problems During the first part of the war, "hanging separately" seemed like a real possibility. When you look at some of the problems the Americans faced, you can see that their chances of winning were not that great.

For one thing, the 13 new states may have been united, but their people certainly were not. Many remained loyal to the king and to Great Britain. These people were called Loyalists. Many of them moved to Great Britain or Canada, but others stayed in America and helped the British. About 50,000 Loyalists actually fought in the war on the side of Great Britain.

For another thing, Great Britain had one of the largest armies in the world. And that was even before you added the 50,000 Loyalists. On top of that the British hired about 30,000 professional soldiers from other countries. Soldiers for hire are called mercenaries. Counting the mercenaries, Great Britain's army was five times larger than the American army. The British could also count on their Indian allies in the West.

The British soldiers were well-trained fighters. Commanders could count on having their soldiers for a

certain number of years and had time to train them for battle.

General Washington would have loved an arrangement like that. You'll remember that he had to build an army from scratch. His army was made up mainly of farmers—amateurs, not professional soldiers.

Also, Washington never knew how many soldiers he could count on at any one time. Some joined the Continental army for a three-year term. Most volunteered to serve for less than a year. And some signed up for only three months. Some would join the Continental army when the fighting got near their village or farm. Then they would leave it once the British troops moved on. Soldiers would often return to their farms at planting time and harvesting time. Lots of men did serve at one time or another, it is true. But with all these comings and goings, can you imagine how difficult it was to train an army?

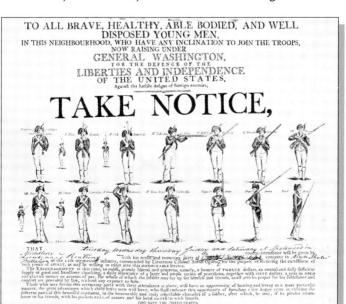

Posters like this one were used to find soldiers for the Continental army.

Then, too, Great Britain was the wealthiest nation in the world. The British could supply their army with whatever it needed. The American army, though, was often short of cannons, gunpowder, food, and other supplies, including uniforms. All through the war, most American soldiers fought in their own clothes. Several times during the war, General Washington had to write Congress that if it didn't come up with money for supplies and pay soon, "the army must absolutely break up."

As for a navy, the British had the greatest in the world. They had 100 times as many warships as the Americans had.

Certainly none of that looked very good for the Americans.

Americans had a few things going for them, though. For one, they were fighting on their own land. Can you see why that was important? It meant that fresh troops and supplies were often available nearby, while the British had to ship everything—including troops—from 3,000 miles away. Also, it makes a difference when one side is fighting to defend its own homes, its families, and its freedom while the other side is just fighting for pay.

Another advantage the American side had was the huge size of the country. Even if the British won in one part of the country, American armies could always retreat to another, where the British could not get them. Tom Paine wrote that the American plan would be like a game of checkers: "We can move out of *one* square to let you come in," he said to the British, "in order that we may afterwards take two or three for one." Since we can keep moving around, he said, "we can always prevent a total defeat."

Support from Women and Black Americans

The Patriot side could also count on important support from women. Women worked in army camps. They washed, cooked, nursed the wounded, and made gunpowder. There were even times when women went onto the battlefields, though they weren't supposed to. In one battle fought under a blazing sun, Mary Ludwig Hays brought her husband's cannon crew water from a nearby stream. She carried so many pitchers of water to the thirsty men that they came to call her Molly Pitcher.

According to legend, Molly's husband became ill during the battle. The other members of his cannon crew had been killed. Molly loaded and fired the cannon by herself

According to legend, Molly Pitcher helped the Patriots at the Battle of Monmouth.

until other soldiers arrived to take over. We don't know if that story is true, but it is certainly true that many American farm women knew how to handle a gun.

One of them was Deborah Sampson. Sampson dressed in men's clothing and joined the army. It was only when she became ill that doctors found out she was a woman. A number of other women served as messengers and spies.

But of course women didn't have to be on a battlefield to help the Patriot cause. They made their greatest contribution at home. In addition to doing the work they had always done, they also did the work of the men who had gone to fight. There were many women who kept the family farm going or the family business running.

About 5,000 blacks fought on the American side in the Revolutionary War. Most of them were free men from the northern states. They took part in almost every battle, starting with the very first at Bunker Hill. There were several black regiments from New England states.

But black Americans were divided over the Revolution, just as white Americans were. In fact, some southern states were even opposed to blacks joining the Continental army. They were always worrying about slave uprisings, and they did not like the idea of black people having guns—even blacks ready to fight for American independence!

In addition, black people knew that even if the United States succeeded in winning independence, that would not end slavery. It is hard to be enthusiastic about fighting for a country that wants to keep people like you in slavery.

The British knew that very well. Soon after fighting started, they offered freedom to any slave who would fight on Great Britain's side. Several thousand slaves risked their lives in running away so they could accept the offer. As fighting during the war reached slaveholding areas of the country, many slaves fled to the protection of the British. The British navy, in fact, carried several thousand of these escaped slaves to Canada, where they started free settlements.

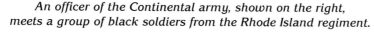

An officer of the Continental army, shown on the right, meets a group of black soldiers from the Rhode Island regiment.

16 Raising America's Spirits

n Early British Victory Things went badly for the Americans during the early part of the war. Hardly three months after Americans lit bonfires to celebrate the Declaration of Independence, a large British army assembled in New York City to do battle with Washington's still untrained army.

The British defeated the Americans easily and almost trapped them. That might have ended the war then and there. Led by Washington, however, the Americans escaped from the city.

It was during that battle for New York City that a 24-year-old Connecticut schoolteacher named Nathan Hale won fame with words that inspired the Patriots. Hale was caught serving as a spy for the Americans and was hanged by the British. His last words have been quoted by patriotic people for more than 200 years: "I only regret that I have but one life to lose for my country."

After their narrow escape from New York, the Americans retreated all the way across New Jersey and into Pennsylvania, with the British close behind. Luckily, it was getting late in the year. Winter was a hard time to fight battles. The British were satisfied to take control of New York and New Jersey, and stop for the winter. There would be time enough in the spring to finish off the Americans. It was at this moment that Washington's leadership began to pay off for the Americans. Other generals might have panicked after facing such a setback. Not Washington. Whether he won a battle or lost, he remained the same steady person. Soldiers admired him, and they were willing to follow him into battle.

Battle, however, was not what Washington wanted. He knew his untrained troops were no match for the experienced British army in big head-on battles. Washington's plan for winning the war required patience. It can be summed up this way: Keep the Continental army moving—there was Tom Paine's checkerboard. Stop and fight the British now and then, but don't get into a major battle. Use the time to build up the army and train it.

This plan meant the American army would not win many battles. But they wouldn't lose many, either. Meanwhile, as the war went on, the British people might tire of paying for it. Then a few big American victories, and who knows? They might stop supporting the war.

The British burned New York City behind the retreating Continental army.

This famous painting by Emmanuel Leutze of Washington crossing the Delaware River was painted many years after the event.

A Surprise Attack

Washington realized that the American people could tire of the war, too. So could his army, if it kept suffering defeats. Washington needed a quick victory or two to raise the spirits of his soldiers and also of the nation.

He therefore planned a surprise attack on British mercenaries—remember the mercenaries, the troops the British hired from other countries? These mercenaries came from the German state of Hesse, so they were called Hessians. The Hessians were camped in Trenton, New Jersey, just across the Delaware River from Washington's troops in Pennsylvania. Washington knew that no one would expect him to move his troops across the ice-filled Delaware River.

That's exactly why he did it. On Christmas night, 1776, shivering American soldiers stepped into the long rowboats that would carry them across the river. By four o'clock in the morning, all 2,400 of Washington's men were on the New Jersey side of the river.

The Continentals marched the nine miles to Trenton in the dark of night. Then, as day broke, they attacked the sleeping Hessians. What a surprise! What confusion! After a short fight, 900 Hessians surrendered. The Continental army captured not only the enemy soldiers but also their weapons and supplies.

Eight days later, Washington won another victory. Again, he surprised British soldiers and defeated them, this time at Princeton, New Jersey. Just as Washington hoped, the victories at Trenton and Princeton raised the spirits of Americans and especially of the army.

ritain's Master Plan Those spirits wouldn't stay high for very long, if the British could help it. In fact, British generals had a plan to knock the Americans right out of the war before the year was over.

This was the plan. The Hudson River runs north and south in New York State. The British aimed to win control of the entire Hudson River valley. That would cut off New England from the other states, dividing the Americans in two. The British would then be able to defeat the rebels one part at a time— first New England, then the rest.

That summer, General John Burgoyne (bur *GOYN*) led a large British army southward from Canada into New York State. The plan was for the main British army in New York City to start moving north soon after Burgoyne entered New York State. At about the same time, a third, smaller British force in western New York State would move east. The three British armies would meet near Albany, on the Hudson River. At that point, it would be all over for the upstart Americans. Only it didn't happen. General William Howe was in charge of the main British army in New York. Howe wanted to capture Philadelphia first before starting north along the Hudson. Philadelphia was America's largest city. It was the meeting place of the Continental Congress. What a blow to American spirits if the British were to take it!

That was General Howe's thinking, anyway. Howe was sure he could capture Philadelphia and still have time to send his armies north to meet Burgoyne. He was

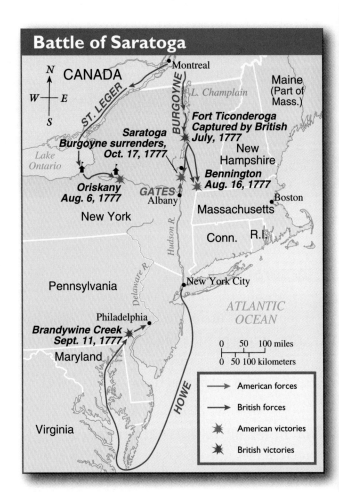

The British plan didn't work because only one British force arrived at Saratoga.

wrong. By the time he captured Philadelphia, there was no time left to get his troops back to New York. Howe didn't even try.

Meanwhile, the third British force—the one moving eastward across New York State— under the command of Barry St. Leger ran into American soldiers along the way. Those British soldiers never made it to Albany either.

So there was Burgoyne, moving south in New York State, suddenly finding his army all alone. The only ones there to meet him were American soldiers under General Gates—thousands and thousands of them. In October 1777, the British and Americans fought at Saratoga, north of Albany. The Americans won, and 6,000 of Great Britain's best soldiers surrendered.

The victory at Saratoga was a great turning point in the war. Not just because it was a great victory but also because it brought us a new ally—France. Do you remember how the French and the English had been fighting for a hundred years? And how the French lost all their North American colonies to Great Britain in the French and Indian War? Well, ever since, they had been burning for revenge.

It was a great moment when General Gates accepted General Burgoyne's surrender after the Battle of Saratoga.

New Allies

One way for France to get revenge on Great Britain was to help the American colonies break away. Soon after the colonies declared independence, France secretly started sending them money and supplies. If they did it openly, Great Britain would probably declare war on France, and the French king did not want that.

The Americans hoped for more. They wanted France to jump into the war with both feet. Every time they asked the French, though, they got the same answer: Show us first that you have a real chance of defeating the British, and then we might consider joining forces with you. The victory at Saratoga showed France that America could win. Several months after Saratoga, the French did come into the war on the side of the Americans. France sent money, equipment, and soldiers. Most important, as you will soon see, France also sent a large naval fleet to help the Americans. It's quite possible that without the French, the Americans would not have won.

Later, Spain and the Netherlands, two more old enemies of Great Britain, entered the war on the American side. These changes meant that Great Britain would have to fight not only in North America but also in Europe and other parts of the world. All because three British armies failed to meet as planned in Albany.

18 Valley Forge

Hard Winter Now came the worst time of the war for the Continental army. It was the winter of 1777–1778. The British had taken Philadelphia.

Twice, General Washington had sent his troops into battle near Philadelphia. Twice the British had defeated them. With cold weather coming on, Washington had to choose a place to camp for the winter. The place he chose was called Valley Forge, an open field about 20 miles from Philadelphia.

Snow was already on the ground when the troops arrived in Valley Forge. They put up their tents and began building huts with whatever wood they could find. Before long they had built 2,000 of them—drafty, dirty, and cold, but at least providing a roof over the heads of the men. Each had a fireplace but no windows. The smoke from the fires made men cough as if their lungs would burst.

The winter at Valley Forge could have broken the spirit of the Continental army.

That winter was a terrible one. Supplies did not arrive. Blankets were scarce. There was not food enough to go around. With no boots or shoes, the men wrapped their feet in rags. General Washington later said, "You might have tracked the army to Valley Forge by the blood of their feet." An officer from Connecticut tells us how bad things were in his diary:

It snows. I'm sick. Eat nothing. No whiskey. No forage. Lord, Lord, Lord . . . cold and uncomfortable. I am sick, discontented, and out of humor. Poor food. Hard lodging. Cold weather. Fatigue. Nasty clothes. Nasty cookery. Vomit half my time. Smoked out of my senses. The Devil's in it. I can't endure it. Why are we sent here to starve and freeze? . . . I have

Courtesy of, The Valley Forge Historical Society

Many Europeans came to support the Patriot cause, including (from left to right) Steuben, Pulaski, Kosciusko, and Lafayette.

left at home a charming wife, pretty children, good beds, good food, good cookery. . . . Here all confusion, smoke and cold, hunger and filthiness. A pox on my bad luck.

At least 2,500 soldiers died of disease or exposure at Valley Forge that winter. That means that every single day, soldiers had to bury 25 or 30 of their comrades. Some men deserted, which means they simply sneaked out of camp and went home. At the start of winter, Washington's army numbered about 7,000 men. At the end of winter, there were only about 4,000 left.

The winter at Valley Forge was a time of testing for the men of the Continental army. They passed the test. Much of the credit has to go to their commander, George Washington.

A Man of Character

Character. What did people mean when they said that George Washington was a man of great character? They meant he was honest. They meant that he cared for his men, and that he was fair with them. They meant that you always knew where Washington stood and that he kept his word. They meant that he respected others and that you could depend on him. They meant that Washington was the kind of man you would always want on your side.

Washington also knew enough to put able men in charge of important tasks. For example,

in February, when things were at their worst, a balding, red-faced man appeared at Washington's headquarters to offer his services. His name was Baron Frederick von Steuben (STOO bun). Washington could tell that this fellow knew how to train men to be soldiers, and that was what Washington needed. He hired von Steuben. The German officer taught the men about soldiering, and he drilled them over and over. By spring, General Washington had a well-trained army for the very first time.

Von Steuben was only one of a number of Europeans who were inspired to help the American cause. Another was a 19-year-old Frenchman named the Marquis de Lafayette. As soon as he heard that fighting had begun in America, Lafayette decided to join the Americans in their fight for liberty. "I am persuaded," he said, "that the human race was created to be free, and that I am born to serve that cause." Washington took a great liking to this daring Frenchman, and Lafayette quickly became one of his most trusted aides.

Others arrived as well to help the American cause. From Poland came Thaddeus Kosciusko and Casimir Pulaski. Pulaski was wounded in battle and died, while Kosciusko later returned to Poland to fight for liberty there. Many others were inspired to fight for American liberty.

Another Plan Meanwhile, the British generals came up with another plan to win the war. For three years, said the generals, we've been fighting the Americans in the North. We've won most of the battles, so we're not losing the war. But we're not winning it either.

To win, we have to beat down the rebellion. That means we have to really defeat the Continental army. Every time we have a chance to do that, though, General Washington and his army slip away from us. The British generals thought: Suppose we shift the battle to the South? That would give us several big advantages. For one thing, most of the Continental army is in the North. We will catch them off guard. Also, there are lots of Loyalists in the South. We can count on them to help us with food and supplies. After we take the South, we'll have the Continental army squeezed between our forces there and our other armies in the North.

The plan turned out to be pretty successful for a while. The British navy brought soldiers from their base in New York to Savannah, Georgia. The soldiers quickly captured that city. Within a year they controlled the whole state of Georgia. Soon after, the British took Charleston, South Carolina, and handed the Americans their worst defeat of the war. From there, British troops successfully went on to control a large part of the South.

However, the British were still not able to crush the enemy. American military commanders in the South followed the George Washington strategy. Small battles, yes. Big battles, no. Never risk the whole army in one big fight. Also, southerners knew their land better than the British did. They set up secret bases in the swamps of South Carolina. They would come out of the swamps to attack small groups of British soldiers. Then, as suddenly as they had appeared, they were gone.

This kind of hit-and-run fighting is called **guerrilla** warfare. A general named Francis Marion was so successful at it that he came to be called the Swamp Fox. So the British armies won many small battles, but they could never catch up to the American troops to defeat them in a big one. And in time, the American troops began to win their share of the battles.

> **vocabulary**
> **guerrilla** a member of an irregular hit-and-run military force

War in the West

Meanwhile, in the West, a young Virginian named George Rogers Clark attacked several British forts near the Great Lakes. The British were using these forts to stir up their Indian allies to attack American settlers.

On July 4, 1778, Clark and a company of 175 Virginia militiamen captured the first of these forts without firing a shot. Later, Clark captured two more. His victories drove the British out of part of the land between the Appalachian Mountains and the Mississippi River.

The sea battle between the Bonhomme Richard *and the* Serapis *took over four hours.*

A Victory at Sea

The tiny American navy, of course, was no match for the great British fleet. But American warships put up a good fight when they met one British ship at a time. John Paul Jones was the commander of the American ship *Bonhomme* (BAHN um) *Richard* when it came upon the British warship *Serapis* off the coast of Great Britain. The two ships opened fire. Soon the deck of the American ship was in flames. The British commander then demanded that Jones surrender. Jones replied, "I have not yet begun to fight!"

And fight he did. His own ship, the *Bonhomme Richard,* sank, but not before Jones and his men climbed aboard the *Serapis* and took it over. This was one of the most famous naval battles in our country's history.

Benedict Arnold

During this time, George Washington suffered one of his greatest disappointments. It was not a defeat on the battlefield. It was a defeat of the spirit. One of his bravest and finest generals, and one of Washington's favorites, went over to the enemy.

His name was Benedict Arnold. He had helped win the battle of Saratoga. He had been promoted to general and his future in the American army was bright. In 1780, General Washington placed Benedict Arnold in command of West Point, a fort on the Hudson River.

But Benedict Arnold still did not feel appreciated enough. And he liked to spend much more money than he could afford on luxuries. So in exchange for a large sum of money, Arnold agreed to turn over West Point to the British.

The plot was discovered in time, but Arnold himself escaped and joined the British forces. Americans were shocked to learn of Benedict Arnold's treason. Even today, the name "Benedict Arnold" is a synonym for a traitor.

20 The World Turned Upside Down

British Mistake Now came the big mistake that cost Great Britain the war. The general in charge of British armies in the South was Lord Charles Cornwallis. Cornwallis had spent a year chasing American troops in the South.

He finally decided to move his army to Virginia. Cornwallis believed that if he could defeat the American soldiers in Virginia, he would crush the rebellion.

In the summer of 1781, Cornwallis chose a small Virginia town called Yorktown for his base. Yorktown is located on the York River, which flows into the sea. Cornwallis chose this place so that the British navy could reach him easily with troops and supplies.

Normally, it's not a good idea to set up a base with a river at your back. If you have to retreat, you have no place to go. But Lord Cornwallis felt safe there. He had one third of all the British soldiers in America with him. And he could count on the British navy to bring him even more, if he needed them.

Washington Responds

At the very moment that Cornwallis was setting up his base at Yorktown, George Washington was meeting with a French general in Rhode Island. The French, you see, had sent an army to help the Americans. There was also a large French fleet on its way to help out.

Washington and the French general Rochambeau (row sham BOW) were making a plan to attack the British armies in New York City when the news about Yorktown arrived.

Washington immediately saw Cornwallis's mistake. Forget about attacking New York, he said. The American and French armies should hurry to Virginia. Together, they had enough men to trap Cornwallis with his army's back against the river. If the French fleet could get there in time, it could keep the British navy from helping Cornwallis. Then Cornwallis would have to surrender. In one single victory, Washington might end the war! Yorktown was 500 miles away. George

Yorktown was on a peninsula that the Americans and the French surrounded on land and on sea.

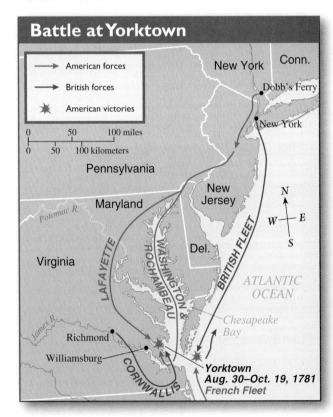

Battle at Yorktown

The American Revolution ended soon after the surrender at Yorktown.

Washington had started his military career with a 500-mile journey. That one ended in disappointment. Now he was to set out on another one, with the chance of winning the victory of a lifetime.

It took more than a month for the armies to get to Yorktown. Then it took a few more days to dig a great half-ring of trenches around the town, surrounding it by land. On October 9, at five o'clock in the afternoon, the first cannon was fired, and the battle had begun. For once, it was General Washington who had the most guns and cannons. For once, it was General Washington who had the most men.

Cornwallis looked out to the sea for help, but none ever came. The French fleet had driven off the British fleet. Cornwallis's army was on its own.

Each day, Washington moved his army closer and closer, tightening the half-ring a little more. Washington rode back and forth among his men, taking his chances like everyone else that a bullet might strike him. The troops cheered and pressed on.

Cornwallis was trapped. For several more days, cannons roared. Finally the British general saw that it was useless to continue. On October 17, Cornwallis surrendered.

Two days later the American and French armies formed two long lines. The defeated British troops marched between them and left the town. As they did, a British army band played a tune that all of them knew. It was a tune that went with a nursery rhyme. A strange tune to play at a time like this, you might think. But the words, which every British soldier knew, were the reason it was chosen:

John Trumbull/Yale University Art Gallery

If buttercups buzzed after the bee,
If boats were on land, churches on sea,
If ponies rode men, and if grass ate the
    corn
And cats should be chased into holes by
    the mouse,
If the mammas sold babies for half a
    crown,
If summer were spring, and the other way
    'round,
Then all the world would be
    upside down.

A ragtag collection of citizen soldiers had defeated one of the world's greatest armies. A group of colonies had succeeded in gaining independence from a mother country for the first time ever. The United States of America had been created, and a great British Empire had been humbled. In the peace treaty that followed, Britain agreed that the colonies were now "free and independent states."

A Final Word

The American Revolution produced many heroes. Some became famous: George Washington, John Paul Jones, Francis Marion.

Most of the heroes, though, were ordinary people. Their names are never written in the history books. They were the Minutemen on Lexington Green. They were the soldiers who shivered at Valley Forge. They were the men who dashed out of their swamp hideouts to strike at the British army.

They were also the women who brought food and water to the men in battle, took care of the wounded and the sick, and kept farms and shops running. They were the farm families who shared their food with the soldiers and the townspeople who gave the soldiers housing. They were the women, children, and old men who made weapons and gunpowder for them. They were the boys and girls who helped produce the food and the clothing that the American soldiers needed.

When the war was over, people everywhere asked, "How could the American colonies have won a war against one of the great military powers in the world?" The answer to this question was really not difficult to find. The main reason the Revolutionary War was won is that ordinary Americans refused to lose it.

There were many steps that led to independence.

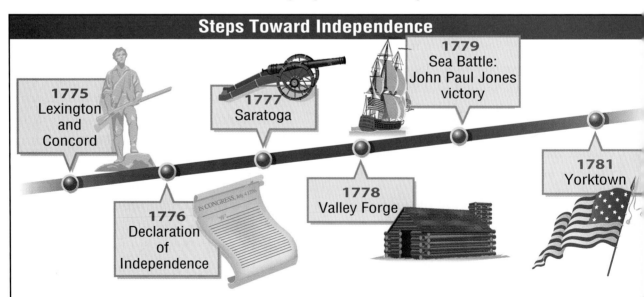

Steps Toward Independence

1775
Lexington
and
Concord

1776
Declaration
of
Independence

1777
Saratoga

1778
Valley Forge

1779
Sea Battle:
John Paul Jones
victory

1781
Yorktown

Glossary

ally a nation that has promised to help another nation in wartime

assembly a group of representatives who gather to make laws

boycott an organized campaign in which people refuse to have any dealings with a particular group or country in order to force a change of policy

frontier the newly settled area on the edge of the unsettled area or wilderness

guerrilla a member of an irregular hit-and-run military force

immigrant a person from one country who comes into another country to live there

militia a body of armed citizens prepared for military service at any time

petition a formal written request signed by several people

repeal to cancel or do away with

We the People
of the U.

insure domestic Tranquility, provide for the common Defence, pro.

Section, in which Case it shall not be a Law.

Every Order, Resolution, or Vote to which the Concurrence of the Senate and House of Representatives may be necessary (except on a question of Adjournment) shall be presented to the President of the United States; and before the Same shall take Effect, shall be approved by him, or being disapproved by him shall be repassed by two thirds of the Senate and House of Representatives according to the Rules and Limitations prescribed in the Case of a Bill.

Section. 8. The Congress shall have Power To lay and collect Taxes, Duties, Imposts and Excises, to pay the Debts and provide for the common Defence and general Welfare of the United States; but all Duties, Imposts and Excises shall be uniform throughout the United States;

To borrow Money on the credit of the United States;

To regulate Commerce with foreign Nations, and among the several States, and with the Indian Tribes;

To establish an uniform Rule of Naturalization, and uniform Laws on the subject of Bankruptcies throughout the United States;

To coin Money, regulate the Value thereof, and of foreign Coin, and fix the Standard of Weights and Measures;

To provide for the Punishment of counterfeiting the Securities and current Coin of the United States;

To establish Post Offices and post Roads;

The
United States
Constitution

Contents

Change in Government Suppose you are watching TV and you hear this news report: "Troops today took over the White House, and the President has resigned. Soldiers have also occupied Congress and sent the members home."

Suppose the report continued, "General John Jones, in charge of the army, has announced that he will be the new President. Congress will no longer meet, and there will be no more elections. Laws will be made by a small group of people to be appointed by General Jones. Also, starting today, all newspapers and television stations must get permission from the government to report any news story. The police and the army will be free to search the homes of citizens without warning. And trial by jury will be suspended until further notice."

How do you think you would feel? Scared? Upset? Angry? That's not surprising. Most Americans would. That kind of thing may go on in other parts of the world but not here in the United States. Americans would never stand for it.

Now, why do you suppose that is? Would you be surprised to know that it has a lot to do with events that happened more than 200 years ago? It does. It's because of what American colonists did when the British government threatened their liberties. It's because of the ideas that Thomas Jefferson wrote about in the Declaration of Independence. It's because of the blood that was shed to defend those liberties and those ideas in the American Revolution. It's also because of

the Constitution of the United States, which you will soon be reading about.

One of the ideas Jefferson wrote about is that "all men are created equal." Of course, Jefferson didn't mean that every person has equal abilities. He certainly didn't mean that all can run equally fast, or jump equally high, or that each person is as good in math or science or music as every other person. No, what Jefferson meant is simply that each person is born with the same **rights** as any other.

Jefferson then wrote that some of these rights are "unalienable." That means that God has given them and that no one—not a king or anyone else—can take them away. He wrote that these unalienable rights include "life, liberty, and the pursuit of happiness."

> **vocabulary**
> **right** something due to one by law, custom, or nature

Now, Thomas Jefferson didn't make up those ideas the day he sat down to write the Declaration of Independence. He had been thinking about them for a long time. So had many other Americans. These ideas were truly revolutionary. They would forever change the way people thought about their government—not just American people but people all over the world.

After writing those things, Jefferson stated three important ideas about government. First, he wrote, the main purpose of government—the reason we have governments in the first place—is to protect the rights of the people. Second, he wrote that if a government fails to protect those rights, or—even worse—takes them away, the people have a right to get rid of that government and create another one. Wasn't that what the American Revolution was about?

The third thing Jefferson wrote about government is this: that governments get "their just powers from the consent of the governed." In other words, the power of government comes from the people themselves—they are "the governed." It is the people who decide what powers their government should have. If the people do not give their **consent** that the government can have this or that power, then the government does not have it.

Now, that is a powerful idea. It is one of the most important ideas in all of human history.

Limited Government

In 1776, when Jefferson wrote the Declaration, the idea of *limited government*—the idea that people should have the right to limit the power of their government was not a brand-new idea. A few people in Europe had written books about it, and a few nations, including England, had taken steps toward limited government. For the most part, however, the idea had not been put into practice. Kings, conquerors, and tyrants of all kinds had been ruling governments for hundreds of years without asking ordinary people for their consent. The needs and wants of ordinary people simply were not important.

> **vocabulary**
> **consent** approval or agreement [consent can also be given in a non-political situation]

But in the Declaration of Independence, Thomas Jefferson said, Oh, yes they do count. And that's exactly what most

---

Three Important Ideas About Government

- **People have rights**

- **People should be able to get rid of a government that does not protect their rights**

- **The power of the government comes from the people**

Thomas Jefferson stated the relationship between government and the people very clearly.

Americans believed. After 1776, Americans were given a chance to take the idea of limited government to a whole new level. The Declaration of Independence announced that the American colonies were no longer a part of Great Britain. Each colony became an independent state, and each state had to create a new government for itself.

What followed was truly amazing. In every state, ordinary people discussed and debated what that new government should be like. How much power should the people give these governments? What is the best way to protect the rights of the people? Which of the old British ways should be preserved? How long should our representatives in government serve? Should our state have a governor? And if so, how long should he serve?

Back and forth the discussions went. Americans exchanged their ideas in newspapers. They debated them in the taverns and in each other's homes. The old colonial assemblies held special meetings to discuss what to do next.

James Madison, whom you will meet later, wrote, "It is the first instance, [since] the creation of the world . . . that free inhabitants have been seen **deliberating** on a form of government." He was right. The world had never seen anything like it.

Americans were well aware that they were doing something new—something that had never been done before. By anybody. They knew that they were engaged in a great experiment. Many of them really didn't expect to get everything right the first time. But that was all right. The important thing was to start. If changes were needed, they could always make them later. After all, they were "the people."

Americans didn't always agree. Debates about the new government often aroused strong feelings.

> **vocabulary**
> **deliberate** to think about and discuss issues before reaching a decision

**New Plan of Government** So, Americans set about making constitutions for their new state governments. A constitution is an overall plan of government, something like an outline. It declares what powers the government will have and will not have.

It says what the different parts of the government will be. It assigns duties and responsibilities to each part. It says that this part of the government will make the laws, and that part of government will see that they are carried out, and this third part will decide arguments about what a certain law means, and so on. So you see, a constitution is like a law. But it is higher than ordinary laws. It's a kind of super law, and ordinary laws must fit in with it—they must "get along with" this super law—or they don't count.

You might think of a constitution as the framework of a house and ordinary laws as the furniture. The outside walls, the roof, and the inside walls give you the basic *form* of the house. That's your constitution. You then put in your furniture—that's your ordinary laws.

From time to time you may need to change the furniture. Maybe your family's needs have changed (like needing a bed instead of a crib). Maybe the furniture is broken and needs to be replaced. You can do that.

The one thing you can't do, though, is bring in furniture that is too big for the room. It has to fit inside the room, or you can't use it.

You get the idea. Like the basic form of the house, the constitution sets limits on what you can put inside. As long as a law—like the furniture—fits inside the constitution, the law is OK. If it doesn't, though, then the law is *unconstitutional*. That means that the law is no longer a law that has to be obeyed.

Does that mean that once you have the basic form, the constitution, you can't change it? No, it doesn't. You can change it, just as you can build an addition on a house or move around some inside walls. But that's a much harder job than changing furniture. It's not a job you do easily or often.

The British government did not have, and still does not have, a written constitution.

"Rights of Englishmen" —and More

In each of the 13 states, the first decision made about a new constitution was to put it *in writing*. That made it a firm contract between the people and the new government. It was how the people—"the governed"—gave their consent. It was like the people saying, "These are the things we agree that the government *may* do. And these are the things it may *not* do." There's that idea of limited government.

After 1776 each former colony wrote a constitution setting up a state government. This was the first constitution of the new state of New Jersey.

Actually, it was quite easy for the writers of the constitutions to list what the new state governments could *not* do. The British king and Parliament had practically written the list for them. The governments could not search a person's home without a good reason. They could not put a person in jail without a good reason, either. And they could not keep him or her there without a trial. They could also not take away a person's right to trial by jury. Finally, they could not stop people from assembling peaceably, and they could not take away the people's right to ask or even demand that their government do something they wanted done.

Do all these sound familiar? They should. They are those "rights of Englishmen" that colonists were fighting a war over at that very time.

Many of these new constitutions added still more rights. One was freedom of speech. That means that people in those states were free to speak their mind without fear of being arrested. To give you an idea how revolutionary an idea that was, there was no other country in the world at that time where the right of

free speech was guaranteed. Even today, more than 200 years later, the great majority of the world's people still do not completely enjoy that right.

It was a lot harder to say what powers the new state governments should have than which ones they should not have. Americans had just gotten rid of a too-powerful government. They certainly didn't want to create another.

At the same time, though, Americans were practical people. They knew it made no sense to assign the government a job and then not give it the power to do the job right. For example, if they wanted their government to provide schools or build roads, they had to give it the ability to *pay* for schools and roads. In other words, they had to give the government the power to collect taxes.

For guidance, Americans turned to their own colonial experience. Each colony had its own assembly, or law-making body. Each had a governor, too. But while the assemblies were elected by the colonists, most governors were appointed by the king.

Colonists understood that the governor was the king's man, not theirs. When the governor appointed people to office, he chose men the king wanted him to appoint. When he decided whether to support an act of the assembly, he checked with the king's advisers first. So colonists depended on their elected assembly, not the governor, to look after them and protect them.

Now that they were independent, they continued to rely on the assembly and to distrust the governor. They gave their assemblies, now called legislatures, most of the power in government. The legislatures made the laws. They created the courts and appointed the judges. They appointed most of the officials in each state, even those who worked for the governor.

What power did the governor have left? Not much. In most states he couldn't even veto, or disapprove, laws passed by the legislature. Mostly, the governor was just a figurehead. That means that he had a title but not much else.

At the same time, Americans wanted to be sure the legislatures didn't misuse their power. So in most states, representatives were elected to the legislature one year at a time. That way, voters could keep a close eye on their representative. If they weren't pleased with his performance, they could replace him promptly. Most governors also had only one-year **terms**.

None of these state constitutions used the word *democracy*. That's because they didn't really create a completely democratic form of government. In a true democracy the people govern directly. Each person can vote on every matter, every proposed law.

vocabulary
term a limited extent of time during which something may last

Now, you can get everyone in a village together in one place to discuss issues and vote. You may even be able to get everyone in a small town together. But you can see how it would be impossible to do that in a large area like a state.

In most states, the real power was in the hands of the legislature, not the governor.

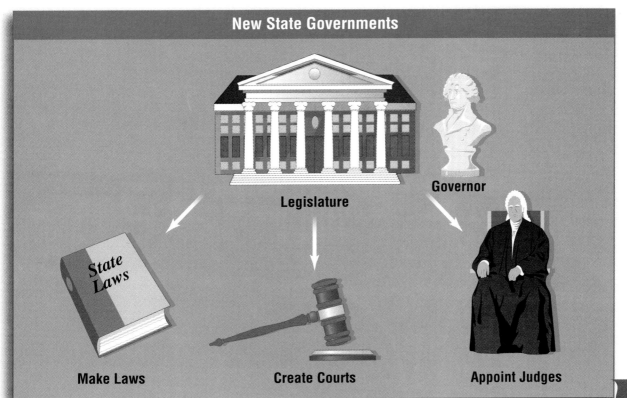

New State Governments

Legislature

Governor

State Laws

Make Laws

Create Courts

Appoint Judges

Here is what you can do, however. You can arrange for people to elect representatives to govern for them. Of course, that's exactly what Americans had been doing for over a hundred years while they were still British colonists. When the people elect representatives to govern them, that is called representative democracy, or republican democracy, as opposed to direct democracy. The resulting government is called a republic. And that's what each state constitution provided for: a republican form of government. (As you'll see a bit later, that's our nation's form of government, too. So when you say the Pledge of Allegiance to the flag of the United States of America, you also say, "and to the republic for which it stands.")

Freedom of Religion

One year after the Declaration of Independence, all but one American state had a brand-new written constitution. In many of them the legislatures guaranteed key freedoms. Nearly every state, for example, passed a law to protect religious freedom.

The most famous of these laws was Virginia's Statute for Religious Freedom. This law was written by—did you guess?—Thomas Jefferson. It said that the state government could not interfere in any way with the religious beliefs of its citizens. As Jefferson said later, "It does me no injury for my neighbor to say there are twenty gods or no god. It neither picks my pocket, nor breaks my leg." And since it does no one any injury, the state should keep its nose out of a person's religious beliefs. Today, we call this idea the *separation of church and state*. It means that the government—the state—has no power to establish an official state religion. Government cannot tell people what church they should belong to or what they

should believe. This is one of the most important freedoms we have.

Also, five northern states passed laws to end slavery. No southern state was willing to do that, but several did make it easier for slave owners to free their slaves, if they wished to.

So state constitution-making was very successful—much more successful than national constitution-making, as you will see.

Thomas Jefferson decided which of his many accomplishments he wanted listed on his tombstone. You can see how important he thought freedom of religion was.

Meeting in Philadelphia The Second Continental Congress was the meeting of delegates from all the colonies that took place in Philadelphia in 1775. Those delegates had been called together to decide what to do about the latest acts of the British government against the colonists' liberties.

If anyone had told those delegates they would still be meeting two years later, probably none of them would have believed it. But in 1777 there they were. And now they weren't just discussing protests against Parliament. They were in charge of a war for independence. And they would keep right on meeting for four more years, still running that war.

The Second Continental Congress was doing one more thing as well. It was trying to agree on a constitution for the new United States of America. Most members of the Congress agreed that the new nation needed *some* kind of a central government—a government for the whole nation. Every time they began to consider *what* kind, though, they ran into a problem. That problem was the fear of a central government with too much power.

In 1777 the Congress voted to approve a constitution for a new central government. This constitution was called the Articles of Confederation, and it went into effect four years later, in 1781.

The Articles of Confederation were very different from the constitutions the states had adopted for themselves. Like those state constitutions, the Articles created a law-making body, which was called Congress. But that's where the similarity ended. The people didn't

elect the members of Congress, the way they elected their state legislatures. Members of Congress were appointed by the states.

In fact, the people of the United States had no direct connection with this new central government at all. You see, the new government didn't represent the people; it represented *the states*. You'll see the importance of that difference in just a little while.

Here was another important difference between the Articles of Confederation and the state constitutions. Those state constitutions gave the legislatures power to do a great many things. The Articles, though, gave Congress power to do very, very few. These were some of the main ones: Congress could declare war and make peace. (You could hardly have one state making peace while the others continued to fight it out against Great Britain!)

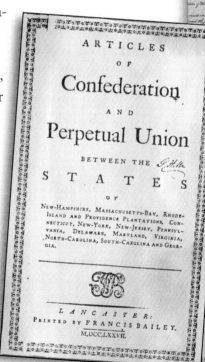

The rules for a new national government were published in 1777 for people in the states to read and discuss.

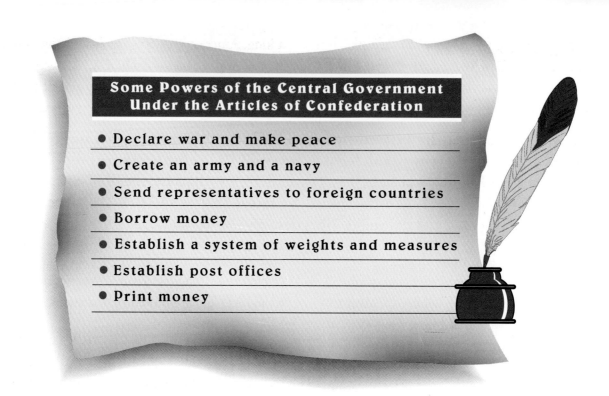

Some Powers of the Central Government Under the Articles of Confederation

- Declare war and make peace
- Create an army and a navy
- Send representatives to foreign countries
- Borrow money
- Establish a system of weights and measures
- Establish post offices
- Print money

The Articles of Confederation gave Congress very little power.

It could make treaties and alliances with other nations. It could settle arguments between the states about their boundaries—about where one state's land ended and another's began. It could borrow money, set up a postal service, and create a currency, or money system.

That was about it. And just to make sure the Congress didn't try to do more than it was supposed to, the Articles of Confederation added this: Unless the Articles *specifically* gave a power to the new Congress, Congress did not have it.

Too Little Power

How did the Articles of Confederation work out in practice? Unfortunately, not very well. There were lots of reasons why. For one thing, each state, whether large or small, had only one vote in Congress. That meant that little Rhode Island, with a population of 68,000, had the same vote as Virginia, which had more than ten times as many people.

Some of the big states became frustrated and felt this voting arrangement was unfair.

Another problem was that Congress was always broke. During the war the Continental Congress had borrowed from other countries and from individual Americans to buy supplies and pay the army. With the war over, it was time to start paying the money back.

Right now you are probably thinking, "Why didn't Congress just pass some laws to collect taxes?" The reason is that the Articles of Confederation did not allow Congress to tax. Only the state governments could do that. There was that problem about a strong central government again.

Then how was Congress supposed to get money? All it could do was tell the states how much was needed and then ask each one to contribute its fair share. If they did, fine. If they didn't, then the central government had no power to make them contribute.

Not surprisingly, perhaps, most didn't. For every $100 Congress asked for, the states contributed just $5. You can't pay off many debts that way.

Even when it became clear that the central government had to have at least some power to raise money, there was not much that could be done about it. That's because of another weakness of the Articles of Confederation: to amend, or change, this constitution, all 13 states had to give their agreement. Twice, those who favored the idea tried to amend the Articles to allow Congress to tax. Each time, 12 states said yes, but one refused to go along. That was the end of the amendment.

While the Articles of Confederation gave Congress the power to declare war, Congress had no power to raise an army. It could ask each state to contribute its fair share of men, but again, it was up to each state to decide whether it would do so.

There were other problems, too. The government of the United States of America had no one at its head. After their experience with a king, Americans decided against giving power to any single person. Each year, Congress elected one of its members to be president of the *Congress*, but that wasn't the same thing as being the head of the whole government. It was just a nice title with no real power.

With such a weak central government, states sometimes just did whatever they wanted, even though they weren't supposed to. For example, the Articles of Confederation said that Congress had the right to raise a navy, but nine states went ahead and had navies of their own.

The central government seemed so unimportant that state legislatures took their good old time electing delegates to Congress. The delegates took even more time getting to its meetings. Some didn't even bother.

Americans had been understandably afraid of creating a central government with too much power. But after six years under the Articles of Confederation, many people believed they had created one with not enough.

The states decided how much they would pay to the central government.

Northwest Ordinance About the last thing you'd expect is that such a weak Congress would pass one of the most important laws in all of American history. But that's just what it did in 1787.

This 1787 law is known as the Northwest **Ordinance**. At that time the United States owned a huge triangle of land in the northwest. It was bordered by the Ohio River, the Mississippi River, and the Great Lakes. Right after the United States became independent, settlers began to pour into this territory.

In those days the usual thing for a country to do was to turn such an area into colonies for its own benefit. That's what Great Britain did. It's what France and Spain did. It's what the Netherlands and Portugal and other European countries did.

Notice which states eventually would be carved out of the Northwest Territory.

> **vocabulary**
> **ordinance** another word for law

It's not what the United States did, though. First, Congress guaranteed everyone who settled in this vast territory the same rights that people in the 13 states had—trial by jury, freedom of religion, and all the rest. Then Congress divided the territory into smaller ones. When a certain number of people settled in a territory, then it could become a state. Not a colony of a mother country, mind you, but a full-fledged state, equal to all the other states. From that time on, that was the plan used to create nearly all the other states in today's United States of America.

There was one more very important part of the Northwest Ordinance. Earlier you read that five northern states had taken steps to end slavery. People in other states, too, were coming to believe that slavery was wrong. Some of these people were slaveholders themselves. They realized

Arthur St. Clair, a leader during the Revolution, was appointed the first governor of the Northwest Territory.

that slavery just did not make any sense when the Declaration of Independence says that "all men are created equal."

Congress could not do anything about slavery in the states where it already existed. But Congress did want to make clear how it felt about slavery. Therefore, the Northwest Ordinance prohibited slavery anywhere in the Northwest Territory. That was an important thing to say then. It would become even more important later on.

A Need for Power

Passing one law, however—even a law as important as the Northwest Ordinance—didn't change the fact that the Articles of Confederation were not working all that well. A growing number of people began to feel that Congress needed more power, more authority, to be effective. Many, though, wanted to keep the Articles of Confederation. They thought that an amendment here or there would be enough to do the trick.

Not James Madison. Madison was from a well-to-do Virginia family. He had spent most of his life studying government and **politics**. People said that Madison knew everything there was to know about governing. When he was still in his 20s, he helped write the new Virginia constitution.

Now in his mid-30s, Madison served as one of Virginia's delegates to the Congress. There, he witnessed firsthand the problems of the struggling young nation. After a few years, Madison decided that no amount of patching and stitching could make the Articles of Confederation work well. There was only one thing to do: scrap that constitution and start all over.

Alexander Hamilton came to the same conclusion. Hamilton's childhood had been far different from Madison's. He had grown up in the West Indies. Hamilton's father was a British merchant who lived very comfortably but who took no responsibility for his son. Hamilton's mother died when he was only 11.

Several years later, Alexander was working as a store clerk when a hurricane swept across his island. He wrote a letter that was printed in the local newspaper describing the hurricane damage. This letter so impressed several wealthy island **planters** that they decided to pay for Alexander to attend King's College in New York.

A strong believer in the Patriot cause, Hamilton joined Washington's army soon after the fighting started. In a short time he became one of General Washington's closest aides. Now, as one of

vocabulary
politics the art or science concerned with guiding or influencing government
planter one who owns and runs a large farm and usually raises one important crop

These men all agreed that the Articles did not give the national government enough power.

New York's delegates to Congress, he too saw how weak the new government was under the Articles of Confederation.

Along with Madison and Hamilton, George Washington felt that the central government simply had to have more power. In 1787 he wrote a friend, "To be fearful of giving Congress . . . [enough] authority for national purposes appears to me . . . madness. What then is to be done? Things cannot go on [this way] forever." Washington feared that people might become so frustrated with the government that they might even start believing the country would be better off with a king!

In 1787, Madison, Hamilton, and several others decided it was time to act. They managed to persuade Congress to call for a special convention of all the states in Philadelphia in May. The purpose of this convention, Congress said, was to recommend changes for *improving* the Articles of Confederation. But for Hamilton and Madison, the real purpose of the convention was not to improve the Articles of Confederation but to *replace* them with an entirely new constitution.

What should that new constitution look like? For more than a year, Madison had been pondering that question. He pored over books on the history of Greece and Rome. He studied the writings of important thinkers on government and politics. He took notes. He thought. Then he read still more books, took more notes, and thought some more.

It was clear to Madison that a new central government must be given more power than the old one had. But here was the big question he had to wrestle with: How do you create a government with enough power to act but not so much power that it threatens the people's liberties? As he studied and thought, his ideas for a plan of such a government gradually began to take shape.

One thing Madison had already figured out: No central government could be successful if it had to depend on the states for everything it needed. It had to be able to raise its own money and enlist its own soldiers and not have to ask the states if they would please contribute. That was the great weakness of the Articles of Confederation.

Meanwhile, as the starting date of the Philadelphia convention drew near, newspapers all over America were filled with stories about what they were calling the "Grand Convention of the States." To us it has become known as the Constitutional Convention.

Readers of those newspapers fully understood that whatever happened in Philadelphia—or didn't happen, if the delegates could not agree—

would have a great effect upon the future of their country.

And not just their own country. One newspaper said, "the Grand Convention of the States will settle forever the fate of republican government." What that meant was this: European governments did not expect the United States to last. They believed that ordinary people could never govern themselves. If the Constitutional Convention failed to create a republican government that worked, then the European governments could say, "See, we told you so."

And it would be a long, long time before anyone else in the world would be willing to try the idea of a republican government again.

Delegates came to the Pennsylvania State House (now called Independence Hall) to try to save the government of the new nation.

263

5 *Waiting in Philadelphia*

Late Start The Constitutional Convention was scheduled to start on May 14, 1787, so when James Madison arrived in Philadelphia on May 3, he figured he was 11 days early. As it turned out, he was actually 22 days early.

That's because the convention could not begin until delegates from at least seven states were present. And as of the morning of Sunday, May 13—the day before the convention was to start—Madison was still the only one from out of state to show up in Philadelphia.

No one was especially concerned, though. In those days, meetings of this sort rarely started on time. Delegates had to come from afar, on horseback or by coach. In the best of weather, the roads were not very good. And the weather in spring of 1787 was anything but the best. In fact, residents of Pennsylvania said it was just about the worst they could remember. Heavy rains turned the roads to puddles and mud.

That Sunday, May 13, though, the weather was dry. In the afternoon the sun came out, as if to greet the arrival of the most famous American of all, George Washington. Philadelphians had eagerly awaited Washington's entry into their city. Now, church bells rang out, and crowds lined the streets to cheer the hero. Men who had served in the American Revolution came out in their old uniforms to greet their commander. The mere presence of Washington was enough to create a feeling of hope and optimism about the Constitutional Convention.

During the following days, other delegates arrived in Philadelphia. Madison put the time to good use. As his fellow delegates from Virginia arrived, he met with them. Together, they came up with a plan of government to

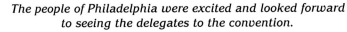

The people of Philadelphia were excited and looked forward to seeing the delegates to the convention.

264

present to the convention. It would be known as the Virginia Plan. Meanwhile, all the delegates got to know each other and discuss the important work that lay ahead. In the evenings, Philadelphia's leading families treated the delegates to entertainment.

It was clear that the states had taken this call for a convention seriously, for they had sent some of the ablest men in America as delegates. The best known of them, next to Washington, was also the oldest. That was Ben Franklin, the man who, with a kite and a key, had shown the world that lightning was electricity. Franklin was Philadelphia's leading citizen. He had founded the first lending library, helped to start a university, and improved life in the city in countless ways. He was also the inventor of numerous items that made life easier for Americans. If anyone deserved the word *practical*, it was Ben Franklin. People counted on his good sense to help the convention succeed.

Franklin was now in his 80s, and not in good health. He was no longer able to walk even the 200 yards from his house to the convention's meeting place. But practical Ben was prepared for everything. He had brought back a sedan chair from France. The sedan chair rested on two long poles and had a

Benjamin Franklin, shown here in a firefighter's helmet, formed the first public fire company in North America.

cover on top to protect the rider from rain or sun. Four men, two on each pole, lifted the chair and its passenger, taking him from place to place. Philadelphians were quite used to seeing four men—in fact, four prisoners from the local jail hired by Ben Franklin—carrying their world-famous citizen around town in this manner.

Three famous Americans were not present for the convention. Thomas Jefferson and John Adams would have loved to be there, but they were serving their country in Europe. Jefferson was our **ambassador** to France, and Adams was our ambassador to Great Britain.

The third was Patrick Henry. People remembered Patrick Henry for his stirring speeches in the Patriot cause. One of the most famous speeches he made before the Revolution started was the one in which he said, "I am a Virginian no more, but an American."

Well, that was then. By the 1780s, Patrick Henry had decided that maybe he was mainly a Virginian after all—that is, his love for his home state was at least as great as his love for

vocabulary
ambassador an official of high rank sent by a country to represent it in another country

People today recreate the Constitutional Convention in the room where it originally occurred.

the United States. He opposed strengthening the central government, and he correctly guessed that that's what the leaders at Philadelphia were up to. Although Virginia chose him as a delegate to the Convention, Henry refused to attend because, he later said, "I smelt a rat."

The Work Begins

Finally, enough delegates arrived for the convention to begin. On Monday, May 25, delegates walked from their hotels and boardinghouses to the handsome Pennsylvania State House. The city was already awake and moving. The clatter of horses' hoofs and the rattle of the iron wheels of wagons traveling over the cobblestone streets was earsplitting. (As a favor to the delegates, the city government later spread a layer of gravel on the cobblestones to reduce the noise.)

The delegates entered the State House and gathered in the east chamber, a large room about 40 feet by 40 feet, with high windows on two sides. In recent years the room had become known as the Independence Room, for it was here that the Declaration of Independence had been signed 11 years earlier.

A number of delegates to the Constitutional Convention were signers of that Declaration. Looking around the room now, they saw familiar sights—the round tables, each covered with a green cloth; the inkwells and quill pens set on each, ready for use; the three or four chairs set around each table. In this room they had helped give birth to a new nation. Now they had come here once more, this time to try to give that young nation a more secure future.

At about 11:00 A.M. the guard closed the doors, and the delegates took their seats. It was time to get to work.

Need for Secrecy Right at the start the delegates made two important decisions. The first was to choose George Washington as chairman of the convention. That was an easy decision because Washington was everyone's first choice.

The second decision was to keep all discussions secret. That way, each person could express his ideas freely. He could even change his mind about a particular issue without having to face public disapproval. The delegates would not have to worry about newspapers or citizens looking over their shoulders and criticizing this or that proposal. Instead, the convention would present its final plan to the people and say, this is the result of our best efforts. Now it is for you, the people, to say yes or no.

The decision for secrecy put a small burden on a few gossipy delegates. It put a big burden of a different kind on the whole convention. Secrecy meant not only closed doors but closed windows. The summer of 1787 was Philadelphia's hottest in nearly 40 years. With not a breath of fresh air entering the hot and sticky convention room, delegates sweltered in the miserable heat. With mosquitoes biting right through clothing, and big bluebottle flies buzzing around their heads, it was a wonder the uncomfortable delegates could concentrate on their work.

If the meetings were so secret, how do we know what was said there? We owe that to several delegates who took notes, especially James Madison. Madison chose a seat at the very front, where he could plainly hear delegates from the right, left, and rear. "I was not absent a single day," Madison wrote later, "Nor more than a . . . fraction of any hour in any day. . . ." Using his own system of abbreviation and symbols, he wrote down in a private journal nearly everything that went on in the secret meetings.

We know from Madison's notes that he himself addressed the convention no fewer than 161 times! Clearly, the quiet, soft-spoken

We know what happened at the Constitutional Convention from the notes kept by James Madison.

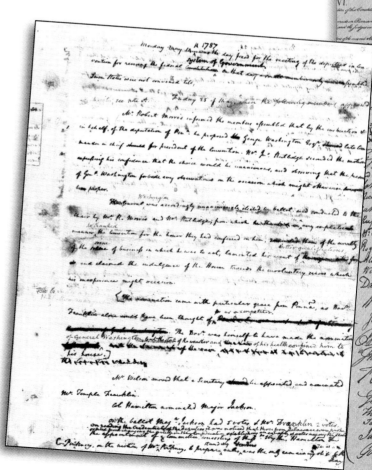

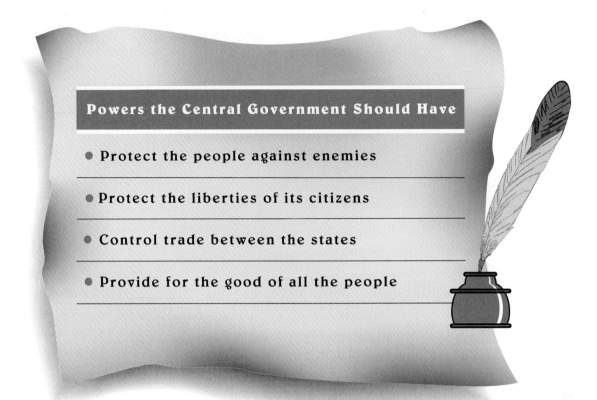

Powers the Central Government Should Have

- Protect the people against enemies

- Protect the liberties of its citizens

- Control trade between the states

- Provide for the good of all the people

These are a few ideas that all of the delegates supported.

James Madison had a lot to say at these meetings, for no one had thought more about constitution-making than he.

With the decision about secrecy out of the way, the delegates turned to the business that had brought them to Philadelphia. That business was to decide the kind of central government the United States of America should have.

The Virginia Plan

Edmund Randolph of Virginia asked to speak first. As governor of the state, Randolph headed the Virginia delegation. It would be his job to present the ideas that Madison and the others had been working on. These ideas came to be called the Virginia Plan.

The Virginia delegation, Randolph told the convention, would offer some proposals shortly. But first, he said, it might be useful to talk generally about the things a central government should be able to do.

A central government, said Randolph, should provide for the common defense. That means it should be able to protect the American people against foreign enemies.

The delegates listened thoughtfully. No argument there.

It should protect the liberties of the American people, continued Randolph.

The delegates continued to listen. No argument there, either.

It should be able to make laws about trade among the states, so that the states would not be taxing each other's citizens.

Again, the delegates agreed, no argument about that.

It should provide for the general welfare of the people. That meant doing things for the good of the whole people and not just the people of one state or another.

Once more, no disagreement from anyone.

But, Randolph continued, under the Articles of Confederation, the central government was not able to do these things. To do them, a government would need the power to raise an army without having to beg the states to contribute soldiers. It would need the power to collect its own taxes, without having to beg the states for money. And it would need many more powers besides. Randolph then continued with a description of what the new government might look like. You'll be reading about that shortly.

By the end of that day, a few delegates were becoming uncomfortable. Yes, yes, they said, the Virginians are probably right. But where is Randolph's argument leading?

Randolph did not leave them to wonder long. The next day he spoke again. The Virginia delegation, he said, believed that the central government must be able to deal directly with the people, instead of depending on the kindness of the state governments. In certain areas it must have powers *higher* than

those of the states. In those areas, the central government must have *supreme* powers.

A Strong Central Government?

But wait—wasn't the whole idea of the Articles of Confederation that the *states* had supreme power? Yes, it was. And now, here was Governor Randolph saying that we needed a national government that would be supreme over the states in some areas.

That last statement of Randolph's was met with a long silence. Remember, Congress had called this convention to revise the Articles of Confederation, not to throw them out. Now, in the very first week of the convention, the Virginia delegation was asking the convention to do just that.

When discussion finally began, it was long and sometimes heated. After a time the delegates put aside this difficult issue to discuss other parts of the Virginia Plan. But the issue had been raised, and it remained in the minds of all.

Edmund Randolph presented Virginia's plan for a change in the government.

Finally, after two weeks, the delegates returned to the issue and made the big decision: No, we are not going to patch and stitch the Articles. Yes, we are going to write a new constitution. We are going to create a new, stronger central government for the United States of America.

The Federal System Still, no one wanted the central government to have all the power and leave the states none. What the delegates created was something in between, where powers are divided between the central government and the states.

This is called a **federal** system. The aim of a federal system is to give each level of government—the national level and the state level—the jobs each can do best. Sound easy? It's not. Getting the right balance between the two is very hard to do. Just think about what was happening under the Articles of Confederation. The Articles let the states keep too much power and gave too little power to the central government. The result was a central government that didn't work well at all.

> **vocabulary**
> **federal** describing a political organization in which power is shared between a central authority and a number of areas or states

As if finding one balance was not hard enough, this convention had to find two. The second was the balance that James Madison had been wrestling with for more than a year. Do you remember it? It was this: How do you create a central government with enough power to act but not so much power that it threatens the people's liberties? That question nagged at the delegates all through the convention. Many delegates were afraid of creating a too-strong central government. You can see what deep scars their experience with the king and Parliament had left on Americans.

Separation of Powers

The Virginia Plan offered an answer to that problem. It proposed to separate the new national government into three equal branches: legislative, executive, and judicial. Each branch would have its own separate duties and powers. This idea is known as the *separation of powers*.

The separation of powers is part of our Constitution today. Here is how power is separated among the three branches of government.

• The legislative branch is Congress. Congress makes the laws for the country.

• The executive branch is headed by the President of the United States. The President sees that the laws are carried out and is responsible for running the government. The President also deals with other countries and serves as commander in chief of the armed forces.

• The judicial branch, or judiciary (it comes from the same word as "judge"), is made up of the Supreme Court and other federal, or national, courts. These courts decide cases involving the Constitution and the laws that Congress passes.

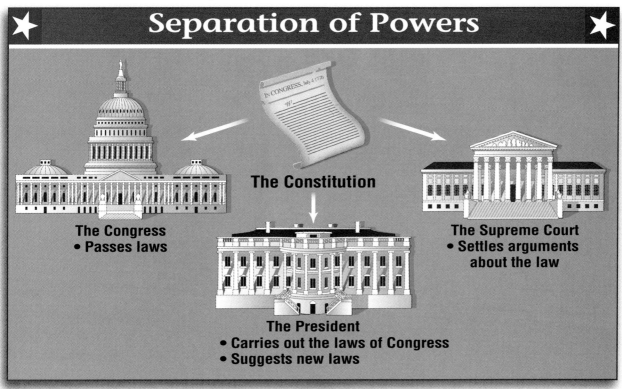

Separation of Powers

The Constitution

The Congress
- Passes laws

The President
- Carries out the laws of Congress
- Suggests new laws

The Supreme Court
- Settles arguments about the law

The new government would be divided into three branches equal in power.

Checks and Balances

Now, each of these branches has a lot of power. But none is completely free to do what it pleases. That's because each branch can check, which means "stop," the others. Each "checks and balances" the other two.

For example, Congress can pass any law it wants, but the President has the right to veto, or disapprove it. The President can make a treaty with another country, but the treaty only goes into effect if the Senate approves it. The President is commander in chief of the armed forces, but only Congress can declare war.

Do you see why this is called a system of checks and balances? Power is spread out and balanced among the three separate branches. Each branch can check, or stop, the other two. You can think of it as a door with three locks. Each of the three branches has the key

to one of them. For the government to use its power, all three have to use their keys to unlock the door.

Compromises

For the first month, the Constitutional Convention made great progress. However, every delegate knew there were several issues certain to cause trouble. If those could not be solved, the whole convention would end in failure.

The first of these was the issue of representation in Congress. How many representatives—that is, how many votes—would each state have in Congress? Do you remember how the Articles of Confederation answered that question? The Articles said, "one state, one vote"—that is, each state had one vote, no matter how big the state or how many people lived in it. Of course, the big states didn't like that. So now the Virginia Plan proposed that representation be based on population. In other words, the more people a state had, the more votes it would have.

It wasn't surprising that Virginia favored this plan. Virginia, after all, was the largest state. And it wasn't surprising that small states like Delaware and New Jersey wanted to keep the one state, one vote rule. They said the Virginia Plan would give the large states too many votes in Congress.

The argument between big states and small states grew more and more heated. Each side said that its own proposal was the only fair one. Each side said it would never agree to the other side's. For a time, it looked like this would be the rock on which the Constitutional Convention would crash.

Then Roger Sherman, a delegate from Connecticut, came forward with a solution. As all the delegates knew, the Virginia Plan actually proposed two separate "houses," or assemblies, in Congress. Why not base the membership of one of them on population? That one would be called the House of Representatives. In the other house, each state, whether big or small, would have an equal vote. That house would be called the Senate. That way, both the large states and the small ones would each get something.

Sherman had proposed a **compromise**. In a compromise, each side gives up something it wants in order to reach an agreement. Delegates on both sides realized they would need a compromise to end the argument, and Roger Sherman's seemed like a reasonable one. Angry words flew back and forth for a few more weeks, but Sherman's idea was finally accepted. This came to be called the Great Compromise. So, the delegates had managed to solve one tough issue. But now they faced another, maybe even tougher—the issue of slavery. It was not a question of getting rid of slavery. Northern states did want to get rid of it, but they knew several southern states would walk out of the convention if they tried. So they didn't try.

Instead, this was the question the convention tried to deal with: Should states be allowed to count slaves as part of their population? If slaves were included in a state's population, then that state would have more votes in Congress.

Roger Sherman of Connecticut presented a plan that shared power between large and small states.

> **vocabulary**
> **compromise** a settlement of differences between two or more sides reached by each side giving up some of what it wanted

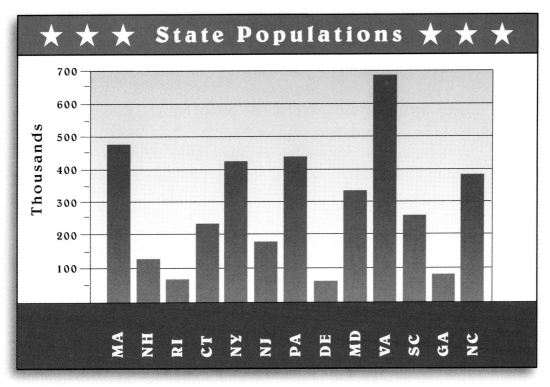

<star> <star> <star> **State Populations** <star> <star> <star>

*The large differences in the number of people who lived in each state
presented a problem to the delegates at the convention.*

(Remember, the bigger a state's population, the more representatives it sent to the House of Representatives.)

The northern states argued that slaves shouldn't be counted. After all, said these states, you southerners claim that the slaves are just property. How can you count property as part of your population? But southern states insisted that the slaves should be counted. Once again, a compromise saved the day. It was agreed that in figuring the number of representatives each state would have in the House of Representatives, five slaves would count as three persons. This came to be known as the Three-Fifths Compromise.

There was one more compromise between northern and southern states involving slavery. Northern states wanted to stop any more slaves from coming into the country. But Georgia and South Carolina threatened to walk out if the convention insisted on stopping the slave trade. In the end the two sides compromised. Slaves could be imported for another 20 years, but after that, Congress could prohibit bringing in any more. (Twenty years later, Congress did just that.)

Making these compromises on slavery was not a proud moment for the Constitutional Convention. Yet all the delegates knew that without them, there would be no new constitution and no new, stronger central government. And slavery would go right on.

Questions Remain With those compromises, the convention moved steadily forward to complete its work. Several important questions remained. Here were a few of them. How shall the new constitution be amended? Will it be necessary to change or add to the new constitution?

You'll remember that amending a constitution should not be done often, or easily. It certainly should be harder than passing an ordinary law. At the same time, it shouldn't be impossible. That was one of the problems of the Articles of Confederation, which required all 13 states to agree to an amendment. The Constitutional Convention's answer was to require two-thirds of each house of Congress and three-fourths of all the states to approve an amendment before it could become a part of the constitution.

Two more questions had to do with ratifying the constitution. To *ratify* means to approve or accept. Everyone agreed that before the new constitution could go into effect, it had to be ratified by the states. But by how many states? And who would speak for each state? Here again, the Articles of Confederation provided an example of what *not* to do. The Articles had let the state legislatures decide for each state and had required all 13 of them to give their approval. It had taken *four years* to get all 13 states to ratify!

The delegates to the Constitutional Convention said: We can't let that happen again. This is also too important to let the state legislatures decide, as though the constitution were just another law. So this is what the convention decided: Each state would call a special ratifying convention. The people themselves would choose the members of these conventions. The ratifying conventions would have only one job: to decide whether to approve the new constitution. When nine of them approved, the new constitution would go into effect.

Ratifying the constitution would not be a simple task.

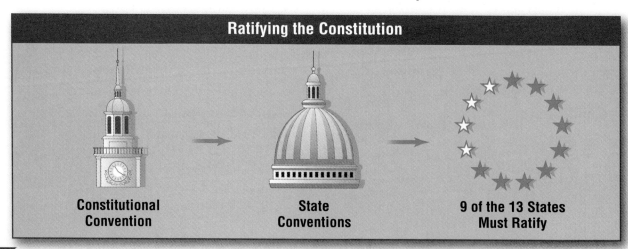

Ratifying the Constitution

Constitutional Convention → State Conventions → 9 of the 13 States Must Ratify

Supreme Law of the Land

Here was another very important question for the delegates: What happens if part of a state's constitution disagrees with the constitution the convention was creating? Or if a state passes a law that disagrees with it? Is that OK? The delegates quickly saw that it certainly would *not* be OK. If that was to be allowed, each state could go its own way and ignore the new constitution altogether. You would not have a real nation at all.

The convention took care of that problem by including these words in the Constitution: "This Constitution, and the laws of the United States . . . shall be the supreme law of the land; . . . anything in the constitution or laws of any State to the contrary notwithstanding." In plain English, that means that whenever a state law or a state constitution says one thing, and the United States Constitution or Congress says another, then what the U.S. Constitution or the Congress says goes.

More Questions

Another important question: Should the new constitution include a bill of rights? A bill of rights would list the rights of citizens that the new national government could not interfere with. This list would include such rights as freedom of speech, freedom of the press, freedom of religion, the right to trial by jury, and other rights you probably remember.

Some delegates thought the new constitution should list each of these rights. Most, though, felt that the state constitutions already guaranteed them, so there was no need to repeat them. In the end the delegates decided not to include a bill of rights. As you'll soon see, that turned out to be a mistake.

The convention had to settle a number of other questions also. Here are some of them, along with the answers the delegates decided on:

- What should the term of office be for a member of the House of Representatives? Answer: Two years

- What should the term of office be for a member of the Senate? Answer: Six years

- How many senators should each state have? Answer: Two.

- How many presidents should there be? Yes, that's right—how many presidents at one time? For a while, the delegates considered dividing the powers of the president among three people. They feared giving all that power (again!) to just one person. Answer: One president, with a term of four years

One reason the delegates finally decided to have a single President was that all of them knew who the first one would be. It was a person they knew they could trust, a person who would not abuse his power. He was the same man they had trusted to lead their armies in war and to be president of this convention. You know who he was.

Success at Last!

The Constitutional Convention was now nearing the end of its work. A committee was appointed to put all the things it had agreed on into language that would be right for a constitution. On September 12 the delegates assembled to hear one of the committee members read the proposed constitution aloud. "We, the People of the United States,"

E PLURIBUS UNUM.

LIBERTY

CONSTITUTION & LAWS

The creator of this cartoon felt the new constitution would guarantee liberty and law and create one nation out of many states.

he began. What words those were! Not "We the States." Not "We the People of the states of New York and Pennsylvania and Georgia." No. "*We, the People of the United States.*"

We, the People of the United States, in order to form a more perfect union [to have a better government than we had under the Articles of Confederation], establish justice, insure domestic tranquility [to keep peace within the country], provide for the common defense, promote the general welfare, and secure the blessings of liberty to ourselves and our **posterity**, do ordain and establish this Constitution for the United States of America.

As they listened, the delegates could not help but marvel at what they had achieved during those four months in Philadelphia. It was, George Washington later said, "little short of a miracle."

vocabulary
posterity
generations to come

There were a few more days of discussion and small changes. Then on September 17—nearly four months after the Constitutional Convention opened—the final document was ready to be signed. The time for secrecy was over. Windows were opened once more, and a cool breeze flowed through the room.

Forty-two delegates had assembled in the Independence Room. Three of them had already decided that they could not support the new Constitution. One of them was Edmund Randolph, the very person who had presented the Virginia Plan to the convention. The other 39, one by one, stepped to the front of the room where the document was ready to be signed.

None of the 39 agreed with everything in the document. None of them believed that it was perfect. But all of them felt it was the best they could do. And all of them believed the Constitution was a great improvement over the Articles of Confederation. So they signed.

As they did, old Benjamin Franklin, unable to rise from his chair, spoke to the delegates one last time. At the start of the convention, said Franklin, he had noted that on the back of the chairman's chair there was a carving of a sun with sunbeams.

> I have often . . . looked at that [sun] . . . without being able to tell whether it was rising or setting. But now at length I have the happiness to know that it is a rising and not a setting sun.

It took many months of hard work, but finally in September the delegates were able to sign a new Constitution for the United States.

The Final Test Now came the final test. Would the people approve what the Constitutional Convention had created or not? It was time to find out. Within days of the convention, newspapers throughout the country printed the entire Constitution.

All Americans, no matter where they lived, were given the opportunity to read every line of the document. And discuss it. And analyze it. And argue about it.

It had been amazing enough to have delegates come together to write a new constitution. It was even more amazing to see people—"We the People"—having a say about their own futures and the future of their country.

It quickly became clear that some Americans wanted the Constitution very much, while others didn't want it at all. Those who wanted to approve it came to be called Federalists. Those who opposed it were known as Anti-Federalists.

Both sides used the newspapers to present their cases to the public. Anti-Federalists had three main arguments. First, they said that the Constitutional Convention was only supposed to recommend changes to the Articles of Confederation. What business did the delegates have throwing out the Articles? They had gone way beyond what they were supposed to do.

Second, Anti-Federalists argued that the convention had created a much too powerful central government. Had they learned nothing from all those years of strong central government in Great Britain?

And third, they complained that the convention had failed to include a bill of rights

These two patriots who fought for independence disagreed completely on how the new nation should be governed.

Patrick Henry   **Alexander Hamilton**

in the Constitution. This, said the Anti-Federalists, was a direct threat to the liberties of the people.

The plan of the Anti-Federalists was delay. They tried to get the states to put off calling a ratifying convention. They tried to get the states and the Congress to call another national convention to fix the problems of this Constitution first. There would be plenty of time, they said, to have ratifying conventions after that.

The Federalists, of course, felt their best chance was to act quickly. Among the leading supporters of the Federalist side were Alexander Hamilton and James Madison. Those two, plus John Jay from New York, wrote 85 separate newspaper articles in which they went over every part, practically every sentence, of the new Constitution. They explained to the American people why each part was important and showed them how the new government would work.

The Struggle for Ratification

You'll remember that each state was to hold a special ratifying convention. It would take a yes vote in nine states to put the new Constitution into effect.

Delaware held the first convention, and it voted yes. Pennsylvania and New Jersey soon followed. That made the score three for yes, zero for no. Yes votes in Georgia and Connecticut in January 1788 made it five.

Federalists were pleased by this good start. But they knew that the hardest battles lay ahead. One of those battles was sure to take place in Massachusetts, where the Anti-Federalists were very strong.

In the Massachusetts ratifying convention, Anti-Federalists fiercely attacked the new Constitution. Here's how one delegate expressed his fear and distrust of it:

> We [fought against] Great Britain—some said for a three-penny [tax] on tea; but it was not that. It was because they claimed a right to tax us and bind us in all cases whatever. And does not this Constitution do the same? Does it not take away all we have—all our property? Does it not lay [impose] all taxes?

Other opponents jumped on the absence of a bill of rights in the new Constitution. Without a bill of rights, they said, the liberties of the people would not be safe.

No one knew for sure if the new Constitution would be ratified by the states.

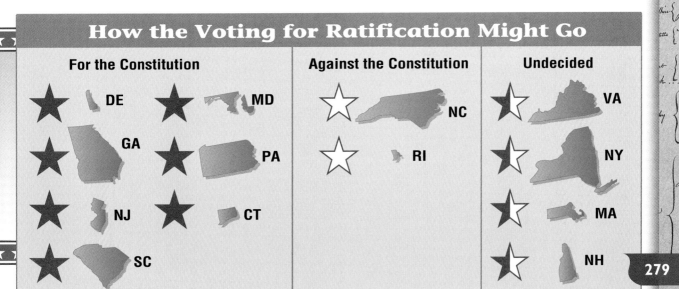

How the Voting for Ratification Might Go

For the Constitution	Against the Constitution	Undecided
★ DE ★ MD	☆ NC	★ VA
★ GA ★ PA	☆ RI	★ NY
★ NJ ★ CT		★ MA
★ SC		★ NH

For a time the Anti-Federalist strategy seemed to work. Then the Federalists hit upon a neat strategy of their own. Instead of trying to explain why no bill of rights was needed, they decided to agree with the Anti-Federalists. You're right, said the Federalists to their opponents. Tell you what: You draw up a list of rights that you think should be in the Constitution. Then join us in ratifying the Constitution, and we promise to work with you to get your list added to the Constitution as amendments. This offer won over enough Anti-Federalists to swing the Massachusetts ratifying convention in favor of the Constitution.

Six down, three to go, said the Federalists. Then Maryland voted yes in April, and South Carolina voted yes in May, making eight states in favor of the new Constitution. Eight—just one more to go. New Hampshire was the next state to have a ratifying convention. If New Hampshire said yes, the Constitution would go into effect.

The only problem was that two of the biggest and most important states, Virginia and New York, were not among the nine.

Without at least one of those two states, the new nation would be very, very shaky.

So even when New Hampshire voted yes in June, supporters of the Constitution could not breathe easily. Their eyes turned to Virginia. There the battle between Federalists and Anti-Federalists raged for nearly a month. Patrick Henry was among the leading Anti-Federalists. He could still win over listeners with his brilliant speeches. James Madison was among the leading Federalists. He could win over listeners with his calm explanation of the Constitution.

And there was Governor Edmund Randolph. Remember him—the man who proposed the Virginia Plan and then refused to sign the Constitution? Randolph had changed his mind once more and was now in favor of the Constitution.

As in Massachusetts and several other states, Anti-Federalists in Virginia pointed to the absence of a bill of rights. Patrick Henry led the charge. Without a bill of rights, roared Henry, our liberty, the "greatest of all earthly blessings," is in danger.

New-York Historical Society

DEL. PEN. N.JER. GEOR. CON. MASSA. MARY. S? CARO. N.HAMP.

The Federalists, however, had an answer, just as they had in Massachusetts. Vote for the Constitution now, they told the Anti-Federalists, and we will work with you to add a bill of rights to the Constitution.

No, said the Anti-Federalists. First, call a new constitutional convention and add a bill of rights. *Then* we'll vote. Amend first, said the Anti-Federalists. Amend later, said the Federalists.

On the day of the vote, Madison promised that once the Constitution took effect, he personally would lead the fight to amend it with a bill of rights. That seemed to do the trick. By a narrow margin, Virginia voted yes.

The Bill of Rights

Madison was true to his word. As soon as a newly elected Congress met under the new Constitution, he proposed a number of amendments to protect the rights of the people. Congress voted to accept them (Do you remember that amending the Constitution requires a two-thirds majority in each house of Congress?) and sent them to the states for their approval. In 1791, ten of these amendments were ratified by the states and added to the Constitution. These first ten amendments are known as the Bill of Rights.

The Bill of Rights says to the national government: These are the basic rights of the people, and you cannot take them away. (Remember those "unalienable rights" that Thomas Jefferson wrote about?) One of those amendments says that Congress may not make any law that interferes with your freedom of speech or freedom of religion. It can't take away the press's freedom to print what it wishes, even if the press is criticizing the government. It can't prevent people from assembling peaceably or from asking the government to do something about their complaints.

Another of those first ten amendments protects you against the government illegally entering and searching your house. (Sound familiar? It should. Many of these are the same "rights of Englishmen" over which a war was fought.) Four other amendments make sure that people accused of a crime get a fair trial.

Taken together, those first ten amendments to the Constitution are the most important protector of our liberties that we have.

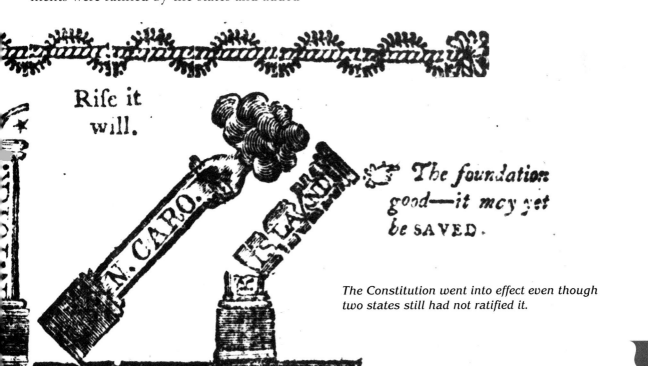

Rise it will.

The foundation good—it may yet be SAVED.

The Constitution went into effect even though two states still had not ratified it.

But we have gotten ahead of our story. After Virginia approved the Constitution, it was clear that the struggle for ratification had been won. Meanwhile, in New York, that state's ratifying convention was meeting. At the start the Anti-Federalists seemed to have a majority. Alexander Hamilton, who had represented New York at the Constitutional Convention, was very worried. However, as soon as Virginia's convention voted yes, a messenger raced to New York with the news. He reached there in early July, and the news he brought had an almost immediate effect. With Virginia voting yes, New Yorkers realized that the new Constitution would definitely go into effect. They decided it would not be wise to be left out of the new nation. By the end of July, New York voted yes also.

Two states, North Carolina and Rhode Island, were still holding out. But they could wait. The constitution drawn up that summer in Philadelphia was now, officially, the Constitution of the United States.

It was time for the nation to celebrate. And did it ever, with bonfires, ringing church bells, and parades in cities, towns, and villages throughout the land.

No celebration was grander than the one in the nation's largest city, Philadelphia. There, the citizens chose to celebrate their nation's new beginning on Independence Day, the Fourth of July. At dawn, church bells and booming cannons from the ship *Rising Sun* in the harbor announced the start of the celebration. Later that morning a mile-and-a-half-long parade set off through the streets of the city. Floats, marching bands, and ordinary citizens offered their welcome to their nation's new beginning. Following that came an afternoon of speeches and picnicking. Nearly half the entire population of Philadelphia turned out for this huge party. At the end of the day, one leading citizen of the city said, "Now it is done. Now we are a nation."

Indeed we were.

Celebrations took place in all the states that ratified the Constitution. This one was in New York City.

Still Going Strong If the Americans who wrote the Constitution could come back today, would they recognize the country they helped create? You can probably list a hundred things that would be totally strange to them. And if that's all they saw, then they wouldn't recognize today's America at all.

What would they say about airplanes flying everywhere, cars and trucks whizzing along paved roads (when they aren't stuck in traffic jams!), tall office buildings in crowded cities, wristwatches, telephones, television, computers?

But if those same earlier Americans could listen to today's citizens debate who to vote for, or argue against the school board's new plan in a public meeting, or discuss the news they'd heard on TV or read in the newspaper —well then, that would be a different story. Choosing our own representatives, meeting publicly to have a say about laws we will live under, exercising our rights to free speech and free press—surely those visitors from the 1780s would find these quite familiar. Chances are, in fact, they would smile, congratulate each other, and say, "The Constitution we wrote more than 200 years ago is alive and well in twenty-first century America."

Indeed it is. Even though the Constitution of the United States is by far the oldest written constitution in the world, it's still going strong. What has allowed this Constitution to last so long? The short answer is that for all of those 200-plus years, the Constitution has served the American people well. But just how, exactly, has it done this?

Modern highways bring people and goods to American cities like Los Angeles shown here.

Not Too Much, Not Too Little

To begin with, one of the great features of the Constitution of the United States is that it doesn't try to say or do too much. Do you remember how a well-made constitution is like the framework of a house, and ordinary laws are like the furniture that fits inside?

That's the goal. However, too often when people actually start writing a constitution—when they start building the framework of the house—they soon fill it up with lots of unnecessary furniture. And before long, they have a very cluttered constitution.

The people who wrote our Constitution, however, never confused the house with the furniture. They didn't try to write rules for every small detail of government. They set down the main framework of government, and that's all.

Why is that important? What's wrong with a constitution that spells out little details of government? What's wrong is that nobody, no matter how wise, can possibly guess what life will be like 100 or 200 years in the future. Remember that a good written constitution should not be too easy to change. If you load up your constitution today with a lot of rules that make no sense tomorrow, your constitution is not going to work well for very long.

Here's an example: How many people should each member of the House of Representatives represent? The Constitution says that each member has to represent

at least 30,000 people. It could be more, though. How many more? The Constitution doesn't try to spell out that detail. It lets each future generation decide for itself. A good thing, too. Suppose the Constitution had said, "each member of the House shall represent exactly 30,000 people, no more and no less." With our population today there would be over *9,000* members sitting in the House of Representatives—that is, if they could find seats!

So one reason the Constitution has lasted all this time is that it does not try to do more than a constitution should. In fact, after tacking on the Bill of Rights—the first ten amendments—in 1791, we Americans have amended our Constitution only 17 more times.

Four Guiding Principles

The Constitution has served the American people well for so long for another reason: It is built on four strong guiding principles. The first of these guiding principles is the one that Thomas Jefferson stated in the Declaration of Independence: *governments get "their just powers from the consent of the governed."*

The 19th Amendment made it possible for women to take an active role in government.

One of the responsibilities of the national government is printing and coining money.

Do you remember what that means? To put it simply, it means that "we the people" rule. We rule by choosing the people who represent us in government. We do this on the national level. We do it on the state level. We do it in the towns and cities in which we live. If we like the job our representatives have done, we can reelect them. If we don't like it, we can choose others to represent us.

The second guiding principle is *limited government*. You'll remember what that means. The Constitution lists many things the national government may do. It can collect taxes and borrow money. It can control trade between the United States and other countries. It can make laws about immigration and citizenship. It can coin and print money, run a postal service, and create new courts. It can create an army and a navy, and it can declare war and make peace. Those are a lot of powers, to be sure.

But the Constitution also states many things the national government may *not* do. Most important of all, the Constitution prevents the government from interfering with the freedoms and liberties of the people. To top it off, the Bill of Rights spells out still other limits on the federal government, as you have read. The principle of limited government is what guarantees our freedoms against the possibility of a too-strong government.

The third guiding principle built into our constitution is the *separation of powers*. You'll remember that the responsibility for government in the United States is split among three branches of government: the legislative branch, the executive branch, and the judicial branch.

The legislative branch, or Congress, makes the laws. The executive branch, headed by the President, carries out the laws. The President is helped by a number of departments, like the Treasury Department and the Department of Defense. The judicial branch handles cases involving federal laws and also cases involving disagreements between the states. Our Supreme Court has the power to decide whether a law passed by Congress is

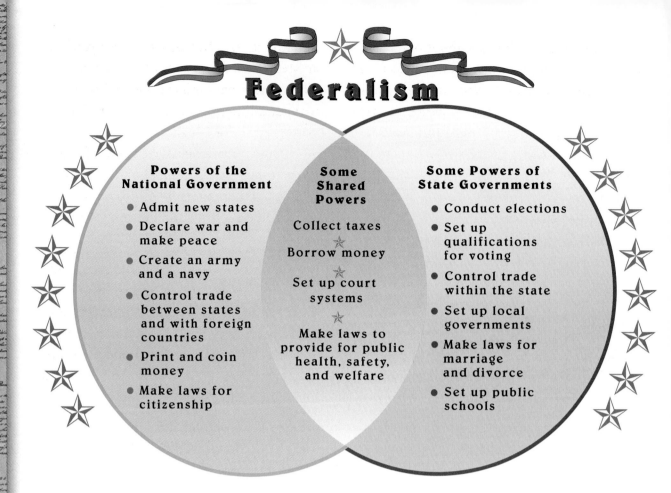

Federalism

Powers of the National Government
- Admit new states
- Declare war and make peace
- Create an army and a navy
- Control trade between states and with foreign countries
- Print and coin money
- Make laws for citizenship

Some Shared Powers

Collect taxes

Borrow money

Set up court systems

Make laws to provide for public health, safety, and welfare

Some Powers of State Governments
- Conduct elections
- Set up qualifications for voting
- Control trade within the state
- Set up local governments
- Make laws for marriage and divorce
- Set up public schools

The states and the federal government share some powers.

permitted by the Constitution. If not, the law is "unconstitutional."

With the powers of government separated in this way, no one branch of government can just do whatever it wants. No one branch can ride roughshod over the other two. Each is checked and balanced by the others.

The fourth guiding principle is *federalism*. As you have learned, federalism is the system of dividing the powers of government between the national government and the state governments. But you'll also realize that the trick to making a federal system work well is to give each level of government the jobs it does best. The men who made our Constitution did a brilliant job of dividing up powers the right way.

For example, take the matter of printing money. Who should that job be given to, the states or the national government? Well, we have 50 states today. If that job had been given to the states, we'd have 50 different kinds of money to deal with today. Clearly, that's a job that's best done by the national government. And that's what the Constitution says.

On the other hand, what about marriage and divorce? You *could* have a single, national law about marriage and divorce, of course. Many countries do. But most Americans feel that in a country as huge as ours, those subjects should be left to the individual states. They generally feel the same way about things like adoption, crime, education, and many, many other things. In our federal system, those matters belong to the states.

Here's an interesting fact about our Constitution. Important as these subjects are, words like *marriage, adoption, education,* and *police* don't even appear in it. That's because the main purpose of the Constitution was to set up a new national government. Remember, each state already had a constitution and a government of its own. They were already doing lots of jobs that governments do. So everyone at the Constitutional Convention understood that unless they said that the new national government should do this or that job, the state governments would go right on doing it.

The chart lists some of the powers the Constitution grants to the national government and some of the powers that remain with the states. On that same chart you'll see an area where the powers of each overlap. That means that both the national government and the states have this power. The power to tax, for instance. The national government needs this power to pay for our armed forces and a hundred other things. The state governments need this power to pay for building roads and running schools.

So now you have an answer to the question about how our Constitution has lasted more than 200 years. Or at least a part of the answer. The rest of the answer, you see, lies in the good sense of the American people. We have respected the Constitution, and we have taken care to preserve it. And in return, it has taken care of us.

Glossary

ambassador an official of high rank sent by a country to represent it in another country

compromise a settlement of differences between two or more sides reached by each side giving up some of what it wanted

consent approval or agreement [consent can also be given in a non-political situation]

deliberate to think about and discuss issues before reaching a decision

federal describing a political organization in which power is shared between a central authority and a number of areas or states

ordinance another word for law

planter one who owns and runs a large farm and usually raises one important crop

politics the art or science concerned with guiding or influencing government

posterity generations to come

right something due to one by law, custom, or nature

term a limited extent of time during which something may last

EARLY PRESIDENTS:
WASHINGTON THROUGH JACKSON

Contents

1 Washington Becomes President

ome at Mount Vernon The candles in the windows of George Washington's home at Mount Vernon shone brightly on Christmas Eve, 1783, as they did every Christmas Eve. This Christmas Eve, though, was different. One month earlier the United States and Great Britain had signed a peace treaty ending the Revolutionary War.

At a dinner in New York soon after, General Washington said his goodbyes to his fellow officers. Later he presented Congress with his resignation as commander in chief of the Continental army. His work was done, he told the Congress, and he was retiring from public life forever—from the army, from government, from all the duties that America had called on him to do.

Now, after nearly nine years of service to his country, Washington was free to return to his beloved Mount Vernon. As he rode up the circular drive to Mount Vernon that Christmas Eve, he could see the candles shining in the windows. In the doorway his wife, Martha, waited to welcome him. At last, America's hero was home.

When Washington told Congress he was leaving public life forever, he meant it. Have you ever noticed, though, how sometimes things happen that make you take back words like *forever, never,* and *always?* That's what happened to George Washington.

First, Virginia asked him to serve as one of the state's delegates to the Constitutional Convention in Philadelphia. How could Washington say no? He had fought to give life to the young nation, but for the last four years, he could only watch helplessly as it struggled under the Articles of Confederation. He could not turn his back on his country. He had to take back that *forever*. He had to serve.

George Washington, the newly-elected President, arrives in New York City.

Then, when the delegates to the Constitutional Convention gathered in Philadelphia in 1787, they needed a strong, steady leader to get them through the hard work ahead. They turned to George Washington to serve as president of the convention. Again, Washington agreed to serve.

And now, with the Constitution **ratified** by the states, Washington knew he would be called to serve again. Just as everyone expected, Washington was everyone's choice to be the nation's first President. Once again, he knew he could not say no. Forever would have to wait.

On April 16, Washington said goodbye to Mount Vernon once again and set out for New York, the nation's temporary capital. There his inauguration would take place. An inauguration is a formal ceremony at the start of a term of office.

The trip from Mount Vernon to New York City took far longer than Washington expected. In every village and town that he went through, he had to attend speeches, parades, and dinners in his honor. Citizens lined the streets to cheer as his carriage passed by. On the country roads, men on horseback rode in front of, behind, and alongside Washington's carriage, filling the country air with dust as they turned the journey into one long parade. After eight days, Washington finally arrived in New York.

detail, Collection of The New-York Historical Society

George Washington is inaugurated on the balcony of Federal Hall.

April 30, 1789, Inauguration Day, dawned bright and sunny in New York City. A crowd of thousands soon assembled in front of the building known as Federal Hall. Shortly after noon, George Washington and a small group of officials stepped out on the balcony. Placing his hand on a Bible, Washington repeated the oath of office written in the new Constitution: "I do solemnly swear that I will faithfully execute the office of President of the United States, and will to the best of my ability, preserve, protect, and defend the Constitution of the United States."

In that day before loudspeakers, few on the street below could hear the words. Nevertheless, they knew they had just witnessed a historic moment. After Washington spoke the final words of the oath, an official called out, "Long live George Washington, President of the United States!" The crowd cheered wildly.

2 The First Year

Setting Precedents With the election of a congress and a president, the new government was ready to start. Washington and Congress wanted to proceed carefully because, as Washington said, "I walk on untrodden ground." He meant that no one had ever done anything like this before.

Almost every action they took might set a **precedent,** that is, a pattern that would be followed in the future.

For example, members of Congress tied themselves into knots over the proper way to address the President. Vice President John Adams suggested that the President be called "His Highness, the President of the United States of America and Protector of Their Liberties." Others said that sounded too much like the way the British addressed their king. A number of congressmen thought "His Excellency" was just about

right. In the end it was agreed to address Washington simply as "Mister President." Today this matter seems more amusing than important. But in 1789 it was taken very seriously.

vocabulary
precedent an example to follow in the future

Other precedents were more important. For example, the Constitution set up three branches of government: the legislative, judicial, and executive branches. The Constitution also said there will be

George Washington is shown here with members of his first Cabinet. Henry Knox is seated next to the President; Alexander Hamilton is standing next to the seated Thomas Jefferson; Edmund Randolph is seated at the right.

"departments" in the executive branch of government to help the President. It doesn't say, though, what those departments will be. And it doesn't say how many of them there will be. It was up to Congress to fill in that empty space in the Constitution.

Congress decided to create three executive departments. One was the Department of State. That department was supposed to help the President in his dealings with foreign countries. Another department was the War Department. That department was in charge of defending the country. A third department was the Department of the Treasury. That one was expected to collect taxes, pay bills, and take care of the government's money. The head of each department was called a *secretary,* like the secretary of state.

Creating these departments led to another precedent. The Constitution says the President may seek advice from his department heads. At first, Washington just talked to each one separately about the work his department was doing. After a while, though, President Washington felt he needed advice on many other matters. He began having all the secretaries meet with him at the same time to get their advice. The department heads came to be called the President's *Cabinet,* which means a "group of advisers." The first Cabinet also included an attorney general who gave the President legal advice, and a postmaster general who ran the post office. The meetings came to be known as *Cabinet meetings.*

The Constitution doesn't say anything about a Cabinet, but every President since Washington has had one. Over the years,

The Cabinet Today: There are 15 members in the Cabinet. The Department of Veterans Affairs (1989) was the latest addition.

Congress has added departments to the executive branch, and the President's Cabinet has grown.

Another of those empty spaces in the Constitution had to do with the courts. The Constitution says that there will be a Supreme Court, but it doesn't say how many judges should serve on it. It says that Congress can establish courts below the Supreme Court, but it doesn't say what those courts should do or how many there should be. All of that was up to Congress.

Therefore, in that very first year under the new government, Congress passed a law filling in the empty spaces in the Constitution about courts and judges. It said the Supreme Court should have six judges. Congress changed that number several times over the years—seven, then eight, then nine, then ten, then eight again, and nine again! (It's been nine for more than 130 years, so it will probably stay that way.) The Supreme Court, of course, is the top court in the country, but Congress also created enough other courts so that people in every part of the country could be served by them.

A United States Tax

Congress passed still another important law in that first year under the new government. In the old days, the central government didn't have a cent. That was because it didn't have the power to tax. Well, the new Constitution changed that. In 1789, Congress placed a tax on more than 80 imported products—that is, products brought into the United States from other countries. It wasn't much of a tax, but it was enough. For the first time, the central government could start paying its bills.

Solid Foundation What a busy year 1789 was for the new government of the United States! New executive departments. A brand new federal court system. Important precedents. The new nation's first-ever tax.

In just six months, President Washington and Congress had laid a solid foundation for a healthy new government of the United States.

What's more, the American people seemed very satisfied. Less than a year before, arguments about the Constitution had raged in the state ratifying conventions. Now, wrote Thomas Jefferson, "the opposition to our new Constitution has almost totally disappeared."

But the harmony didn't last. Differences soon arose among Washington's closest advisers and in Congress. The differences grew into angry debates. Before long they threatened to tear apart Washington's **administration.**

At the very start of his administration, President Washington had chosen Alexander Hamilton to head the Department of the Treasury. He chose Thomas Jefferson to head the Department of State. Hamilton and Jefferson were two of the most capable people ever to serve in government. They were both great patriots. But they disagreed on almost everything. At times, President Washington felt as if he were driving a coach with horses pulling in opposite directions.

Scholars believe that the two men had never met before Washington appointed them to his Cabinet. James Madison, who

> **vocabulary**
> **administration** a group making up the executive branch in a presidential government; also its term of office

TWO GREAT PATRIOTS

Alexander Hamilton

Thomas Jefferson

Thomas Jefferson wanted an America of small towns and farms.

knew both men well, introduced them to each other. Madison thought they would get along just fine. Was he ever wrong! In just a few months, conflict between the two men grew.

Different Hopes for the Nation

Hamilton and Jefferson had almost completely opposite hopes and plans for America's future. Hamilton wanted to encourage the growth of manufacturing. He pictured great numbers of Americans being employed at machines, producing goods for sale in America and other countries. Jefferson agreed that the country needed some manufacturing and trade. However, he wanted America to remain mainly a nation of small farmers.

Hamilton hoped the United States would soon have many large cities. Jefferson did not want to see cities grow. He had seen Europe's large cities, with their masses of poor and hungry people, and he wanted no part of that for America.

Hamilton favored a stronger central government than the one the new Constitution created. Jefferson said, "That government governs best, which governs least." That is, the smaller the government, the better.

Who should run this government and make decisions? Here again, Hamilton and Jefferson came down on opposite sides. For Hamilton, government should be in the hands of "the rich, the well-born, and the able." *Well-born* means they should come from important, aristocratic families. These people, he said, would make wise decisions. Ordinary people aren't steady, Hamilton believed. They are always changing their minds. And when they do make decisions, they usually make bad ones.

Jefferson, though, believed that ordinary people were quite capable of governing themselves. "Whenever the people are well-informed," he wrote, "they can be trusted with their own government."

With such opposite beliefs, it's no wonder that Hamilton and Jefferson disliked each other so strongly. In fact, each one regarded the other as dangerous to the future of the young republic. They were wrong about that. Both contributed greatly to the nation's growth and health in its early years.

The many disagreements between Hamilton and Jefferson led to the birth of political parties in America. A political party is a group of people who share certain beliefs about how the government should be run and what it should do and not do. These people join together to elect representatives who share their beliefs.

In the 1790s those Americans who favored Hamilton and his ideas called themselves *Federalists*. Supporters of Thomas Jefferson called themselves *Democratic-Republicans*.

The Whiskey Rebellion

Under the Articles of Confederation, Congress couldn't raise money to pay the nation's debts. Alexander Hamilton proposed a plan to do this. Hamilton's idea was to raise money by putting a tax on certain goods, including whiskey. People disagreed with other parts of Hamilton's plan, but almost everyone thought the tax on whiskey was reasonable, and Congress passed it.

Almost everyone, that is, except certain settlers on the western **frontier**. Many of those farmers raised corn as their main crop. Although farm families used most of what they grew to live on, they planned to sell the remainder. But the cost of shipping corn to eastern cities by wagon added so much to its price that few buyers could be found for it.

Whiskey can be made from corn. Shipping a barrel of whiskey cost less than shipping the corn it was made from. So farmers often turned their corn into whiskey.

For these farmers, paying a tax on whiskey was like having to pay a tax on the corn itself. Since money was scarce on the frontier, frontier farmers often used jugs of whiskey as a substitute. For farmers who used whiskey that way, taxing whiskey was like taxing money itself!

> **vocabulary**
> **frontier** the border region between settled areas and unsettled wilderness

In 1794, farmers in western Pennsylvania banded together and refused to pay the tax. They even threatened tax collectors. President Washington had some sympathy for the farmers, but he felt that the law is the law. He also felt it was especially important for the new government to show it could enforce its laws. Washington put on his old general's uniform and led 13,000 troops to western Pennsylvania to put down the Whiskey Rebellion, as it was being called. Happily, there was no need to fire a shot. When farmers heard that troops were coming, they dropped their guns and fled. That ended the rebellion. Washington had shown that the new government could not only pass laws but also make people obey them.

Still, the use of troops to put down the Whiskey Rebellion left a bitter taste in the mouths of many farmers. They turned against the Federalist party. They knew that Jefferson supported farmers, and so they supported the Democratic-Republican party.

New President Twice the American people had chosen George Washington to be their President. Twice he had served, even though he would rather have returned to his beloved Mount Vernon. If Americans had their way, Washington would go right on serving as President.

Washington, however, decided that eight years in the presidency was enough. Not just enough for him, but enough for the country. He believed that if the new government was to succeed, the people must not depend on just one man. America needed a President, not a king. Washington returned to his home at Mount Vernon.

With Washington out of the picture, the United States had its first real contest for the presidency. John Adams, who had been the Vice President under Washington, was the candidate of the Federalist party. The Democratic-Republicans soon named Thomas Jefferson as their choice for President. John Adams won, but just barely. In those days the person who came in second became the Vice President, even though he might be from the other political party. So Thomas Jefferson became Vice President of the United States.

Election of 1796: the first election in which political parties played a role

John Adams was a greatly respected American. But he was not loved as Washington was. And he was not especially popular. While he was President, he had to make a decision that made him even less popular. But it was the right decision for the country.

An Old Problem

The problem actually began while Washington was still President. Those old enemies, France and Great Britain, were back at war again. During our War for Independence, France had been America's best friend. The French navy and army had made possible the victory at Yorktown, which ended the war.

Now the French thought it was America's turn to help them fight against Great Britain. Some Americans agreed. They were even more in favor of France because the French people had just had a revolution of their own. They had overthrown their king and set up a republic. Many of the Americans who wanted to help France were Democratic-Republicans. Other Americans, though, thought the United States should side with Great Britain. Those people were usually Federalists. President Washington decided that the United States must remain neutral, which means it would not take sides. It would stay out of the fighting. Even when the British navy began to seize American ships carrying goods to France, the President was determined to keep the United States out of war. He knew that the young nation needed time to grow and become stronger. He feared that

By the time John Adams became President, there were 16 states.

talk to the Americans. The Americans returned empty-handed and angry.

When others heard their story, they became angry, too. "Millions for defense," they shouted, "but not one cent for **tribute!**" Some leading Federalists, especially Alexander Hamilton, wanted to go to war against France right then and there. Congress created a navy department and paid for building a number of ships. It looked like war for sure.

A Tough Decision

President Adams knew that war would make him popular. But like President Washington before him, he also knew that the young republic needed peace. He decided he must try once more to keep the peace. He sent a new ambassador to France. This time the French government talked with the American ambassador, and the two reached an agreement.

war might destroy the modern world's first great experiment with republican government.

John Adams also believed it was important to keep the United States out of war. However, by the time he became President, that was becoming even more difficult. The reason was that by then, the French navy had also started to seize the ships of American merchants. At the same time, the French government was threatening the United States. President Adams hoped to keep America at peace. He sent three personal representatives to France to get the French to stop. But the French officials they met insisted on a bribe before they would even

President Adams had done the right thing. He had kept America out of war.

But in doing so, he lost a lot of popular support. Federalists who wanted war turned against him. Democratic-Republicans weren't going to support him anyway. When Adams ran for reelection to the presidency, he lost. The new President was none other than the leader of the Democratic-Republicans, Thomas Jefferson.

ederal City Here is a puzzler to stump your friends with: What do the following cities have in common—Philadelphia, Pennsylvania; Lancaster, Pennsylvania; York, Pennsylvania; Princeton, New Jersey; Trenton, New Jersey; Annapolis, Maryland; and New York, New York?

The answer is that each was once the capital of the United States of America. Several served as the capital while the Second Continental Congress was running the War for Independence. Several others served during the days of the Articles of Confederation. In each of those cities today you will find a historical marker proudly stating that it was once the capital. The truth is, though, that when the central government was weak and unimportant, none of those places cared much one way or the other about being the capital.

However, once the new Constitution set up a strong national government, people cared very much about its location. New York, where President Washington took the oath of office, was just a temporary capital. The Constitution expected that a state, or several states, would

give the new government a chunk of land for a permanent capital. Several states offered land. They wanted to have the capital nearby.

In 1790, Congress accepted an offer of land from Maryland and Virginia. The land was just about in the middle of the states that then made up the United States. Congress also made Philadelphia the temporary capital for the next ten years, while the new capital was being built.

It was left up to President Washington to choose the exact piece of land, which was to be called the Territory of Columbia. (It is now known as the District of Columbia.) The President selected a site just across the Potomac River from his own home at Mount Vernon. The plan was for the government

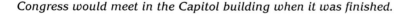

Congress would meet in the Capitol building when it was finished.

buildings to be located in one part of the District. That part would be known as the Federal City or the City of Washington. Later on, it all came to be known as Washington, District of Columbia, or D.C.

Designing the City

President Washington hired a well-known **surveyor,** Andrew Ellicott, to map out the area. Ellicott needed a scientific assistant for this work, someone who knew a lot about mathematics. The man he chose was a self-taught African American named Benjamin Banneker. Together, Ellicott and Banneker surveyed the District, noting every feature of the land.

Pierre L'Enfant shows his plan for the Federal City to President George Washington.

To design the Federal City, President Washington hired an engineer named Pierre L'Enfant (pyer lahn FAHN). He was a French army officer who came to America in 1776 and fought with the American army. He first met George Washington at Valley Forge.

L'Enfant was a brilliant engineer and **architect** (AHR kuh tekt). Unfortunately, he had a terrible temper. And he always had to have his way. This got him in trouble with a lot of people—including Washington and Jefferson. He lasted on the job less than a year before he was fired.

During that year, though, L'Enfant used Ellicott and Banneker's survey to lay out the basic plan for the city of Washington. He adopted Jefferson's idea for a grid system for the city's streets. A grid system looks like the lines on a checkerboard. Then he added several broad avenues that spread out from the center, like spokes on a wheel. His plan set aside spaces for the main government buildings. The Capitol would be set on a hill (*Capitol* is the building where the members of the Senate and the House of Representatives meet. *Capital* is the city). The "President's Palace" was to be located on lower ground, with a fine view of the Potomac River. (The President's Palace was later called the President's House, and still later simply the White House.) L'Enfant also reserved open spaces for parks, monuments, and fountains. It was a beautiful plan.

Designing the Buildings

After L'Enfant left, the government decided to hold contests for the best designs for the Capitol and for the

> **vocabulary**
> **surveyor** one who measures the size, shape, length, and width of a piece of land
> **architect** one who designs buildings

President's Palace. It turned out that the winners presented handsome drawings of what the buildings should look like, but they didn't know how to draw up the actual construction plans. Before those buildings came to look like they do today, many other people would contribute their ideas, and many more years would pass.

Nevertheless, by 1800 those buildings, and several others, were ready enough to be used. So in that year, right on schedule, the government moved from Philadelphia to its new home. Washington looked nothing like the beautiful city it is today. Most of the District of Columbia remained what it had been—a wilderness area of trees and swamps.

A few people had bought land in the part known as the Federal City or Washington and built homes, boarding houses, and other places of business. They were looking ahead to the time when the government would move there. But the buildings were far apart, and there were tree stumps everywhere. None of the roads were paved, so when the rains came, you can just imagine what they were like.

An Uncomfortable Home

President Adams and his family moved into the President's House in November 1800. We don't have to guess what the Adams family thought about their new home, for we have the letters that Abigail Adams, the President's wife, wrote to members of her family. Abigail Adams reported that on the day they arrived, not a single room had been completely finished. In some, the plaster walls were still damp. The main staircase to the second floor was also unfinished. Abigail Adams turned one of the large

unfinished rooms into a laundry room where the family wash was hung to dry.

This was before the days of furnaces, so people depended on fireplaces for warmth. There was a fireplace in each room of the President's House to take the chill off and keep the house dry. That was fine, but nobody had thought to supply firewood. It turned out that the President was responsible for supplying his own. There was also no well for water, so servants had to carry water from a distance of five city blocks.

Still, Abigail Adams found much to like about the house. She could see its possibilities, as she could see the possibilities for the young republic. Unfinished? Yes. They both were. But Abigail was sure the new house, like the new nation, would become great. She knew this house was not built for a year or a decade. She wrote to her sister, "This House is built for ages to come."

Abigail Adams found the White House a difficult place in which to live.

An Unusual Person Here's another puzzler for you: Soon after Thomas Jefferson became President, all of the following lived in the White House: an architect, a lawyer, a scholar, an inventor, an author of books, a scientific farmer, and a politician. How many people lived in the White House?

The answer is one—Thomas Jefferson. You see, Jefferson was all those things. Like his countryman, Benjamin Franklin, Jefferson was a man of endless curiosity. He was a **philosopher.** He owned more than 6,500 books, on almost every subject imaginable.

Like Franklin, Jefferson applied a scientific approach to everything. All his life he recorded his observations of the weather, the stars, and the world of nature around him. On his plantation he continually experimented to discover which plants and trees from around the world would grow well in Virginia. He even wrote a book about his state's animal and plant life and its geography.

While still in his early twenties, Jefferson designed and supervised the construction of his home and of everything in it, right down to the furniture and curtains.

> **vocabulary**
> **philosopher** one who seeks wisdom; a thinker

The house sits on a mountain top in western Virginia, so Jefferson called it *Monticello,* which is Italian for "little mountain." Over the years he invented many gadgets for Monticello that still delight the thousands who visit there each year. Later, Jefferson designed the campus and first buildings of the University of Virginia.

Jefferson's main interest, though, was in making life better for all. He believed that "the pursuit of happiness" was only possible when the rights and freedoms of ordinary people were protected. And this was only

possible when they governed themselves. Jefferson's faith in ordinary people, though, came with one very big condition: the people must be educated. An ignorant and uneducated people would never remain free for long. Years before Jefferson became President, he tried to get his state of Virginia to provide free education for all. But this idea was too advanced for people at that time. Jefferson's attempt was unsuccessful.

Sadly, Jefferson also failed to persuade his state to accept another of his ideas. Jefferson viewed slavery as evil. He tried to get Virginia to pass a law that children born to slaves would be automatically free at birth. This plan for gradually ending slavery is one of the great "might have beens" in our history. Just think of how many millions would have enjoyed freedom if all states had adopted such a law. Just think how our nation could have been spared the pain of a terrible civil war over slavery. It was not to be.

Yet Jefferson himself owned many slaves, as nearly every well-to-do southern family did. Jefferson had an interesting exchange of letters on the subject of slavery with Benjamin Banneker, the man who helped

survey the Federal City. Banneker reminded Jefferson of his own words in the Declaration of Independence—that all men are created equal, and that one of their unalienable rights is liberty. Why then, Banneker asked, was slavery allowed to continue? And how could Jefferson himself continue to hold slaves?

In his reply, Jefferson agreed that slavery was wrong. He said that Banneker himself was proof that black Americans could achieve much, if given their freedom. But he had no good answers to Banneker's questions, especially about his own slaves. Those questions troubled Jefferson to the end of his days.

Mr. President

This is the man who prepared to take the office of President of the United States on March 4, 1801. That morning, Jefferson rose early as usual, wrote letters, and read in his room at a Washington, D.C., boardinghouse. He had breakfast with the other guests, as he had done for many days before. He was dressed in a plain suit, like those worn by plain citizens.

Shortly before noon, Thomas Jefferson stepped out of the boardinghouse, where he was met by a small group of officials. Together they walked briskly through the muddy streets to the Capitol, where Jefferson would take the oath of office. No elegant uniform. No special badges. No ceremonial sword at his side. No elegant horse-drawn coach to carry him. No big parade. That was Thomas Jefferson.

The soil around Monticello was heavy with clay. Jefferson invented this plow to make farming easier.

That was Jefferson's White House, too. All visitors were treated the same. The British ambassador was offended that the President of the United States greeted him in slippers. At dinner, there was no special seating plan for guests. The first ones to the table, whoever they might be, could sit next to the President if they wished. When Jefferson had to go anywhere outside the President's House, he rode on horseback by himself—no splendid presidential coach, no guards. President Jefferson did these things because he wanted to make a point. In a republic, all are equal. No one should have privileges above anyone else.

The Louisiana Purchase

President Jefferson and the members of his Democratic-Republican party in Congress quickly changed many of the laws the Federalists had made. They got rid of the hated whiskey tax. They cut government spending. For example, they reduced the size of the army and the navy.

Jefferson had planned to make all those changes when he became President, so no one was surprised by them. His greatest achievement, however, was one he hadn't planned on at all. In fact, it came about through an incredible stroke of luck. Because he acted quickly when this lucky situation arose, President Jefferson was able to double the size of the United States.

Back in the 1700s, France had once claimed all the land between the Mississippi River and the Rocky Mountains. France called this area Louisiana, after King Louis of France. After one of its wars with Great Britain, France gave Louisiana to Spain.

To American farmers who lived in the West, the most important part of Louisiana

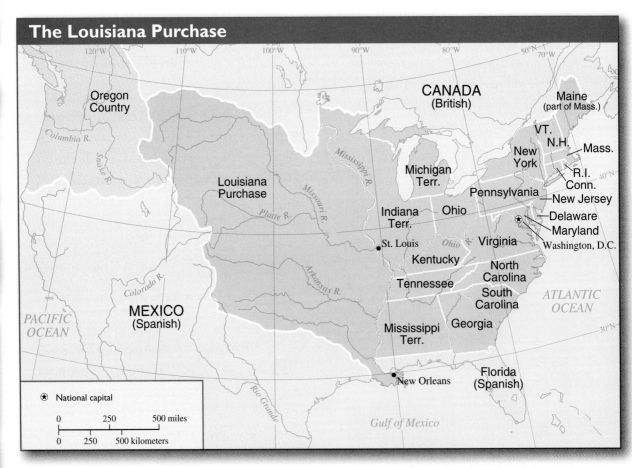

The Louisiana Purchase doubled the size of the new nation.

was the port city of New Orleans, near the mouth of the Mississippi River. When you look at a map, you see why. If you are a western farmer growing corn or wheat, how do you send your crops to markets in the eastern cities or in Europe? Not by wagon. That would be far too expensive. You put them on rafts and floated them down rivers. All the rivers in that part of the country eventually flow into the Mississippi River. So New Orleans would be the end of the line for your crops. There you would sell them to a merchant, who would then put them on ships bound for the eastern cities, or Europe, or perhaps the West Indies.

This cartoon celebrated the Louisiana Purchase on its 100th anniversary.

What would happen, though, if the country that owned New Orleans stopped allowing Americans to use it? American farmers would not be able to get their crops to market. They would go broke.

In 1802, it looked like that might happen. Spain suddenly announced that western farmers could no longer use New Orleans. Even worse, President Jefferson learned that Spain had secretly given back all of Louisiana, including New Orleans, to France. Jefferson knew that the French emperor, Napoleon Bonaparte (nuh POH lee un BOH nuh pahrt), wanted to build a new empire in the Americas. This was serious trouble.

Jefferson sent two representatives to France and instructed them to offer $10 million for New Orleans. Here is where luck entered the picture. You remember how France and Great Britain were always going to war against each other. Well, they were about to do that again. France needed money. Also, Napoleon had given up his ideas about starting a new French empire in North America.

When the American representatives offered France $10 million for New Orleans, they were amazed by France's reply. No, said the French, we're not interested in selling New Orleans by itself. But if you'd like to buy all of the Louisiana Territory, including New Orleans, for $15 million, we can make a deal.

The Americans quickly accepted. The Louisiana Purchase, as it was called, doubled America's territories at a cost of a few pennies an acre. It was the biggest bargain in American history.

Neither Jefferson nor anyone else knew exactly what he had bought. No one could know that until explorers went to see for themselves. They soon did. But that is a story for another time.

ar in Europe You won't be surprised to learn that soon after the Louisiana Purchase, France and Britain were at war again. Once again the United States was determined not to get involved. That was very hard to do.

The United States, you see, had already become an important trading nation. Both France and Great Britain were eager to buy our goods. That was fine with us. But each side wanted to keep the other from buying our goods. And that wasn't so fine with us. France said it would seize any ship trading with Great Britain. And Great Britain said it would seize any ship trading with France. Soon the British and the French navies were taking turns capturing American ships. Great Britain's navy was larger, so it seized the most ships.

That was bad enough. But the British also did something worse. Sometimes they took American sailors right off American merchant ships and forced them to serve in the British navy. Why would the British want Americans to serve in their navy? The reason was that being a sailor on a British naval ship was no picnic. Conditions were terrible, and captains were often cruel. A lot of sailors took any opportunity to desert, or run away. As a result, the British navy was always short of sailors.

Many of those British deserters took jobs on American merchant ships. The British captains wanted to get those men back. Can you see what is coming? The British navy began stopping American merchant ships to search for these deserters. Sometimes by accident and sometimes on purpose, the British carried off American as well as British seamen. No matter—all were forced to serve in the British navy. This practice was called *impressment*.

You can imagine how angry Americans were about impressment. They demanded that their government do something. Even if it meant war.

War was the last thing that President Jefferson wanted. There must be some other way to make Britain and France stop seizing our ships and our seamen, he thought. The idea he hit upon was this: stop trading. Stop trading altogether. Don't allow any ships—neither ours nor any other country's—to leave American ports and don't permit any ships to enter them.

Such a complete stopping of trade is called an **embargo.** Jefferson proposed that the embargo would continue until Great Britain and France agreed to leave our ships

> **vocabulary**
> **embargo** a government order forbidding trading ships to enter or leave a nation's ports

alone. You see, Jefferson believed that those countries needed American trade so badly that they would have to agree to stop seizing our ships. Congress thought the idea was a good one, and the embargo began.

American sailors are forced to board a British ship.

Jefferson didn't expect what happened. The embargo wound up hurting Americans more than it hurt Great Britain and France. American merchants couldn't sell their goods. Farmers couldn't sell their crops. Shipbuilders lost business. Sailors lost jobs. Americans hated the embargo. And worst of all, Great Britain and France did not promise to change.

The embargo was a failure. After one year, Congress repealed—in other words, canceled—the embargo law. Ships once again entered and left American ports. The British and French went right back to seizing American ships, and the British impressed American sailors again. Nothing had changed.

Madison for Peace

By this time, Thomas Jefferson's term had ended and a new President was in the White House: James Madison.

People were already calling him the Father of the Constitution because of his contributions to the Constitutional Convention. He had served in the Congress for many years. He had helped get the Bill of Rights added to the Constitution. He had helped Thomas Jefferson form the Democratic-Republican party. He had served as Jefferson's secretary of state.

As President, Madison was no more successful than Jefferson had been in dealing with Great Britain and France. Once, France tricked him into believing that they would leave our ships alone. Madison wanted so badly to believe the French that even after everyone else saw they were not keeping their word, Madison still said they were.

Americans were angry at France, but they were especially angry at Great Britain. Great Britain was not only seizing our ships but also impressing our seamen. They were angry for another reason, too. In the Northwest Territory, Native Americans were attacking American settlements, killing some settlers and driving away others. Why should Americans blame Great Britain for that? Because the Native Americans were getting their guns from the British government in Canada. Some westerners said the only way to stop the attacks was to drive the British out of Canada.

In Congress there was more and more talk about war with Great Britain. Some said the United States must defend its honor against the British navy. There were even people who wanted the United States to have Canada for itself and were willing to go to war to get it.

James Madison was reluctant to have the United States declare war on Great Britain.

Congressmen who talked this way became known as the War Hawks. Most of them were younger men. They had not fought in the American Revolution. Some had not even been born by then. They didn't know—at least not from their own experience—how terrible war can be. To them, war was all about glory. They were eager to fight. It would all be so easy, they thought. Why, the Kentucky militia could take Canada all by itself, said one of them. (He was from Kentucky, of course!)

War Is Declared

Older Americans like James Madison knew more about war. They really hoped to avoid it. But in the end, the pressure from his own party was too much for President Madison. In 1812 he asked Congress to declare war against Great Britain. Congress quickly did. Those who opposed the war called it "Mr. Madison's war."

You might think that if a country plans to go to war, it would at least prepare for it. The United States, though, was almost completely unprepared. There we were, talking about taking on the British navy with its 600 ships, while we had only 16. There we were, talking about driving the British out of Canada while we had only 7,000 soldiers.

It's not surprising, then, that at first things did not go well for Americans in the West. American troops not only failed to take Canada but also were forced to surrender some American land.

Then came a big surprise: America's first victory came on the water rather than on the land. The United States had a small fleet on Lake Erie, one of the Great Lakes. Great Britain had a larger one. The American fleet was commanded by Oliver H. Perry. Perry was only 28 years old, but he had served in the navy since he was 14. In September 1813, Perry's fleet defeated a British naval force on Lake Erie, forcing it to surrender. Perry then sent this message to the American general in the region: "We have met the enemy and they are ours."

The Burning of Washington

The next year, 1814, started out badly for the Americans. Great Britain's main enemy had always been France, and in 1814 the French armies surrendered to the British. That was not good news for the United States. It meant that the British could now turn their full attention to those upstart Americans.

That summer a British fleet sailed into Chesapeake Bay in Maryland with several thousand troops. Their mission was to destroy the American capital city, Washington.

Residents of Washington fled into the countryside, ahead of the arrival of the British troops. But Dolley Madison, the wife of the President, coolly remained at the White House until she had arranged to save important government records and a fine painting of George Washington. Only then did she and the last of the White House guards leave—just hours before the redcoats arrived!

When British soldiers burst into the empty White House, they found a dinner that had been prepared for the Madisons. British officers enjoyed the fine food. Then the troops went through the place, destroying everything in their path. Finally, they set fire to the White House, the Capitol, and many other government buildings. The next day a hurricane hit Washington, adding to the damage. Luckily, a heavy rainstorm put out most of the fires.

From Washington the British marched on to Baltimore. At the same time, the British fleet bombarded Fort McHenry, at the entrance to Baltimore's harbor. The attack lasted all day and all night, but the Americans held out. That was the attack that led Francis Scott Key to write our national anthem, the "Star-Spangled Banner."

O say, can you see,
by the dawn's early light,
What so proudly we hail'd
at the twilight's last gleaming?
Whose broad stripes and
bright stars,
thro' the perilous fight,
O'er the ramparts we watch'd,
were so gallantly streaming?
And the rockets' red glare,
the bombs bursting in air,
Gave proof thro' the night
that our flag was still there.
O say, does that star-spangled
banner yet wave
O'er the land of the free
and the home of the brave?

Dolley Madison is honored on a U.S. dollar coin for her actions when the British set fire to government buildings in Washington, D.C.

The Battle of New Orleans

Near the end of 1814, the British tried to capture the city of New Orleans, at the mouth of the Mississippi River. A British fleet landed 7,500 soldiers near the city. General Andrew Jackson, commanding a tough band of 5,000 militia and frontiersmen, was waiting to meet them.

Pirates also helped to defend New Orleans. Jean Lafitte was the leader of a band of pirates. Lafitte persuaded General Jackson to use his men and their cannons against the British.

The last attack of the battle began on January 8, 1815. Wave after wave of redcoats attacked the American defenses. Each wave was thrown back, with heavy losses to the British. After the defeat, the British retreated to their ships and left.

The War Is Over

The Battle of New Orleans was the final battle of the War of 1812—in fact, it actually took place *after* the war officially ended. News traveled so slowly in those days that the warring armies didn't know that the two sides had signed a peace treaty two weeks earlier!

In that peace treaty, each side kept the same territory it had had before the war. So one way of looking at the outcome of the war is to say that neither side won.

That's true. Neither side did win. But the Americans did have some gains to show for it all. They had shown themselves and the world that even if they couldn't defeat mighty Great Britain, they could certainly hold their own. In addition, the British stopped providing guns to the Native Americans in the West, and that was one of the goals of the United States. So all in all, the United States could feel satisfied with the outcome of the war.

Many battles were fought near or on the Great Lakes.

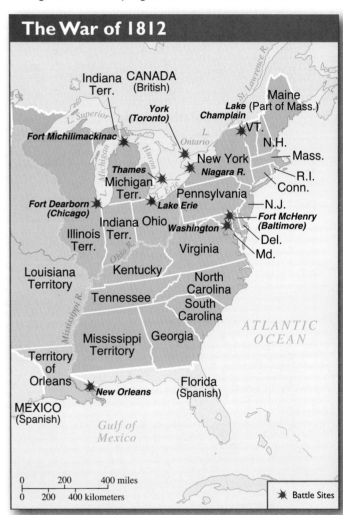

The War of 1812

ames Monroe Have you noticed that, except for John Adams of Massachusetts, all of America's early Presidents came from the state of Virginia? The man who followed James Madison in the presidency was still another Virginian. His name was James Monroe.

Monroe was the last President to come from the generation that had taken part in the birth of our nation. Like those other Virginian Presidents, he came from a well-to-do family. He was a college student when fighting broke out between the colonies and Great Britain. He promptly left his studies and joined General Washington's army. He fought in a number of important battles.

After the war, Monroe studied law and then held a number of important jobs in the national government. He was one of the people President Jefferson sent to France to buy Louisiana. He later served as Madison's secretary of state.

There was a lot about James Monroe that seemed old-fashioned. He even dressed in an old-fashioned way, wearing knee pants long after most men had switched to trousers. He wore shoes with silver buckles, which had gone out of style many years before.

Still, people seemed to like James Monroe. Perhaps they felt comfortable with him. Perhaps it was because he didn't lecture them. Like those earlier Presidents, he knew a lot about farming. Like them, he loved books and learning. And like them, he believed in duty to his community and his country. Also, everyone agreed that he was as honest as the day is long. That's a lot of things to like about a person.

James Monroe may have been old-fashioned in his dress but he was up-to-date in his thinking.

When Monroe ran for reelection in 1820, no one ran against him. However, that wasn't just because he was well-liked. It was because of an important change in the political parties. The Federalists had not won an election

Andrew Jackson led the troops into Pensacola, which was then a part of Spanish Florida.

since John Adams was President, before 1800. Over the years, the Federalist party had become less and less popular. Many Federalists had opposed the War of 1812, and some even sounded like they'd be happier if the union of states broke up.

That's not a good way to win elections. When Monroe ran for his first term, the Federalist party wasn't able to offer much opposition. By the time he ran for a second term, the Federalist party was no more.

Spain Loses Power and Colonies

Spain once had the largest colonial empire in the world. The Spanish had controlled all of Central America, nearly all of South America, and a big chunk of North America as well. But those days were long gone by now. In the 1800s, Spain was a weak nation. Nearly all its colonies in the Americas were overthrowing Spanish rule.

Spain still claimed Florida, but it had only a handful of settlements there, and it was

clear there would never be more. Most of Florida was home to the Seminoles, a large group of Native Americans. Sometimes Seminoles would cross the border into the state of Georgia and raid Georgians' farms. The Spanish government had promised to prevent those raids, but it didn't have nearly enough soldiers in Florida to do so. Slaveholders in southern states were also upset. Their slaves often ran away to Florida, and because Florida wasn't part of the United States, they couldn't get them back.

After another Seminole raid into Georgia, President Monroe sent General Andrew Jackson to deal with them. Jackson's army pursued the Seminoles into Florida, battled them, and burned their villages and crops. Jackson also marched into several of the Spanish forts and took them over.

General Jackson had gone much farther than he was supposed to, and Spain protested. President Monroe ordered Jackson to pull his forces out of Florida. But by then everyone could see how weak Spain was. America knew that Spain could not hope to hang on to Florida. Spain knew it, too.

Monroe's secretary of state was John Quincy Adams, son of the second President of the United States. Adams offered Spain $5 million for Florida, and Spain accepted. In 1821, Florida was officially added to the ever-growing United States.

By that time, nearly all of Spain's colonies had won their independence. Many of these newly independent nations, such as Argentina and Bolivia in South America, looked to the United States as an example of how to set up new governments. They wrote constitutions that used many of the same ideas, and even some of the same words, as the Constitution of the United States. That made Americans feel good. It's always a nice feeling when someone wants to imitate you. For their part, North Americans were enthusiastic about independence in South America. They even named some towns after newly liberated

South American countries—for example, Peru, Illinois; and Chile, New York.

Some European countries, though, were not happy about this. They didn't want their own colonies getting ideas about independence. Perhaps, they thought, the best way to keep that from happening would be to help Spain get back its South American colonies.

Now it was America's turn to be unhappy. President Monroe and Secretary of State Adams wanted each new nation to shape its own future. They believed it was important for the United States to take a strong stand against any interference in the Americas from European countries.

So in 1823, President Monroe declared that European countries must not try to regain control of Spain's colonies. The United States was not interfering in Europe's affairs, said Monroe, so Europe should not interfere with the affairs of the Western Hemisphere. President Monroe's message to Europe was sweet and simple: Hands off! This policy became known as the Monroe Doctrine.

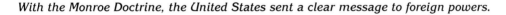

With the Monroe Doctrine, the United States sent a clear message to foreign powers.

President John Quincy Adams

You'll remember that the only party left by this time was the Democratic-Republican party, or just the Republican party, as it was usually called. The Federalist party had died. Don't think for a minute, though, that there weren't any more contests for the presidency. In 1824 there were four candidates for the presidency. Two of them were Andrew Jackson and John Quincy Adams. The election was very close, but Adams won, even though many of Jackson's supporters charged—wrongly—that he had won unfairly.

John Quincy Adams certainly was well trained for the presidency. His parents, John and Abigail Adams, saw to it that he was well educated. He could translate Greek, and he could speak French. When he was only 14 years old, he was already serving his country as a secretary to the United States ambassador to Russia. After that, he continued to serve his country in one important job after another. As you have read, he was President Monroe's secretary of state.

During all those years, and as President too, John Quincy Adams followed a daily routine. He rose at 5:00 A.M. He built a fire in the fireplace, read his Bible, and then went out to the Potomac River and bathed. After that, he was ready to start his workday.

Adams was very bright, hardworking, and honest. Like his father, he believed in doing what was right, not just what was popular. And he had many good ideas, like building a national university and better roads to tie the nation together.

Unfortunately, he was unable to get support for them. Partly that was because many members of Congress were still supporters of Andrew Jackson and opposed anything that Adams wanted. Partly it was because other

Even though they were political enemies, President Adams (left) and Andrew Jackson (center) would meet socially.

congressmen just did not agree with his ideas. And partly it was because John Quincy Adams did not believe the President should try to persuade members of Congress to follow him. He believed the President should just present his ideas, and then it was up to Congress to consider them. But that's really not the way to be a successful President.

Even if Adams had tried to persuade members of Congress to support his ideas, he probably would not have been good at it. He was not an easy man to warm up to. It may have been all right for George Washington to be that way, but John Quincy Adams was not George Washington. Besides, the times had changed since Washington's day, as you will soon learn. Presidents could no longer be chilly and expect to be successful.

So even though John Quincy Adams had great training and great ability, he did not become a great President. Like his father, he was unable to get reelected. When he ran for a second term, he was again opposed by Andrew Jackson. This time, Jackson won.

Different President "I never saw anything like it before," wrote an amazed United States senator. Neither had anyone else. The senator was writing about the crowds in Washington, D.C., on March 4, 1829. That was the day Andrew Jackson took the oath of office as President of the United States.

Twenty thousand Americans—farmers, frontier people, ordinary folks from towns and countryside—had flocked to the capital to witness the event. And to celebrate, too. After Jackson took the oath at the Capitol, the crowds followed him to the White House. In they went, walking across the carpeted floors in muddy boots, standing on chairs and furniture to get a good look at their President. Dishes were broken and punch bowls were knocked over as people helped themselves to refreshments. A woman who was there reported later that "those who got in could not get out by the door again, but had to scramble out the windows."

President Jackson himself had to escape by a side door and spend his first night as President at a hotel. Someone finally got an idea for getting the crowd to leave the White House. They carried the tubs of punch out to the lawn, and the people followed.

What happened at the White House that day was a result of an important change that had taken place in the United States. The American people had long been choosing representatives to make their laws and to carry them out. In the early years, however, only adult white males who owned property could vote.

Thousands came to celebrate with the new President.

Election Day has been important throughout our history, and by the 1820s more people could vote.

Rise of the Common Man

As time went on, Americans began to ask why it should be necessary to own property to vote. If all men are created equal, why shouldn't all have the right to vote, whether they own property or not? Those questions were part of a larger democratic spirit that had been sweeping America since the early 1800s.

Where did this new democratic spirit come from? Partly from the West. People who moved to the frontier were used to relying on themselves, and on neighbors like them. They were used to making their own decisions. They expected to make decisions about who would serve in their governments.

The new democratic spirit also came from eastern cities. Many workers in the cities did not have much money or property, but they felt they should have as much say in government as property owners did.

As a result, by the late 1820s, except in a handful of states, the laws were changed so that *all* adult white males could vote, whether they owned property or not. This change has been called "the rise of the common man."

Of course if only white males could vote, that still left out a lot of people. It left out women. It left out Native Americans. It left out African Americans—although five states did allow free black Americans to vote. With all those people left out, the changes of the early 1800s don't seem so great today. In fact, though, they were a big step toward greater democracy in America. There was more democracy in the United States than in any other country in the world.

Along with the growth of democracy came a spirit of equality. Americans believed that every person was as good as the next. Earlier, when Americans voted for their representatives in government, they usually chose people who were well educated and owned property. Those were the people who were considered leaders. Now, though, they began to ask why ordinary Americans like themselves couldn't do just as good a job running the country.

When voting for President, they no longer looked for philosophers, like Thomas Jefferson or James Madison. They wanted a person who had things in common with themselves. They liked the idea of a President who had started life as a common person.

For many Americans, Andrew Jackson was just such a person. He was born in a log cabin on the frontier. His father died two months before he was born, and his mother died when he was just 14. Andrew had to make his own way in life. He had little schooling. As an adult, however, he became a lawyer. (In those days, there were no special law schools. You could become a lawyer by studying for a while with someone who was already a lawyer.) Jackson also served as a judge and was a member of Congress for a short time. He bought a lot of land in Tennessee and raised tobacco and cotton.

Most Americans, though, knew Andrew Jackson as a soldier. They remembered him as a hero in the Battle of New Orleans. And they had cheered when General Jackson helped the United States gain Florida. Andrew Jackson was the first President from the West. Ordinary Americans thought of Jackson as one of them. They felt close enough to call him Andy or to refer to him by his nickname, Old Hickory —a fitting name since the hickory tree was the hardest and strongest of the woods of Tennessee. (For many years, baseball bats were made of hickory.) Can you imagine anyone calling President Washington "Georgie" or President Jefferson "Tommy" or some other nickname? So you see, those thousands of people who filled Washington, D.C., to celebrate Jackson's victory were also celebrating their own triumph.

Jackson returned to his home in Tennessee after his presidency.

Jackson and Native Americans

Jackson was a successful President in many ways. But his treatment of Native Americans was awful. In this, though, he was probably reflecting the attitudes of most white Americans of the times.

Although most eastern Native Americans had already been forced to move west across the Mississippi River, a number of tribes remained in the East. White settlers wanted their land for farming, and Jackson and Congress were determined that they should have it.

In 1830, Congress passed the Indian Removal Act. This law allowed the federal government to force the remaining Native Americans out of the eastern United States. They had to move to land set aside for them in present-day Oklahoma.

Some Native Americans resisted, but the United States Army was too much for them. Finally, they moved. By the time Andrew Jackson left the presidency, nearly all Native Americans had been forced to move west of the Mississippi River. You will read more about that next year. For now, we can simply say that this was not a proud page in the history of the United States.

Washington, John Adams, Jefferson, Madison, Monroe, John Quincy Adams, and Jackson: these were America's first Presidents. In personality they differed greatly, some as much as night and day. They were not all from the same political party. They did not all favor the same programs. They did not all share the same vision of what America of the future should be. But these seven Presidents were alike in several important ways. Each was dedicated to helping the new country grow and to helping its people prosper. Each did everything he could to make the country safe from possible enemies. Each was determined to bring success to the world's first great experiment in republican government. In all these ways, they succeeded. The United States was fortunate to have their leadership.

The Cherokees, forced from their homeland, had to leave behind homes, farms, and stores.

Glossary

administration a group making up the executive branch in a presidential government; also its term of office

architect one who designs buildings

embargo a government order forbidding trading ships to enter or leave a nation's ports

frontier the border region between settled areas and unsettled wilderness

philosopher one who seeks wisdom; a thinker

precedent an example to follow in the future

ratify to give formal approval to

surveyor one who measures the size, shape, length, and width of a piece of land

tribute a payment by one nation to another as the price of peace

American Reformers

Contents

Springtime of Reform

aking Life Better How can we make life better for people less fortunate than ourselves? Chances are you have heard that question many times—at home, at school, or perhaps at your family's place of worship. You've probably thought a lot about it. Maybe you've shared your ideas on that subject with others.

Did you know, though, that that question is a very American question? It doesn't mean that only Americans are concerned about the less fortunate. That would be a silly thing to say. No, what it means is this: before you even bother to ask such a question, you first have to believe that things can be made better. You have to believe that the lives of people can be improved. Otherwise there would be no point in asking *how* it can be done, would there?

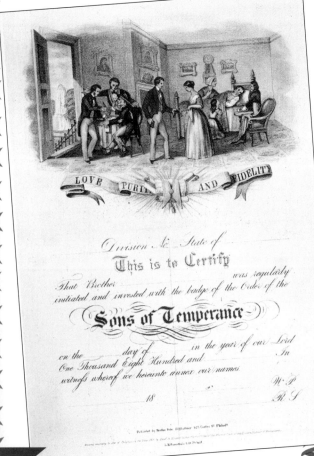

And that's what makes the question so very American. Americans have always been interested in trying to improve things and make life better for more people—and that's also what reform is all about. About progress. About making lives better for more and more people.

A reform is an attempt to change society for the better. People who spend a lot of time and effort trying to make things better are called reformers. Someone once said, "Scratch an American and you will find a reformer." Can you figure out what is meant by that?

There have always been reformers in America, but there have been more at some times in our history than at others. During the time you are reading about right now, the 1830s and 1840s, reformers were especially active. In this land of growing democracy and equality, Americans believed that everything was possible.

Thousands of Americans took part in reform movements. Many of the reformers were inspired by their strong religious faith. They believed they could help individuals change their behavior and become better

Many young men, seeing the dangers of alcohol, signed pledges promising to limit how much they would drink in the future.

persons. They believed they could help the less fortunate by bringing the sad facts of their situation to the attention of citizens of good will. They believed they could make life more fair by changing attitudes and changing laws. And they believed that by doing all these things, they would make the United States a better country.

The Temperance Movement

One group of reformers was concerned about people who drank too much liquor. You probably know that there are many Americans today with drinking problems. Believe it or not, it was even worse in the early 1800s. Americans then drank *three times* as much alcohol per person as they do today. A lot of people then had the notion that liquor was good for them. Some started the day with a glass of whiskey before breakfast! Instead of the coffee breaks we take in the mid-morning and mid-afternoon, they took whiskey breaks.

Most of the heavy drinkers were grown men, but a large number were teenagers. On the frontier, women also drank heavily. Drinking ruined many a home and many a life. It contributed to poverty, and it contributed to crime.

This heavy drinking gave rise to one of the important reform movements of that time, the temperance movement. *Temperance* means "drinking little alcohol, or none at all." Reformers believed that if people would give up alcohol, they would improve their own lives and save their families from pain and poverty as well.

Children who joined the Cold Water Army signed a pledge and recited a poem, shown on this poster. The Cold Water Army was a powerful weapon of the temperance movement.

Reformers used many methods to carry their message to people. They wrote songs, put on plays, handed out pamphlets, and delivered sermons in church. They organized huge parades of children who carried banners begging grownups to give up drink. (Reformers called the children who paraded the Cold Water Army. Can you see why?) Reformers also got drinkers to sign a pledge, or promise, that they would cut out or at least cut down on their drinking. More than a million people took the pledge.

The temperance movement was very successful. In just ten years, Americans were drinking less than half as much alcohol as before. As the years passed, it is true that a number of people who signed the pledge went right back to drinking. That's probably not surprising, but what is more important is that a great many did not.

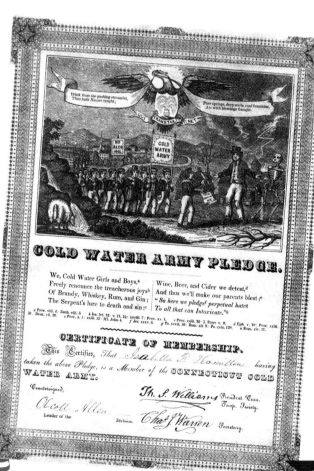

Dorothea Dix Temperance reformers tried to improve people's lives by getting them to change their own behavior. Other reformers tried to help the insane and mentally ill. Those reformers believed that others would do something to help if they only knew about the sad conditions in which the mentally ill lived.

Dorothea Dix was one of those reformers. She worked very hard to get kinder treatment for the insane and mentally ill. Dorothea Dix hadn't always been a reformer. She started teaching school in Boston at the age of 14— you could do that in those days. After working for 25 years, she became ill and had to stop. Soon after, a friend asked if she could teach a Sunday-school class for women prisoners in the East Cambridge jail, near Boston.

Dix went. What she saw changed her life. Of course she had expected to find women charged with committing crimes, and she did. But she was completely unprepared to find mentally ill and insane inmates, clothed in rags and kept in a single filthy and unheated room.

These people had committed no crime. They were simply ill. In those days there were no effective treatments for mental illness. Most towns and cities just wanted to get mentally ill people out of the way. A few states had hospitals which were called **asylums**. Massachusetts was one of them, thanks to the efforts of a reformer named Horace Mann. (You'll be meeting Horace Mann again when you read about another important reform.) But the Massachusetts hospital was a small one. Most states just put the mentally ill in jails or in almshouses, which were places where the extremely poor were sent to live. Often they were just locked up and forgotten. Their "keepers" often treated them with great cruelty.

A Life's Work

Dorothea Dix was so upset that Sunday morning in 1841, she spent the rest of her life working to improve conditions for the mentally ill. She started by visiting jails and almshouses all over her state. Dix took careful notes on the conditions she found. In one of her notebooks she wrote that people were held "in *cages, closets, cellars, stalls, pens!*" "*They were chained naked, beaten with rods,* and *lashed* [whipped] into obedience!"

Dorothea Dix knew that only the state government could change these conditions. She arranged to speak before the Massachusetts state legislature. She began: "I come to present the strong claims of suffering humanity. I come to place before the Legislature of Massachusetts the condition of the miserable, the desolate, the outcast. I come as the **advocate** of helpless, forgotten, insane . . . men and women, . . . wretched in our prisons, and more wretched in our almshouses."

Then she described the hopeless conditions she had found.

> **vocabulary**
>
> **asylum** a hospital for the care of the mentally ill
>
> **advocate** someone who speaks for the cause or benefit of others

This was the kind of situation that caused Dorothea Dix to fight for reform of the treatment of the mentally ill.

Of course the people in charge of the jails and almshouses denied everything. People accused of wrong doing often do. They accused Dix of making up lies. But Dorothea Dix's evidence was so convincing that the legislators believed her. The lawmakers agreed to make the state hospital bigger so that it could take in more of the mentally ill.

Dorothea Dix then carried her work to other states. She went as far west as Illinois. She went as far south as Alabama. Almost none of those states had even one hospital for mentally ill people. Wherever she went, Dorothea Dix followed the same plan that had worked in Massachusetts. She would visit as many jails and almshouses as she could.

She would fill her notebooks with information about the treatment of the insane in that state. Then she would present her findings to the public and the state legislature. Finally, she would recommend that the legislature create special hospitals where trained people would treat the mentally ill like human beings instead of animals.

Altogether, Dorothea Dix visited more than 800 jails and almshouses. She persuaded more than a dozen states to improve care for the insane. In the 40 years after Dix visited that jail in East Cambridge, 110 new mental hospitals were built in the United States. Most of the credit for that belongs to the brave and determined reformer, Dorothea Dix.

chool for Everyone When you were reading about Dorothea Dix, you met Horace Mann. He was the person who got the state of Massachusetts to build the first hospital for the mentally ill. He became most famous, though, for another great reform. He led the movement to provide free public school education for all.

In Horace Mann's time there were few free public schools outside New England. They were mainly for poor children, and the schools were usually as poor as the children they served. Wealthy families either hired private tutors for their children or sent them to private schools. What about the many who were between the poor and the well-to-do—in other words, the majority of children? Their parents either taught them at home or got together with other parents and hired someone to teach them.

Even in the New England states, where the taxpayers provided free public education, the schools were not very good. Take Massachusetts, for example. In many towns the school "year" was only two months long. School buildings were often run down and unheated. Teachers had no training for the difficult tasks they had to do. (That's how Dorothea Dix could become a teacher at age 14.) As in other states, wealthy families in

Massachusetts paid for private tutors or sent their children to private schools.

As a boy, Horace Mann went to one of those two-months-a-year schools. In later years he studied a lot on his own. He then became a lawyer and was elected to the Massachusetts legislature. In the legislature, and later as a state official, he worked to provide a good education for every child in the state.

Mann began to speak at many public meetings to get support for his ideas. He told his listeners how education could improve the lives of their children. He told them how it would help their children get better jobs than their parents had. He told them how Thomas Jefferson believed that only an educated people could expect to remain free. And he told them how democracy and education go hand in hand. For a democracy

Horace Mann led the campaign for public schools.

to succeed, all children, not just the children of the wealthy, must be educated to become good citizens and wise voters.

Making a Difference

Horace Mann soon found support from many different people. Business people needed workers who could read, write, and do math. Working people knew that education was the key to a better life for their children. Those who had thought a lot about how to preserve freedom and democracy in America also knew that Mann was right. All these people realized that the best hope for providing all children with a good education was free public schools.

Of course not everyone agreed. Some said that if you "give away" education free to the children of the poor, they will grow up lazy! Others grumbled that they would have to pay taxes to educate other people's children.

But most Americans realized that spending money to educate children was a wise investment for the whole country.

Under Horace Mann's leadership, the state of Massachusetts created schools for training teachers. The state provided enough money to pay for six months of school each year for all boys and girls. It divided schools into grades instead of having children of all ages trying to learn different things in the same classroom. It also passed a law saying that all children must attend a school.

Massachusetts became a model for other states which asked Horace Mann to help them make the same school reforms. Most northern and western states started free public schools. (Southern states did not do the same until many years later.) That's why Horace Mann is known in history as the Father of the American Public School.

Educational reform depended on well-trained teachers.
Here young women learn how to teach science.

4 Abolitionism

The Crusade Against Slavery The biggest and most emotionally-charged reform movement of the 1830s and 1840s was the abolitionist movement. This was the movement to put an end to slavery in the United States. Many Americans were coming to believe that slavery was wrong.

"All men are created equal," says the Declaration of Independence. All have the **unalienable right** to life and to liberty. All of our early Presidents—Washington, Adams, Jefferson, Madison, Monroe—felt slavery was wrong and believed it would end in time. But saying that slavery is wrong was one thing. Actually doing something to **abolish** it was another. In fact, all of those early Presidents except John Adams owned slaves themselves. Several northern states did pass laws to end slavery. But no southern state did, and that is where most slaves lived.

Some slaveholders in the South freed their own slaves. George Washington did. One slaveholder in North Carolina gave these four reasons for freeing his slaves.

Reason the first: every human being . . . is entitled to freedom.

Reason the second: my conscience condemns me for keeping them in slavery.

Reason the third: the golden rule directs us to do unto every human creature, as we would wish to be done unto.

Reason the fourth and last: I wish to die with a clear conscience that I may not be ashamed to appear before my master in a future world.

But these were all individual deeds by kind owners. They were never more than a small minority of all slaveholders. The flame of antislavery feeling had never burned strongly in the South. By the early 1800s, it flickered and died out.

Abolitionists wanted to light that flame again. Most abolitionists were religious people. They believed that slavery was not just wrong. They believed it was a great sin in the eyes of God. They thought the way to end slavery was to appeal to the conscience of slave owners. They thought that once masters understood how sinful it was for one person to own another, they would give up their slaves, just the way that North Carolina slaveholder did.

But things didn't work out as they hoped. Slave owners were not interested in hearing the abolitionists' message. In fact, they even said that slaves benefited from slavery! Slaves were happy to be taken care of, said the owners. How then could slavery be a sin? In their eyes, abolitionists were nothing but a bunch of troublemakers.

So abolitionists turned their efforts to educating northerners on the evil of slavery. They formed antislavery organizations. They

> **vocabulary**
> **unalienable right**
> a right that cannot be given away or taken away
> **abolish** to do away with

328

handed out over a million pamphlets. They gave public lectures.

One of the leading abolitionists was William Lloyd Garrison. Garrison published an abolitionist newspaper called *The Liberator*. He also started the American Anti-Slavery Society, which was the main organization of abolitionist reformers. Another important abolitionist was Frederick Douglass. Douglass had escaped from slavery. When he gave a lecture about slavery, his listeners knew that he was talking from real experience. Douglass later wrote a book about his life as a slave and his escape. In addition, he published an abolitionist newspaper.

At first there were only a few abolitionists. Only a few thousand people in the whole country bought *The Liberator*. Even in the North, where most people didn't like slavery,

abolitionists were not popular. That's because abolitionists weren't just saying they didn't like slavery. They were saying that the country should *do* something about it—abolish it, not at some time in the distant future but *now, right away.*

Abolitionists believed deeply in their cause, and they kept working to achieve freedom for the slaves. In public meetings they told their listeners about the cruel treatment of slaves. They told them of the whippings. They told them of husbands separated from wives and of children being sold and separated from parents. In time, a growing number of people came to understand the true horrors of slavery. Some came over to the abolitionists' side and supported their arguments. And even those who didn't come all the way over believed more strongly than ever that slavery was evil and must not be allowed to spread.

William Lloyd Garrison used his newspaper **The Liberator** *to inform people about the evils of slavery.*

Women as Second-Class Citizens

Women Speak Out Angelina and Sarah Grimké were sisters who had grown up in South Carolina. They had lived with slavery, and they hated it. They felt so strongly about slavery that they left the South.

In the 1830s the Grimké sisters began giving talks about **plantation** life and slavery to audiences of men and women in northern towns and cities. Many people were shocked to hear the sisters lecture on the evils of slavery. You might be surprised to learn what shocked them, though. It wasn't *what* the sisters said about slavery. It was the fact that these women were speaking in public *at all*. At that time women, like children, were supposed to be seen and not heard. Most men agreed with the old saying, "A woman's place is in the home." Women might speak to groups of other women. But they should not be speaking at public meetings where men were in the audience. That was for men only.

Are you surprised? That's what the world was like for women in the first half of the 1800s. And that was just one of the ways in which women lacked equal rights. Women also lacked equal opportunity in education.

> **vocabulary**
> **plantation** a large farm on which one main crop is grown

In the 1800s most people believed that women should stay home and care for their children.

In those days few people—male or female—got more than a few years of schooling. But a man was much more likely to finish high school or go to college than a woman. And you never heard of a woman who became a doctor or a lawyer. When women did work they usually earned very low wages.

There's more. When a woman married, in most states everything she owned, even money or property given her by her parents, became the property of her husband. If she worked, her earnings belonged to her husband. If she got divorced, it was usually the father, not the mother, who got the children. That was the law. And because women couldn't vote or hold office, the laws would not be changed unless men voted to change them. In time, men did. But the changes were few, and they came very slowly.

Sarah Grimké became so angry about these unfair laws and attitudes, she wrote a pamphlet to express her outrage. "Men and women are CREATED EQUAL," she wrote. "Whatever is *right* for man to do, is *right* for woman." She refused to surrender woman's claim to equality. "All I ask of [men] is, that they will take their feet from off our necks and permit us to stand upright on that ground which God designed us to occupy."

Those were very angry words, but you can certainly understand why Sarah Grimké wrote them.

You might think that men who were reformers would have a different attitude about women. Some did, but not most. One woman who joined a temperance organization found that men held all the offices and made all the speeches. She was told that "the sisters were not invited there to speak but to listen and learn." Women in the antislavery movement were treated the same way, even though they made up more than half its members. Ministers who strongly supported abolition refused to allow women to speak at antislavery meetings in their churches.

That was the attitude in most parts of the world. Women **delegates** to a World Anti-Slavery Convention in London, England, were not allowed to take part in the meeting. They could only watch from a balcony. So you see, even when working for the cause of freedom, women were expected to take a back seat—or, in this case, an upstairs seat—to men.

> **vocabulary**
> **delegate** a person sent to speak and act for his or her group

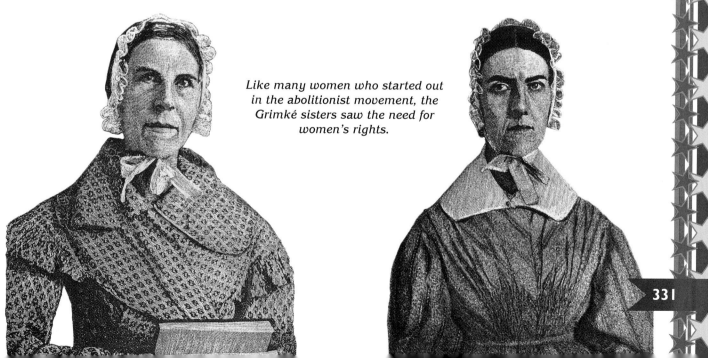

Like many women who started out in the abolitionist movement, the Grimké sisters saw the need for women's rights.

Woman's Rights Convention In July 14, 1848, this notice appeared in the *Seneca Country Courier* newspaper: "Woman's Rights Convention—a Convention to discuss the social, civil, and religious conditions and rights of woman—will be held in the Wesleyan chapel, at Seneca Falls, N.Y."

A woman's rights convention? No doubt some readers wondered, what will they think of next? Few would have guessed that this short announcement would be the start of one of the biggest reform movements in our history.

The idea for a convention on women's rights had been born eight years earlier. You remember that World Anti-Slavery Convention in London—the one where women delegates were told they could watch from the balcony but not take part? Two of those women sitting in the balcony were Lucretia Mott and Elizabeth Cady Stanton.

Lucretia Mott and her husband, James, were active in many of the reform causes of the day. Mott once organized a campaign asking people not to buy products made or raised by slave labor, such as cotton clothing, sugar, and rice. She hoped that would cause plantation owners to give up slavery. Despite her work in good causes, Mott always felt put down as a woman. She later said that women's rights "was the most important question of my life from a very early day."

As for Elizabeth Cady, she had learned about the unequal treatment of women very early in life. Her father was a lawyer and a judge. "Oh, my daughter," he had said on one occasion, "I wish you were a boy." For as

Lucretia Mott, and other women supporting equal rights for women, often needed protection from angry groups of men.

a girl, Elizabeth could never become a lawyer as her father was.

Elizabeth Cady resolved to show her father that she could be every bit as good as a boy. She learned to play chess and other games that men said were beyond the mental powers of girls and women. She studied Greek, Latin, and mathematics. Still, no matter how well she did, the rule at colleges then was "men only." Cady had to be content with attending a school for women in Troy, New York.

After graduating, Cady became active in a number of reform movements. She soon met Henry B. Stanton, who was a leader in the antislavery movement, and the two decided to marry. In those days, women promised to "love, honor, and obey" their husbands in the marriage vow. However, Elizabeth Cady insisted on removing the word *obey*. The Stantons spent their honeymoon in London, England so that they could attend the World Anti-Slavery Convention.

Lucretia Mott was a good deal older than Elizabeth Cady Stanton. The two had never met before the London meeting. But both were angered by the way they were treated. By the time they left London, these two reformers promised each other to hold a convention on women's rights when they returned to the United States.

For eight years nothing came of the promise. Elizabeth Cady Stanton was busy raising a family, and Lucretia Mott was involved in other activities. Then on July 13, 1848, Mott visited the town of Seneca Falls, New York, where the Stantons lived. That afternoon, over a cup of tea with Stanton and three local women, it was decided to hold the long-delayed convention. They would have it in Seneca Falls six days from that day.

Six days! So much to do, and so little time. Still, when 300 men and women showed up at the Wesleyan chapel on July 19, the two reformers were ready. Elizabeth Cady Stanton read aloud a Declaration of Sentiments she had written. You will see what famous document she used as a model when you read her words: "We hold these truths to be self-evident: that all men and women are created equal." Stanton went on to list 15 ways in which women were treated unequally. She could have listed a hundred.

At the end of the declaration, Elizabeth Cady Stanton shocked the audience when she demanded that women be given the right to vote. Even for some reformers, that was going too far. Lucretia Mott tried to discourage

Women, and some male supporters, gathered at Seneca Falls to hold a convention on women's rights.

her friend. Demanding the vote "will make us look ridiculous," she said. "We must go slowly." But Mott eventually agreed, and so did a majority of the convention.

Today, it's hard to imagine anyone disagreeing with the goals of the Seneca Falls Convention. However, that was a different time. The few newspapers that paid any attention at all to the meeting made fun of it. One laughed at the women's demand that they be allowed to vote, become lawyers, and keep their own property. While they were at it, said the newspaper, they should have voted to make men "wash dishes, . . . handle the broom, darn stockings, . . . wear trinkets, [and] look beautiful."

None of this ridicule stopped the women's movement. After the Seneca Falls meeting, women in a half-dozen other states organized similar meetings.

The movement for women's rights had other heroines besides Elizabeth Cady Stanton and Lucretia Mott. There was Lucy Stone, the first American woman to deliver a public lecture on women's rights. When Lucy Stone married, she kept her own name because she didn't wish to be Mrs. anybody. There

was Elizabeth Blackwell, who became the first woman graduate of a medical college. There was Amelia Bloomer, who wore large, roomy trousers with a short skirt over them because they were more comfortable than the heavy dresses women were expected to wear.

And then there was a remarkable former slave named Sojourner Truth. Nearly six feet tall and wearing a white turban, Sojourner Truth became a familiar person at public meetings on women's rights. She could neither read nor write, but she certainly could speak. To those who said women were weak, Sojourner said, "I have as much muscle as any man, and can do as much work as any man. I have plowed and reaped and husked and chopped and mowed, and can any man do more than that?" When Sojourner Truth was speaking at another convention, a few rowdy men showed up to jeer. Sojourner Truth had these words for them: "I am sorry to see [some men] so short-minded. But we'll have our rights; see if we don't; and you can't stop us from them; see if you can. You may hiss as much as you like, but it is comin'."

Sojourner Truth was right. But as things turned out, it was a long, long time in comin'.

Sojourner Truth felt strongly about two things: the end of slavery and the need for equal rights for women.

Glossary

abolish to do away with

advocate someone who speaks for the cause or benefit of others

asylum a hospital for the care of the mentally ill

delegate a person sent to speak and act for his or her group

plantation a large farm on which one main crop is grown

unalienable right a right that cannot be given away or taken away

Index

Credits

All photographs and artwork © Pearson Learning unless otherwise noted.

COVER: *top left to top right, counterclockwise:* Seaver Center for Western History Research, Los Angeles County Museum of Natural History. Trustees of the Royal Watercolour Society, London, UK/The Bridgeman Art Library. Hirmer Fotoarchive. Library of Congress. Bettmann/Corbis. The Granger Collection. Culver Pictures, Inc. SuperStock. Pearson Learning. Earl & Nazima Kowall/Corbis.

USING MAPS
Photos: *Unit Opener:* The Mariners Museum/Corbis.
2: Bettmann/Corbis. 5: Jan Butchofsky-Houser/Corbis.
8: *t.l.* AFP/ Corbis; *t.r.* Morton Beebe/Corbis. 10: Philip Gould/Corbis.
11: The Granger Collection. 14: Courtesy Albrecht-Kemper Museum of Art.
Illustrations: 20: Pat Grush. 21, 22: Jim O'Shea.
Maps: 2, 4, 5, 6, 9, 10, 12, 14, 16–17, 19: Mapping Specialists, Ltd.
Border Art: Joe LeMonnier.

WORLD MOUNTAINS
Photos: *Unit Opener:* SuperStock, Inc. 29: Paul Lally/Stock Boston.
30: *t.* Kent & Donna Dannen/Photo Researchers, Inc.; *b.* Richard & Susan Day/Animals Animals/Earth Scenes. 31: St. Meyers/Okapia/Photo Researchers, Inc. 33: John Elk III/Stock Boston. 34: Galen Rowell/Bettmann/Corbis. 36: Stephen Simpson/FPG International.
37: Jess Stock/Stone. 38: l. Galen Rowell/Mountain Light/PictureQuest; r. Hulton-Deutsch Collection/Corbis.
Map: 28: Mapping Specialists, Ltd.

EUROPE IN THE MIDDLE AGES
Photos: *Unit Opener:* Musee Conde, Chantilly/The Bridgeman Art Library. 44: Scala/Art Resource. 45: Corbis. 47: The Bridgeman Art Library. 48–49: Ruggero Vanni/Corbis. 50: Archivo Iconografico, S.A./Corbis. 51: Fulvio Roiter/Corbis. 53: Giraudon/Art Resource.
54: Gianni Dagli Orti/Corbis. 56: Art Resource. 60–61: Karen Minot.
62: The Granger Collection. 64: Harry Bliss/© National Geographic Society. 65: The Granger Collection. 67: Gianni Dagli Orti/Corbis.
68: Archivo Iconografico, S.A./Corbis. 70, 71: The Granger Collection.
72–73: Historical Picture Archive/Corbis. 74: AKG London.
75: ScalaArt Resource. 76: Bibliotheque Municipale, Castres, France/The Bridgeman Art Library. 77: The British Library.
78-79: The Bridgeman Art Library. 80: Stone. 81–82: AKG London.
83: The Granger Collection. 86: l. Leonard de Selva/Corbis; r. Museum of London/© Dorling Kindersley. 89: Jean Francois Amelot/AKG London. 91: l. Dept. of the Environment, London, UK/The Bridgeman Art Library; r. Bettmann/Corbis. 93: The Granger Collection.
95: Bibliotheque Nationale, Paris, France/The Bridgeman Art Library.
96: The Granger Collection. 98: Musee du Louvre/AKG London.
99: Musee des Beaux-Arts, Orleans, France/The Bridgeman Art Library. 100: Leonard de Selva/Corbis. 102: The Granger Collection.
Maps: 42, 57, 47: Mapping Specialists, Ltd.
Chart: 58: Robert LoGrippo.
Border Art: Michael Storrings/Artville/ PictureQuest.
Initial Capital Art: Aridi Computer Graphics, Inc.

THE SPREAD OF ISLAM
Photos: *Unit Opener: bkgd.* PhotoDisc, Inc.; *frgd.* Nabeel Turner/Stone. 108: Christophe Boisvieux/Corbis. 109: AFP/Corbis.
111: Bruno Hadjih/Liaison International. 112: Werner Forman Archive/Biblioteca Nacional, Madrid/Art Resource, New York.
115: Corbis. 116: l., r. British Library, London UK/The Bridgeman Art Library. 117: Richard T. Nowitz/Corbis. 118: Archivo Iconografico, S.A./Corbis.
Illustrations: 107, 110: Jose Miralles.
Map: 113: Mapping Specialists, Ltd.

AFRICAN KINGDOMS
Photos: 124: Jose Fuste Raga/Leo de Wys. 125: Harvey Lloyd/FPG International. 126: Daryl Balfour/Stone. 127: Gisela Damm/eStock Photography/PictureQuest. 128: Harvard University—Museum of Fine Arts Expedition/Courtesy, Museum of Fine Arts, Boston. Acc # 20.276.
130–131: Mike Yamashita/Woodfin Camp and Associates.
132–133: James Stanfield/National Geographic Society Image Collection. 136: Lee Boltin/Boltin Picture Library. 137: Wolfgang Kaehler/Corbis. 140: Courtesy of Department of Library Services/American Museum of Natural History. 141: The Granger Collection. 145: Glen Allison/PhotoDisc, Inc. 146: Courtesy of Department of Library Services/American Museum of Natural History. 148–149: Burt Silverman/National Geographic Society Image Collection. 149: inset. James Stanfield/ National Geographic Society Image Collection.
Illustrations: *Unit Opener*, 135, 138–139, 142: Jose Miralles.
Maps: 123, 131, 134: Mapping Specialists, Ltd.
Border and Initial Capital Art: Aridi Computer Graphics.

DYNASTIES OF CHINA
Photos: *Unit Opener:* Picture Finders, Ltd./eStock Photography/ PictureQuest. 154: l. Lowell Georgia/Corbis. 154–155: Lee Foster/Bruce Coleman/PictureQuest. 156: Bibliotheque Nationale, Paris/The Art Archive/The Picture Desk. 157: Picture Finders, Ltd./eStock Photography/PictureQuest. 161: Dagli Orti/Golestan Palace, Teheran/The Art Archive/The Picture Desk. 163: British Library/ The Art Archive/The Picture Desk. 166: D. E. Cox Photo Library/ ChinaStock. 167: British Library/The Art Archive/The Picture Desk.
168: Bettmann/Corbis. 169: Burstein Collection/Corbis. 171: Royal Ontario Museum. 172: Pierre Colombel/Corbis. 173: Bibliotheque Nationale, Paris/The Art Archive/The Picture Desk. 174: Royal Ontario Museum/Corbis. 175: National Palace Museum, Taipei, Taiwan/The Bridgeman Art Library. 176: Private Collection/The Bridgeman Art Library. 178: British Museum, London, UK/The Bridgeman Art Library. 179: Bibliotheque Nationale, Paris, France/The Bridgeman Art Library. 180: Private Collection/The Bridgeman Art Library .
181: Bibliotheque Nationale/The Art Archive/The Picture Desk.
182: D. E. Cox Photo Library/ChinaStock. 183: The Granger Collection.
184–185: Keren Su/Corbis. 185–186: D. E. Cox Photo Library/ChinaStock. 187: North Wind Picture Archives. 188: Royal Ontario Museum/Corbis. 189: British Library, London, UK/The Bridgeman Art Library. 190: The Granger Collection.
Illustrations: 162: Siok Sodbinow. 164: Dick Smolinski.
Maps: 159, 177: Mapping Specialists, Ltd.
Border Art: Gary Torrisi.

THE AMERICAN REVOLUTION

Photos: *Unit Opener:* Courtesy of, The Valley Forge Historical Society. 195: Culver Pictures. 197: The Granger Collection. 198: Christie's Images/SuperStock, Inc. 200: Culver Pictures. 201: The Granger Collection. 203: The Stapleton Collection/The Bridgeman Art Library. 205: Junius Brutus Stearns/SuperStock, Inc. 210–212: The Granger Collection. 214–215: Library of Congress. 216: Bettmann/Corbis. 219–220: The Granger Collection. 222: Library of Congress. 223–224: The Granger Collection. 227: *l.* Library of Congress; *r.* SuperStock, Inc. 228–229: The Granger Collection. 230: *r.* Library of Congress. 231: *frgd.* Library of Congress; *bkgd.* Bettmann/Corbis. 232: Library of Congress. 233: Bettmann/Corbis. 234: Library of Congress. 236: Engraving by Andre Besset/Library of Congress. 237: SuperStock, Inc.
Illustrations: 217, 246: Argosy.
Maps: 196: Patricia Dewitt Grush. 208, 238, 244: Mapping Specialists, Ltd.
Initial Capital Art and Borders: Gary Torrisi.

THE UNITED STATES CONSTITUTION

Photos: *Unit Opener:* *l.* Library of Congress; *r.* The Granger Collection. 252: The Granger Collection. 254: New Jersey State Archives, Department of State. 256: Buddy Mays/Corbis. 257: The Granger Collection. 261: Bettmann/ Corbis. 262: *l., r.* Library of Congress; *m.* Corbis. 263: Kelly Harriger/ Corbis. 264: North Wind Picture Archives. 265: Courtesy Cigna Corporation Museum. 266: Ted Spiegel/ Corbis. 267: Library of Congress. 269: Library of Congress. 272: Corbis. 276: Bettmann/ Corbis. 277: The Granger Collection. 278: *l.* Corbis; *r.* Library of Congress. 280-281: *b.* Collection of The New-York Historical Society. 282: Library of Congress. 283: Richard A Cooke/ Corbis. 284: *l.* Corbis; *r.* AP/Wide World Photos. 285: Paul Conklin/PhotoEdit.
Illustrations: 255, 271, 274, 279: Argosy. 259: Brian Lies.
Map: 260: Mapping Specialists, Ltd.
Border Art: Library of Congress.
Initial Capital Art: Gary Torrisi.

EARLY PRESIDENTS:
WASHINGTON THROUGH JACKSON

Photos: *Unit Opener:* © National Geographic Society. 290: © National Geographic Society. 291: detail, Collection of The New-York Historical Society. 292: Library of Congress. 294: Courtesy, Independence National Historical Park. 295: Prints Collection, Miriam and Ira Wallach Divison of Arts, Prints and Photographs. The New York Public Library. 298, 299: Library of Congress. 300: Architect of the Capitol. 301: Bettmann/Corbis. 302–303: Joseph Sohm/ChromoSohm/Corbis. 303: Jefferson Memorial Foundation/Smithsonian Institution. 305, 307: The Granger Collection. 308: Courtesy, Independence National Historical Park. 309: *l.* Library of Congress; *r.* Bettmann/Corbis. 311: Library of Congress. 312: Bettmann/Corbis. 313: Library of Congress. 314: Bettmann/Corbis. 315, 316: Library of Congress. 317, 318: The Granger Collection.
Maps: 296, 302: Mapping Specialists, Ltd.
Border and Initial Capital Art: Gary Torrisi.

AMERICAN REFORMERS

Photos: *Unit Opener:* The Granger Collection, New York. 322: The Granger Collection, New York. 323: The New-York Historical Society. 325: The Granger Collection, New York. 326: Kevin Fleming/Corbis. 327, 329: *l.:* Corbis; *r.:* The Granger Collection, New York. 330: Historical Picture Archive/Corbis. 331: The Granger Collection, New York. 332: Bettmann/Corbis. 333: The Granger Collection, New York. 334: Library of Congress.